W9-BST-889

GREENBOOK

Guide to

The Enesco

PRECIOUS MOMENTS

Collection

Fifth Edition

GREENBOOK™

Old Coach at Main, Box 515
East Setauket, New York 11733
(516) 689-8466
FAX (516) 689-8177

Library of Congress Catalog Number 90-080129

ISBN 0-923628-05-3

Photography by Anthony Lopez, East End Studio, Miller Place, NY

Printed and bound by Searles Graphics, East Patchogue, NY

Published in East Setauket, NY

GREENBOOK Secondary Market Prices published in *The GREENBOOK Guide To The Enesco PRECIOUS MOMENTS Collection, The GREENBOOK Guide To The MEMORIES OF YESTERDAY Collection by Enesco*, and *The GREENBOOK Guide To Ornaments Including The Enesco Treasury Of Christmas Ornaments And Hallmark Keepsake Ornaments* are obtained from retailers and collectors. Enesco Corporation and Hallmark Cards, Inc. verify factual information only and are not consulted or involved in any way in determining GREENBOOK Secondary Market Prices.

All line drawings in this book are copyrighted by Samuel J. Butcher, 1975-1990. PRECIOUS MOMENTS, PRECIOUS MOMENTS COLLECTORS' CLUB, and PRECIOUS MOMENTS BIRTHDAY CLUB are trademarks and service marks of Mr. Butcher. ENESCO CORP. is the licensee under Mr. Butcher's rights and is also the registered owner of the ENESCO trademark.

©1990 GREENBOOK. All rights reserved. All names and illustrations contained herein are copyrighted. Their reproduction or use elsewhere without the written permission of the copyright owners is strictly forbidden. No part of this book may be reproduced or utilized in any way electronic, mechanical, photocopying or by information storage and retrieval system without the written permission of the GREENBOOK.

ACKNOWLEDGEMENTS

The GREENBOOK would like to thank -

Sam Butcher, for approving the use of his copyrighted line drawings.

Enesco, for assisting in the compilation of the factual information contained in this Guide.

The dealers and collectors across the country who supply us with information including secondary market status and prices.

NOTE FROM THE PUBLISHER

I'm often asked if I collect PRECIOUS MOMENTS. It's difficult for me to say yes, knowing there are a couple dozen or so treasured pieces at home, when, everyday, I talk to those who own every piece in the Collection!

We got to wondering, if you did own every piece in the Collection, how many pieces would you have? Nobody knew. It seemed like a simple straightforward task. So we decided to complicate it by breaking it down by year of introduction and product type. Working independently, three people put together the data - and when they sat down to compare notes they had three different interpretations of the facts. The all-new, exclusive GREENBOOK "WHAT & WHEN - An Introductions Cross Reference Table" is the end result of two inter-office wars and a debate with someone I consider to be a PRECIOUS MOMENTS scholar. The remarks that preface the chart will give you a clue as to the where we had our differences of opinion.

Also new in this, the Fifth Edition, is "WE JUST WANTED YOU TO KNOW..... " This new feature includes color photographs and the story behind pieces we felt many collectors have not had the opportunity to see - the Retailer's Dome (E-7350) and the Damien-Dutton figurine, We Belong To The Lord (103004). We've illustrated the evolution of the box and the difference in coloration between a "No Mark" and subsequent annual symbols with color photographs as well.

The ART CHART and ALPHA-LOG have a new category; a diamond designates a "Two-Year Collectible." The concept of One, Two, and Three-Year Collectibles first made its debut with the Enesco Treasury of Christmas Ornaments and was extremely well received by retailers and collectors alike. The new Four Seasons dolls and musical jack-in-the-boxes have been introduced as Two-Year Collectibles.

In response to your comments and letters, the Listings have undergone a major re-organization. Series and annual pieces that were previously pulled out and grouped together in the front of the listings have been dispersed into the main section and now appear in Enesco Item Number order. A new feature of the QUICK REFERENCE SECTION itemizes the individual pieces that comprise each series.

I've talked to a collector who had a truck crash through his living room, not stopping as it passed through the curio cabinet and another who had pieces packed in moving barrels explode from intense heat. I remember these because they were so unusual, but what about the more common perils including breakage, theft, fire, flood, or even earthquake? How do you go about protecting yourself against damage or loss? The best advice is to consult with your insurance agent. However, in "Insuring Your PRECIOUS MOMENTS Collectibles" we give you a place to start.

Invariably when they meet me, collectors expect that I'm a walking PRECIOUS MOMENTS encyclopaedia. Actually, I'm not. I feel my area of expertise is the Guide. I've done my job, if, Guide in hand, an average collector could hold their own against the walking encyclopaedias!

Simply put, GREENBOOK is a clearing house for information. Two people who have shared their considerable knowledge over the years are contributing editors for this edition.

Sheryl J. Williams is both the before-mentioned PRECIOUS MOMENTS scholar and walking encyclopaedia. What do you say about someone who can discuss, off the top of her head, the different prints of the laundry in the basket as they vary with the six annual symbols on *Be Not Weary In Well Doing*? In addition to her affiliation with GREENBOOK, Sheryl publishes a newsletter, PRECIOUS INSIGHTS. If you're interested, the address for PRECIOUS INSIGHTS is Box 130275, Roseville, MN 55113. The article on page 213, "Advice to the New Collector," is from the newsletter.

If Sheryl is a first lady of PRECIOUS MOMENTS, Juan Carlos Silva is a new kid on the block. Yet I am constantly amazed at his uncanny ability to zero in on trends and, in general, what's happening. At times I think Juan invented networking. Compiling bits and pieces from all over the country, he has a beat on the secondary market unlike any other individual I know. Juan's article, "Insights on Oversights" is on page 217. If you'd like to correspond with Juan, his address is 301 N.W. 58 Ct., Miami, FL 33126.

THE YEAR IN REVIEW

In a single sentence?......What we said last year only more so! The older suspended pieces, new introductions in their original annual symbol, and ornaments are hot.

Educated speculation says the older suspended pieces are, for all intents and purposes, retired. Contributing to this theory are the following thoughts; a) should a piece be "brought back," it most likely would not be identical to the original suspended piece, b) the only reason E-7156 was returned to production was its importance to the Make-A-Wish Foundation, c) there is no dearth of new artwork, and, perhaps most importantly, d) Sam Butcher has grown as an artist and prefers his newer work.

At this writing, all but two of the Spring 1990 introductions have been found with 1989's Bow & Arrow. However, as with last year, some appear to be extremely rare and are already commanding premium prices on the Secondary Market. This information is reflected in the Listings.

Industry-wide, ornaments have to be considered the fasted growing, hottest collectible category. And PRECIOUS MOMENTS ornaments are no exception. I've heard the story more than once - a collector contacting a secondary

NOTE FROM THE PUBLISHER CONTINUED

market dealer wanting to purchase one of every ornament in the Collection - name the price.

What else? In general, people are pleased with the affordable Suggested Retails on the new introductions, particularly the Fall 1990 pieces. Even the higher price points constitute value. Most of the grumbling we heard was about the reproduction of porcelain bisque subjects in painted pewter and art-plas. In particular, the announcement of the pewter *God Loveth A Cheerful Giver* figurine sent collectors scurrying for the exact definition of "Retired." Collectors don't object to the medium, just the duplication of cherished subjects.

Since this is a note and not a letter, I'll stop here. Again, we welcome all your questions and comments. I personally read each and every letter that comes into this office and we answer all correspondence. On occasion, if we get behind, we'll pick up the phone and call. So it would be helpful, if you do write asking for a response, to include a daytime phone number.

We appreciate your support, thank you for buying the Guide, and will do our very best to continue to live up to your high expectations.

Sincerely,

Louise L. Patterson Langenfeld
Publisher

TABLE OF CONTENTS

INTRODUCTION

The GREENBOOK provides information about The Enesco PRECIOUS MOMENTS®
Collection in the form of GREENBOOK Secondary Market Prices plus factual
information describing each piece. The factual information includes:

- Inspirational Title
- Descriptive Title
- Type of Product
- Enesco Item Number
- Year of Issue
- Edition Size
- Issue Price When First Issued as well as each year the annual symbol
  is/was changed
- Size
- Certification
- Is it individually numbered?
- Is it part of a set or series?
- Annual Symbol

The factual information is compiled by the GREENBOOK with assistance from
Enesco. It appears in the Guide in many different forms making it possible for
a new collector as well as the experienced collector to identify the pieces in
their collection or the pieces they wish to buy or sell. The inclusion of Secondary Market prices, as reported by retailers and collectors, make it possible to
determine the value of each piece.

Market prices are important for insurance purposes as well as buying and
selling.

The GREENBOOK also affords collectors an opportunity to become familiar
with the *entire* PRECIOUS MOMENTS Collection - not just the pieces that are
currently available at Suggested Retail and displayed in stores. Current,
Retired, Suspended, Discontinued, Annuals, Two-Year Collectibles, Limited
Editions, and earlier issue figurines, plates, bells, musicals, ornaments, etc. are
included.

The GREENBOOK's exclusive ART CHART contains authorized reproductions of
521 line drawings. In addition, it lists the Enesco Item Number for the figurine,
plate, bell, musical, ornament, doll, thimble, frame, candle climber, box and
nite lite derived from each drawing. Also, it is noted if each piece is an
Annual, a Two-Year Collectible, a Limited Edition, Retired, Suspended, has a
special Inspirational Title or is derived from only a portion of the line drawing.

The ART CHART is designed to provide a graphic illustration of how individual
pieces relate to each other and to the entire Collection as well as add to the
fun of collecting PRECIOUS MOMENTS.

The GREENBOOK's exclusive ALPHA-LOG lists PRECIOUS MOMENTS Inspirational
Titles alphabetically cross-referencing the Descriptive Title, GREENBOOK ART
CHART Number, and Enesco Item Number for each figurine, plate, bell,

musical, ornament, doll, thimble, frame, candle climber, box, and nite lite with that Inspirational Title. In addition, it is noted if each piece is an Annual, a Two-Year Collectible, a Limited Edition, Retired, or Suspended.

Many times certain pieces become important as part of a group. PRECIOUS MOMENTS groups that have become important are included in the QUICK REFERENCE SECTION. Groups included are The "Original 21," Limited Editions, Two-Year Collectibles, the Re-introduced piece, Retired pieces, Suspended pieces, Dated Annuals, Annuals, The Enesco PRECIOUS MOMENTS Birthday Club pieces, and The Enesco PRECIOUS MOMENTS Collectors' Club pieces.

In addition, the OUTLINE OF ANNUALS Section groups annual collectibles by series and product type. The OUTLINE OF THE SERIES Section itemizes the individual pieces that comprise each series.

There's a QUICK REFERENCE CALENDAR as well. It's a summary, by year, of Retired, Suspended, and Annual pieces.

WHAT & WHEN - AN INTRODUCTIONS CROSS-REFERENCE TABLE is a table of introductions, broken down by year and product type. It answers questions such as "How many pieces in the Collection?," or "How many ornaments were introduced in 1986?" Another chart takes the data one step further, exploring the current market status of the yearly introductions.

The GREENBOOK LISTINGS are where specific factual information as well as Secondary Market Prices for each collectible can be found. GREENBOOK Listings are in Enesco Item Number order. The Enesco PRECIOUS MOMENTS Collectors' Club and The Enesco PRECIOUS MOMENTS Birthday Club pieces are in separate sections at the end of the Listings. Enesco Item Numbers can be found on the understamp of most pieces produced from 1982 to the present. If you don't know the Enesco Item Number, but you do know the Inspirational Title, use the ALPHA-LOG to obtain the Enesco Item Number. If you don't know the Enesco Item Number or the Inspirational Title, use the ART CHART to obtain the Enesco Item Number.

Since mid-1981 Enesco has indicated when PRECIOUS MOMENTS collectibles were produced by including an annual symbol as part of the understamp. Pieces crafted prior to 1981 have no annual symbol and have become known as "No Marks."

The GREENBOOK lists the year of issue, issue price and a GREENBOOK Market Price for each change in annual symbol.

Knowing issue prices for each PRECIOUS MOMENTS collectible when it was first issued as well as the current issue price or suggested retail can also be important when investment potential is evaluated. Many PRECIOUS MOMENTS collectibles have been produced for years and collectors who purchased the piece earlier are enjoying an increase in value even though the piece is still being produced.

A very common error made by collectors is to mistake the copyright date for the year of issue because the copyright date appears on the understamp written out as ©19XX. In order to determine what year your piece was produced, you must refer to the annual symbol, not the © date.

Another area of confusion for collectors also pertains to information found on the understamp. Prior to 1985, Jonathan & David was the licensor. Pieces produced prior to 1985 have the Jonathan & David logo on the bottom and "© 19XX Jonathan & David - Lic. Enesco Imports Corp. " Pieces which were in production prior to 1985 and are still in production today still bear the Jonathan & David information. In 1985, the Samuel J. Butcher Company became the licensor. Pieces introduced from that point on have the PRECIOUS MOMENTS logo on the bottom and "©19XX Samuel J. Butcher - Licensee Enesco Corp." It was at this time that the "Sam B" began being incised in the base of the pieces.

In addition to indicating when pieces were produced by an annual symbol on the understamp, Enesco periodically retires and suspends individual pieces. As a result, the GREENBOOK contains eight different classifications of Market Status. They are:

PRIMARY   Piece available from retailers at issue price.

SECONDARY   Piece *not* generally available from retailers at issue price.

RETIRED/PRIMARY   Piece with specific Enesco Item Number will never be produced again. Piece still available from retailers at issue price.

RETIRED/SECONDARY   Piece with specific Enesco Item Number will never be produced again. Piece *not* generally available from retailers at issue price.

SUSPENDED/PRIMARY   Piece with specific Enesco Item Number not currently being produced but may be produced in the future. Piece available from retailers at issue price.

SUSPENDED/SECONDARY   Piece with specific Enesco Item Number not currently being produced but may be produced in the future. Piece *not* generally available from retailers at issue price.

DISCONTINUED/PRIMARY   Production ceased on piece with specific Enesco Item Number. Piece still available from retailers at issue price.

DISCONTINUED/SECONDARY   Production ceased on piece with specific Enesco Item Number. Piece *not* generally available from retailers at issue price.

The eight Market Status classifications have a major effect on the value of

PRECIOUS MOMENTS collectibles. This is reflected in the GREENBOOK Secondary Market Price.

Factors other than current availability that affect Secondary Market prices include rarity, year of issue, condition, and general appeal.

Because there are so many factors based on individual judgements, and because prices can vary from one section of the country to another, Secondary Market prices **are never an absolute number**.

Two questions that come up frequently in regard to their effect on Secondary Market prices are 1) boxes and 2) Sam Butcher signing the piece.

In general, the newer the piece the more important it is to have the box. On hard-to-find, scarce, older pieces, not having a box usually does not subtract from Secondary Market price. On the other hand, pieces that are easier to come by are a tough sell without the box, because one with a box can always be found.

To date, Sam Butcher signing a piece has not added appreciably to its Secondary Market price. Once again, it varies with the raritiy of the piece. Not surprisingly, the value in most signed pieces to a collector is if it was signed by the artist for you.

Variations and Production Rarities (sometimes called errors) are included in the NOBODY'S PERFECT! Section of the Guide. GREENBOOK Secondary Market Prices are included where appropriate. Some pieces are so rare, it's a buyer-willing/seller-willing market. If you have one of these pieces or any one-of-a-kind piece and need a Secondary Market Price for insurance purposes, write to us.

NOTES

GREENBOOK ART CHART

The GREENBOOK ART CHART contains authorized reproductions of 521 line drawings. In addition, it lists the Enesco Item Number for the figurine, plate, bell, musical, ornament, doll, thimble, frame, candle climber, box, and nite lite derived from each drawing. Also, it is noted if each piece is an Annual, a Two-Year Collectible, a Limited Edition, Retired, Suspended, has a special Inspirational Title, or is derived from only a portion of the line drawing.

The ART CHART is designed to provide a graphic illustration of how individual pieces relate to each other and to the entire Collection as well as add to the fun of collecting PRECIOUS MOMENTS.

#	DESCRIPTIVE TITLE	FIG.	PLT.	BELL	MUSC.	ORN.	DOLL	THMBL.	FRAME	CNDL. CLMB.	BOX	NITE LITE
1	Boy with Teddy	E-1372B E-9278	E-9275	E-5208		E-5631*			E-7170		E-9280	
2	Girl with Bunny	E-1372G E-9279 104531	E-9276	E-5209		E-5632*			E-7171		E-9281	
3	Boy with Black Eye	E-1373B										
4	Girl with Doll & Candle	E-1373G										
5	Girl with Goose	E-1374G 520322	E-7174			522910						
6	Boy & Girl on Seesaw	E-1375A										
7	Boy & Girl with Bluebirds	E-1375B										
8	Boy & Girl Sitting/Stump	E-1376	E-5215			522929						
9	Boy Leading Lamb	E-1377A										
10	Boy Helping Lamb	E-1377B										
11	Boy with Turtle	E-1379A										
12	Boy with Report Card	E-1379B		E-5211								
13	Indian Boy	E-1380B										
14	Indian Girl	E-1380G										
15	Boy Patching World	E-1381										
16	Boy Holding Lamb	E-2010		E-5620		E-6120						
17	Boy & Girl Playing Angels	E-2012			E-2809							
18	Boy & Girl Reading Book	E-2013			E-2808							
19	Boy with Dog	E-1374B										
20	Girl with Puppies	E-1378										

BOLD = Suspended   *Italics* = Limited Edition   Shaded Area = Retired   Enclosed in a box = Annual

1. Jesus Loves Me
* Baby's First Christmas

2. Jesus Loves Me
*Baby's First Christmas

3. Smile, God Loves You

4. Jesus Is The Light

5. Make A Joyful Noise

6. Love Lifted Me

7. Prayer Changes Things

8. Love One Another

9. He Leadeth Me

10. He Careth For You

11. Love Is Kind

12. God Understands

13. O, How I Love Jesus

14. His Burden Is Light

15. Jesus Is The Answer

16. We Have Seen His Star

17. Jesus Is Born

18. Unto Us A Child Is Born

19. Praise The Lord Anyhow

20. God Loveth
A Cheerful Giver

#	DESCRIPTIVE TITLE	FIG.	PLT.	BELL	MUSC.	ORN.	DOLL	THMBL.	FRAME	CNDL. CLMB.	BOX	NITE LITE
21	Boy with Manger Baby	E-2011										
22	Nativity Set	E-2800	E-5646		E-2810*	E-5633*						
	E-2395 also includes a camel, donkey, and Three Kings											
23	Angels in Chariot	E-2801										
24	Boy Giving Toy Lamb	E-2802			E-2806							
25	Boy Kneel Manger/Crown	E-2803			E-2807							
26	Boy on Globe with Teddy	E-2804										
27	Boy in Santa Cap with Dog	E-2805										
28	Rocking Cradle	E-3104				E-0518 E-5392			E-0521			
29	Boy with Bible/Crutches	E-3105										
30	Mother Needlepointing	E-3106	E-5217	E-7181	E-7182	E-0514	E-2850	13293	E-7241			
31	Boy Holding Cat/Dog	E-3107										
32	Girl Rocking Cradle	E-3108	E-9256		E-5204							
33	Grandma in-Rocker	E-3109	E-7173	E-7183	E-7184	E-0516		13307	E-7242			
34	Boy Sharing with Puppy	E-3110B										
35	Girl Sharing with Puppy	E-3110G										
36	Girl Helper	E-3111										
37	Boy Writing in Sand/Girl	E-3113										
38	Bride 'N Groom	E-3114	E-5216	E-7179	E-7180	E-2385*			E-7166		E-7167	
39	Boy/Girl Angels on Cloud	E-3115 E-0001	E-0102 E-0202 } Plaques									E-5207*
40	Boy Carving/Tree for Girl	E-3116										

BOLD = Suspended   *Italics* = Limited Edition   Shaded Area = Retired   Enclosed in a box = Annual

(21) Come Let Us Adore Him	(22) Come Let Us Adore Him *4 main pieces	(23) Jesus Is Born	(24) Christmas Is A Time To Share	(25) Crown Him Lord Of All
(26) Peace On Earth	(27) Wishing You A Season Filled With Joy	(28) Blessed Are The Pure In Heart *Baby's First Christmas	(29) He Watches Over Us All	(30) Mother Sew Dear
(31) Blessed Are The Peacemakers	(32) The Hand That Rocks The Future	(33) The Purr-fect Grandma	(34) Loving Is Sharing	(35) Loving Is Sharing
(36) Be Not Weary In Well Doing	(37) Thou Art Mine	(38) The Lord Bless You And Keep You *Our First Christmas Together	(39) But Love Goes On Forever *My Guardian Angel	(40) Thee I Love

#	DESCRIPTIVE TITLE	FIG.	PLT.	BELL	MUSC.	ORN.	DOLL	THMBL.	FRAME	CNDL. CLMB.	BOX	NITE LITE
41	Boy Pulling Wagon w/Girl	E-3117										
42	Boy with Books	**E-3119**										
43	Girl with Box of Kittens	**E-3120**				E-0534						
44	Boy Jogging with Dog	E-3112										
45	Girl with Fry Pan	E-3118										
46	Boy Graduate	**E-4720**		E-7175					E-7177			
47	Girl Graduate	E-4721		E-7176					E-7178			
48	Girl with Piggy Bank	**E-4722**										
49	Boy Reading Holy Bible	**E-4723**										
50	Christening	E-4724	E-7172									
51	Choir Boys w/Bandages	**E-4725**			E-4726							
52	Sad Boy with Teddy	**E-5200**										
53	Boy Helping Friend	**E-5201**										
54	Lemonade Stand	**E-5202**										
55	Boy with Dog on Stairs	**E-5203**										
56	Boy Angel on Cloud		E-6901** (Plaque)		E-5205	E-5627*				**E-6118*** (set)		
57	Girl Angel on Cloud				E-5206	E-5628*						
58	Girl Praying in Field	**E-7155***		E-5210								
59	Boy in Dad's Duds	E-5212				E-0515						
60	Girl with Goose in Lap	**E-5213**										

BOLD = Suspended *Italics* = Limited Edition Shaded Area = Retired Enclosed in a box = Annual

41	42	43	44	45
Walking By Faith	It's What's Inside That Counts	To Thee With Love	God's Speed	Eggs Over Easy

46	47	48	49	50
The Lord Bless You And Keep You	The Lord Bless You And Keep You	Love Cannot Break A True Friendship	Peace Amid The Storm	Rejoicing With You

51	52	53	54	55
Peace On Earth	Bear Ye One Another's Burdens	Love Lifted Me	Thank You For Coming To My Ade	Let Not The Sun Go Down Upon Your Wrath

56	57	58	59	60
My Guardian Angel *But Love Goes On Forever **Collection Plaque	My Guardian Angel *But Love Goes On Forever	Prayer Changes Things *Thanking Him For You	To A Special Dad	God Is Love

#	DESCRIPTIVE TITLE	FIG.	PLT.	BELL	MUSC.	ORN.	DOLL	THMBL.	FRAME	CNDL. CLMB.	BOX	NITE LITE
61	Boy & Girl/Praying/Table	**E-5214**										
62	Manger with Child	**E-5619**										
63	Donkey	E-5621										
64	Shepherd	E-5624		**E-5623**		**E-5630***						
65	Three Kings on Camels	E-5624 / 108243										
66	Three Kings	E-5635	*E-0538*		**E-0520**	**E-5634**						
67	Angel with Trumpet	E-5636 / 520268			E-5645	113980						
68	Angel with Flashlight	E-5637										
69	Cow with Bell	E-5638										
70	Boy Angel Praying w/Harp	**E-5639**										
71	Girl Angel Praying w/Harp	**E-5640**										
72	Follow Me Angel w/3 Kings	**E-5641**										
73	Boy Angel and Knight				**E-5642**							
74	Two Section Wall	E-5644										
75	Mikey						**E-6214B**					
76	Debbie						**E-6214G**					
77	Praying Angel			*E-5622*		*E-5629*						
78	Boy on Telephone	PM-811										
79	Boy Angel Playing Trumpet					**E-2343**				**E-2344** (pair)		
80	Boy in Pajamas w/Teddy	**E-2345**										

BOLD = Suspended   *Italics* = Limited Edition   Shaded Area = Retired   Enclosed in a box = Annual

23

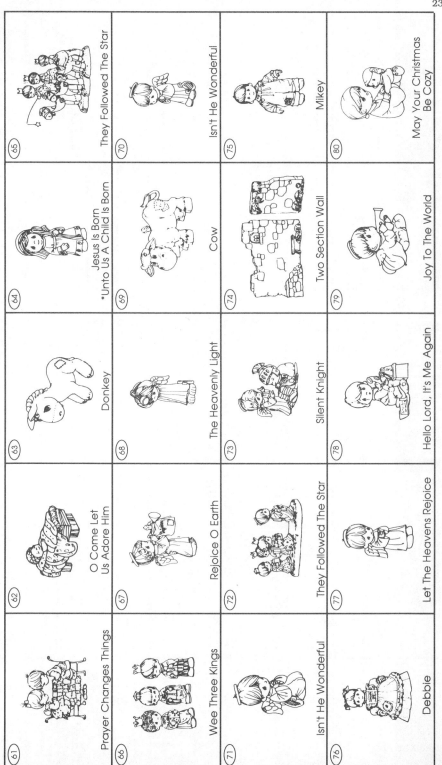

61. Prayer Changes Things
62. O Come Let Us Adore Him
63. Donkey
64. Jesus Is Born *Unto Us A Child Is Born
65. They Followed The Star

66. Wee Three Kings
67. Rejoice O Earth
68. The Heavenly Light
69. Cow
70. Isn't He Wonderful

71. Isn't He Wonderful
72. They Followed The Star
73. Silent Knight
74. Two Section Wall
75. Mikey

76. Debbie
77. Let The Heavens Rejoice
78. Hello Lord, It's Me Again
79. Joy To The World
80. May Your Christmas Be Cozy

#	DESCRIPTIVE TITLE	FIG.	PLT.	BELL	MUSC.	ORN.	DOLL	THMBL.	FRAME	CNDL. CLMB.	BOX	NITE LITE
81	Angel w/Friends Caroling		*E-2347*		**E-2346**	E-0532*						
82	Boy Next to Pot Belly Stove	**E-2348**										
83	Girl w/Doll Reading Book	**E-2349**	15237			**E-0533***						
84	Boy Ice Skater/Santa Cap	**E-2350**				E-2369						
85	Two Angels with Candles	E-2351										
86	Boy Caroling next to Lamp Post	E-2353			**E-2352**	E-0531*						
87	Drummer Boy with Manger	**E-2356**	E-2357	E-2358*	**E-2355**	E-2359*						
		E-2360*										
		E-5384*										
88	Girl with Stocking	**E-2361**										
89	Baby in Christmas Stocking					**E-2362**						
90	Camel	E-2363										
91	Goat	**E-2364**										
92	Boy Angel with Candle	**E-2365**				**E-2367**						
93	Angel Praying	**E-2366**				E-2368						
94	Unicorn					E-2371						
95	Boy Holding Block					**E-2372**						
96	Girl with Presents	E-2374										
97	Girl with Pie	E-2375				E-2376*						
98	Girl Knitting Tie for Boy	**E-2377**	E-2378									
99	Mouse with Cheese					**E-2381**						
100	Camel, Donkey, Cow					**E-2386**						

BOLD = Suspended   *Italics* = Limited Edition   Shaded Area = Retired   Enclosed in a box = Annual

81. Let Heaven And Nature Sing
*without animals

82. May Your Christmas Be Warm

83. Tell Me The Story Of Jesus
*without tree & gifts

84. Dropping In For Christmas

85. Holy Smokes

86. O Come All Ye Faithful
*without lamp post

87. I'll Play My Drum For Him
*without manger

88. Christmas Joy From Head To Toe

89. Baby's First Christmas

90. Camel

91. Goat

92. The First Noel

93. The First Noel

94. Unicorn

95. Baby's First Christmas

96. Bundles of Joy

97. Dropping Over For Christmas
*without dog

98. Our First Christmas Together

99. Mouse With Cheese

100. Baby's First Christmas
Camel, Donkey, Cow

#	DESCRIPTIVE TITLE	FIG.	PLT.	BELL	MUSC.	ORN.	DOLL	THMBL.	FRAME	CNDL. CLMB.	BOX	NITE LITE
101	Mini Houses w/Palm Tree	E-2387										
102	Boy Holding Heart	**E-7153**							12017*			
103	Girl Holding Heart	**E-7154**						100625	12025*			
104	Girl with Shopping Bag	E-0005 E-0105										
105	Boy Holding Chick	**E-7156**	*E-9257*									
106	Waitress Carrying Food	E-7157										
107	Nurse Giving Shot to Bear	E-7158										
108	Bandaged Boy by Sign	**E-7159**										
109	Grandpa in Rocking Chair	**E-7160**				E-0517*						
110	Shepherd Painting Lamb	**E-7161**										
111	Girl at School Desk	**E-7162**			E-7185							
112	Boy with Ice Bag on Head	**E-7163**										
113	Boy/Girl Paint'g Dog House	**E-7164**										
114	Boy/Girl Baptism Bucket	**E-7165**			**E-7186**							
115	Groom Doll						*E-7267B*					
116	Bride Doll						*E-7267G*					
117	Girl with Curlers	PM-821										
118	Boy Pushing Girl on Sled	**E-0501**			E-0519							
119	Boy w/Candle & Mouse	**E-0502**				E-0537*						
120	Girl/Snow Look'g Birdhouse	**E-0503**										

BOLD = Suspended   *Italics* = Limited Edition   Shaded Area = Retired   Enclosed in a box = Annual

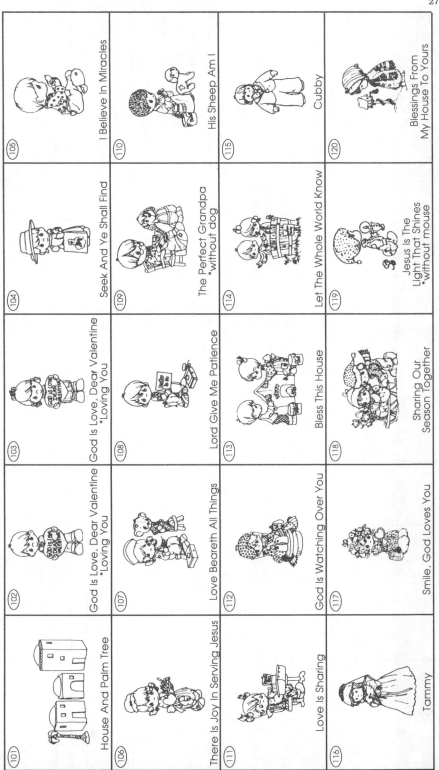

(101) House And Palm Tree	(102) God Is Love, Dear Valentine *Loving You	(103) God Is Love, Dear Valentine *Loving You	(104) Seek And Ye Shall Find
(106) There Is Joy In Serving Jesus	(107) Love Beareth All Things	(108) Lord Give Me Patience	(109) The Perfect Grandpa *without dog
(111) Love Is Sharing	(112) God Is Watching Over You	(113) Bless This House	(114) Let The Whole World Know
(116) Tammy	(117) Smile, God Loves You	(118) Sharing Our Season Together	(119) Jesus Is The Light That Shines *without mouse

| (105) I Believe In Miracles |
| (110) His Sheep Am I |
| (115) Cubby |
| (120) Blessings From My House To Yours |

#	DESCRIPTIVE TITLE	FIG.	PLT.	BELL	MUSC.	ORN.	DOLL	THMBL.	FRAME	CNDL. CLMB.	BOX	NITE LITE
121	Boy Giving Teddy/Poor Boy	E-0504	E-0505									
122	Boy with Wreath	E-0506		E-0522		E-0513*						
123	Girl Looking into Manger	E-0507										
124	Boy/Girl Preparing Manger	E-0508										
125	Girl Angel Push Jesus/Cart	E-0509										
126	Rooster & Bird on Pig	E-0511										
127	Boy Angel/Red Cross Bag	E-0512				102415*						
128	Knight in Armor	E-0523										
129	Boy & Dog Running Away	E-0525										
130	Angel Catch Falling Skater	E-0526										
131	Girl with Bird in Hand	E-0530										
132	Boy with Slate					E-0535						
133	Girl with Slate					E-0536						
134	Baby Collector's Doll						E-0539					
135	Boy Hold Board/Girl/Chalk	E-9251										
136	Boy & Girl with Bandage	E-9252										
137	Boy with Dog Rip'g Pants	E-9253										
138	Girl at Typewriter	E-9254										
139	Groom Carrying Bride	E-9255										
140	Bonnet Girl with Butterfly	E-9258										

BOLD = Suspended   *Italics* = Limited Edition   Shaded Area = Retired   Enclosed in a box = Annual

* = Special Inspirational Title or piece derived from a portion of the line drawing

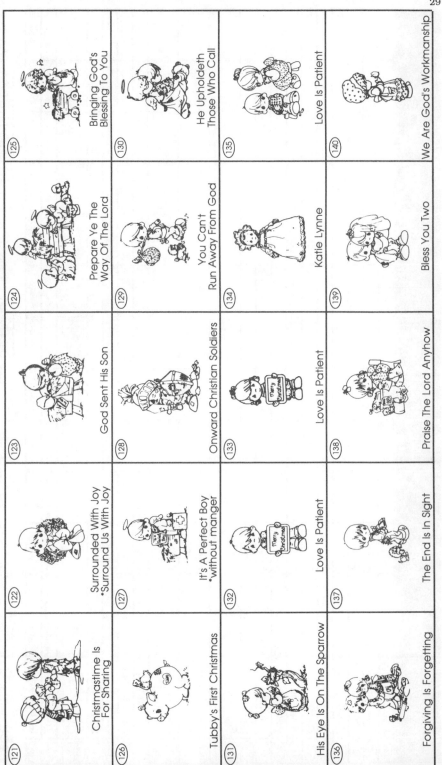

121

Christmastime Is
For Sharing

122

Surrounded With Joy
*Surround Us With Joy

123

God Sent His Son

124

Prepare Ye The
Way Of The Lord

125

Bringing God's
Blessing To You

126

Tubby's First Christmas

127

It's A Perfect Boy
*without manger

128

Onward Christian Soldiers

129

You Can't
Run Away From God

130

He Upholdeth
Those Who Call

131

His Eye Is On The Sparrow

132

Love Is Patient

133

Love Is Patient

134

Katie Lynne

135

Love Is Patient

136

Forgiving Is Forgetting

137

The End Is In Sight

138

Praise The Lord Anyhow

139

Bless You Two

140

We Are God's Workmanship

#	DESCRIPTIVE TITLE	FIG.	PLT.	BELL	MUSC.	ORN.	DOLL	THMBL.	FRAME	CNDL. CLMB.	BOX	NITE LITE
141	Boy with Piggy	E-9259										
142	Boy Angel Wind'g Rainbow	**E-9260**										
143	Boy Graduate with Scroll	**E-9261**										
144	Girl Graduate with Scroll	**E-9262**										
145	Boy & Girl/Horse Costume	**E-9263**										
146	Girl Ironing Clothes	E-9265										
147	Animals	E-9267 (Also see ART CHART Numbers 407, 408, 409, 412, 413 & 414.)										
148	Boy with Dunce Cap	E-9268										
149	Girl with Chicks in Umbrella	E-9273										
150	Girl Angel Making Food	E-9274										
151	Pig	E-9282 / E-9282B										
152	Bunny	E-9282 / E-9282A										
153	Lamb	E-9282 / E-9282C										
154	Boy at Pulpit	**E-9285**										
155	Girl with Lion & Lamb	**E-9287**										
156	Girl Angel w/Sprinkl'g Can	**E-9288**										
157	Boy Angel /Flying Lessons	**E-9289**										
158	Club Meeting	E-0103 / E-0303										
159	Boy Clown Holding Mask	PM-822										
160	Girl Covering Kitten	PM-831										

BOLD = Suspended   *Italics* = Limited Edition   Shaded Area = Retired   Enclosed in a box = Annual

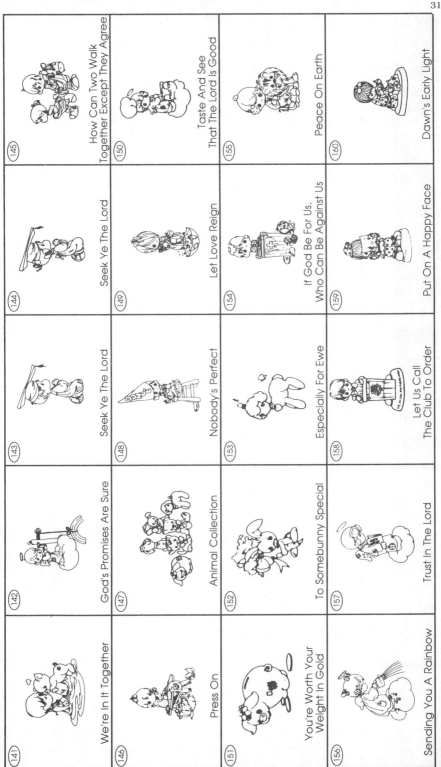

(141) We're In It Together

(142) God's Promises Are Sure

(143) Seek Ye The Lord

(144) Seek Ye The Lord

(145) How Can Two Walk Together Except They Agree

(146) Press On

(147) Animal Collection

(148) Nobody's Perfect

(149) Let Love Reign

(150) Taste And See That The Lord Is Good

(151) You're Worth Your Weight In Gold

(152) To Somebunny Special

(153) Especially For Ewe

(154) If God Be For Us, Who Can Be Against Us

(155) Peace On Earth

(156) Sending You A Rainbow

(157) Trust In The Lord

(158) Let Us Call The Club To Order

(159) Put On A Happy Face

(160) Dawn's Early Light

#	DESCRIPTIVE TITLE	FIG.	PLT.	BELL	MUSC.	ORN.	DOLL	THMBL.	FRAME	CNDL. CLMB.	BOX	NITE LITE
161	Girl with String of Hearts	E-2821 *523283*			112577	112356						
162	Girl Polishing Table	E-2822										
163	Boy Holding Picture Frame	**E-2823**										
164	Girl with Floppy Hat	E-2824										
165	Girl Put'g Bows/Sister's Hair	E-2825										
166	Girl at Table with Dolls	**E-2826**										
167	Girl with Bucket on Head	**E-2827**										
168	Girl/Trunk/Wedding Gown	E-2828										
169	Girl Mailing Snowball	E-2829	101834		112402	112372						
170	Bridesmaid	E-2831										
171	Bride with Flower Girl	E-2832										
172	Groomsman with Frog	E-2836										
173	Angel Carrying Baby	**E-2840**										
174	Baby's First Photo	E-2841										
175	Boy & Girl on Swing		E-2847									
176	Mother Wrapping Bread		E-2848									
177	Baby Collector Doll						E-2851					
178	Baby Figurines	E-2852 (Also see ART CHART Numbers 401-406.)										
179	Happy Anniversary	E-2853										
180	1st Anniversary	E-2854										

BOLD = Suspended *Italics* = Limited Edition Shaded Area = Retired Enclosed in a box = Annual

161	162	163	164	165
You Have Touched So Many Hearts	This Is Your Day To Shine	To God Be The Glory	To A Very Special Mom	To A Very Special Sister
166	167	168	169	170
May Your Birthday Be A Blessing	I Get A Kick Out Of You	Precious Memories	I'm Sending You A White Christmas	Bridesmaid
171	172	173	174	175
God Bless The Bride	Groomsman	Baby's First Step	Baby's First Picture	Love Is Kind
176	177	178	179	180
Loving Thy Neighbor	Kristy	Baby Figurines	God Blessed Our Years Together With So Much Love & Happiness	God Blessed Our Year Together With So Much Love & Happiness

#	DESCRIPTIVE TITLE	FIG.	PLT.	BELL	MUSC.	ORN.	DOLL	THMBL.	FRAME	CNDL. CLMB.	BOX	NITE LITE
181	5th Anniversary	E-2855										
182	10th Anniversary	E-2856										
183	25th Anniversary	E-2857										
184	40th Anniversary	E-2859										
185	50th Anniversary	E-2860										
186	Girl w/Long Hair & Bible	**E-5376**										
187	Girl with Mouse	E-5377										
188	Boy with Harp	**E-5378**				E-5388						
189	Girl with Broom	E-5379 522988										
190	Boy w/Butterfly at Manger	**E-5380**										
191	Boys at Manger	**E-5381**										
192	Deluxe 4-Piece Nativity	**E-5382**										
193	"1984" Girl in Choir	E-5383		E-5393		E-5387						
194	Boy Angel with Candle	**E-5385**										
195	Girl Angel Praying	**E-5386**										
196	Boy in Choir					**E-5389**						
197	Girl in Scarf & Cap					**E-5390**						
198	Girl with Gift					**E-5391**						
199	Angel Behind Rainbow											16020
200	Carollers with Puppy				E-5394							

BOLD = Suspended   *Italics* = Limited Edition   Shaded Area = Retired   Enclosed in a box = Annual

* = Special Inspirational Title or piece derived from a portion of the line drawing
♦ = Two Year Collectible

181

182

183

184

185

186
God Blessed Our Years Together
With So Much Love & Happiness

187
God Blessed Our Years Together
With So Much Love & Happiness

188
God Blessed Our Years Together
With So Much Love & Happiness

189
God Blessed Our Years Together
With So Much Love & Happiness

190
God Blessed Our Years Together
With So Much Love & Happiness

186
May Your Christmas
Be Blessed

187
Love Is Kind

188
Joy To The World

189
Isn't He Precious

190
A Monarch Is Born

191
His Name Is Jesus

192
For God So Loved The World

193
Wishing You A
Merry Christmas

194
Oh Worship The Lord

195
Oh Worship The Lord

196
Peace On Earth

197
May God Bless You With
A Perfect Holiday Season

198
Love Is Kind

199
God Bless You
With Rainbows

200
Wishing You A
Merry Christmas

#	DESCRIPTIVE TITLE	FIG.	PLT.	BELL	MUSC.	ORN.	DOLL	THMBL.	FRAME	CNDL. CLMB.	BOX	NITE LITE
201	Nativity Scene		*E-5395*									
202	Boy Pull Sled w/Girl & Tree		E-5396									
203	Boy Jogger						*E-5397*					
204	Girl with Present & Kitten	**E-6613**										
205	Girl with Dues Bank	E-0104										
		E-0404										
206	Boy Angel with Flashlight	PM-841										
207	Boy with Racing Cup	PM-842										
208	Ringbearer	E-2833										
209	Flower Girl	E-2835										
210	Junior Bridesmaid	E-2845										
211	Boy Sitting with Teddy	**100021**										
212	Boy/Bow & Arrow/Cloud	100056										
213	Girl Kneel/Church Window	100064										
214	Two Girls with Flowers	100072				113956						
215	Baseball Player with Bat	100110										
216	Ballerina	100129				102423*						
217	Mother with Babies	100137										
218	Tennis Girl	100161				**102458***						
219	Kids in Boat	100250				522937						
220	Girl in Old Bath Tub	100277				112380						

BOLD = Suspended   *Italics* = Limited Edition   Shaded Area = Retired   Enclosed in a box = Annual

(201)

Unto Us A Child Is Born

(202)

The Wonder Of Christmas

(203)

(204)

God Sends The Gift
Of His Love

(205)

Join In On The Blessings

(206)

God's Ray Of Mercy

(207)

Trust In The Lord
To The Finish

(208)

Timmy

(209)

Flower Girl

(210)

Junior Bridesmaid

(211)

To My Favorite Paw

(212)

Sending My Love

(213)

Ringbearer

(214)

To My Forever Friend

(215)

Lord I'm Coming Home

(216)

Lord, Keep Me On My Toes
*without bar

(217)

The Joy Of The Lord
Is My Strength

(218)

Serving The Lord
*Serve With A Smile

(219)

Friends Never Drift Apart

(220)

He Cleansed My Soul

#	DESCRIPTIVE TITLE	FIG.	PLT.	BELL	MUSC.	ORN.	DOLL	THMBL.	FRAME	CNDL. CLMB.	BOX	NITE LITE
221	Baby w/Bunny & Turtle	520934			100285							
222	Tennis Boy	100293				102431*						
223	Boy Kneel/Church Window	102229										
224	Girl Holding Cross	103632				522953						
225	Girl Making Heart Quilt	12009						12254				
226	Girl by Fence	12068	12106		408735•		408786•					
227	Girl with Crossed Arms	12076	12114		408743•		408794•	100641				
228	Girl with Hands Behind Her	12084	12122		408751•		408808•					
229	Girl w/Scarf & Hat/Birds	12092	12130		408778•		408816•					
230	Angel Boy in Devil's Suit	**12149**										
231	Boy Playing Piano				12165							
232	Girl Playing Triangle	12173										
233	Nun	**12203**										
234	Angel Cutting Baby's Hair	**12211**										
235	Mini Clowns	12238 (Also see ART CHART Numbers 416-419)										
	• Girl Clown w/Balloon					15822*		100668 (Set of the two with balls)				
	• Boy Clown w/Cap & Ball					15830**						
236	Clown Holding Balloons	12262										
237	Policeman Writing Ticket	**12297**				102377*						
238	Teacher w/Report Card	12300										
239	Boy & Girl/Sandcastle	12319										
240	Mary Knitting Booties	**12343**										

BOLD = Suspended   *Italics* = Limited Edition   Shaded Area = Retired   Enclosed in a box = Annual

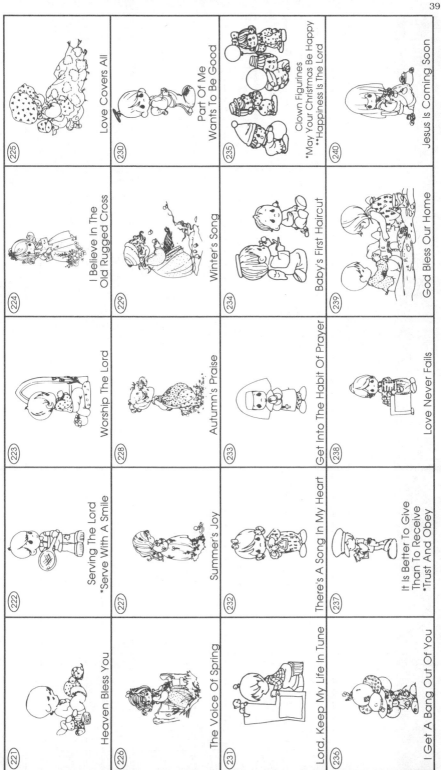

(221) Heaven Bless You	(222) Serving The Lord *Serve With A Smile	(223) Worship The Lord	(224) I Believe In The Old Rugged Cross	(225) Love Covers All
(226) The Voice Of Spring	(227) Summer's Joy	(228) Autumn's Praise	(229) Winter's Song	(230) Part Of Me Wants To Be Good
(231) Lord, Keep My Life In Tune	(232) There's A Song In My Heart	(233) Get Into The Habit Of Prayer	(234) Baby's First Haircut	(235) Clown Figurines *May Your Christmas Be Happy **Happiness Is The Lord
(236) I Get A Bang Out Of You	(237) It Is Better To Give Than To Receive *Trust And Obey	(238) Love Never Fails	(239) God Bless Our Home	(240) Jesus Is Coming Soon

#	DESCRIPTIVE TITLE	FIG.	PLT.	BELL	MUSC.	ORN.	DOLL	THMBL.	FRAME	CNDL. CLMB.	BOX	NITE LITE
241	Angels Make Snowman	**12351**										
242	Boy Playing Banjo	12378										
243	Girl Playing Harmonica	12386										
244	Boy Playing Trumpet/Dog	12394										
245	Two Angels Sawing Star				12408							
246	Boy in Airplane					12416						
247	Boy Angel						12424					
248	Girl Angel						12432					
249	5th Anniversary Piece	12440										
250	Girl Clown w/Bskt/Goose	12459				112364						
251	Clown with Dog on Mud	12467										
252	Baby Boy						12475					
253	Baby Girl						12483					
254	Boy Tangled in Christmas Lights	15482				15849						
255	Mother Goose/Bonnet/ Babes	15490				15857*						
256	Boy Clown Holding Jack-in-the-Box				15504	113972						
257	Baby Boy Holding Bottle	15539				15903						
258	Baby Girl Holding Bottle	15547				15911						
259	Angel with Holly Wreath	15881		15873		15768						
260	Mother with Cookie Sheet	15776						15865				

BOLD = Suspended   *Italics* = Limited Edition   Shaded Area = Retired   Enclosed in a box = Annual

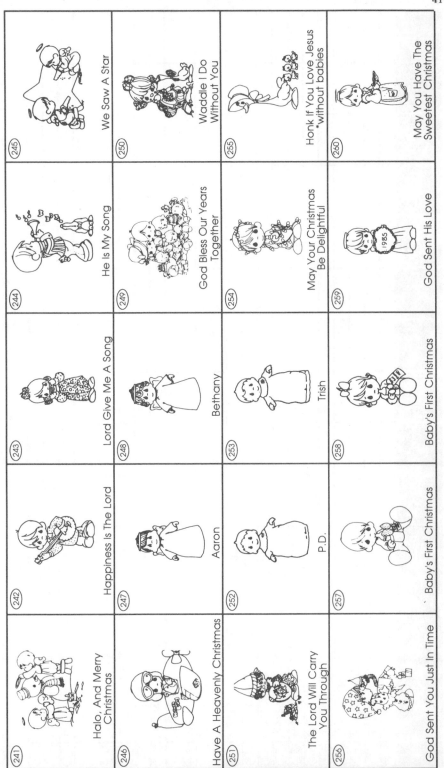

241 Halo, And Merry Christmas	242 Happiness Is The Lord	243 Lord Give Me A Song	244 He Is My Song	245 We Saw A Star
246 Have A Heavenly Christmas	247 Aaron	248 Bethany	249 God Bless Our Years Together	250 Waddle I Do Without You
251 The Lord Will Carry You Through	252 P.D.	253 Trish	254 May Your Christmas Be Delightful	255 Honk If You Love Jesus *without babies
256 God Sent You Just In Time	257 Baby's First Christmas	258 Baby's First Christmas	259 God Sent His Love	260 May You Have The Sweetest Christmas

#	DESCRIPTIVE TITLE	FIG.	PLT.	BELL	MUSC.	ORN.	DOLL	THMBL.	FRAME	CNDL. CLMB.	BOX	NITE LITE
261	Father Reading Bible	15784										
262	Boy Sitting Listen to Story	15792										
263	Girl with Ornament	15806										
264	Christmas Tree				15814							
265	Boy Angel								**E-7168**			
266	Girl Angel								**E-7169**			
267	Angel Pushing Buggy	**16012**										
268	Bridesmaid with Kitten	E-2834										
269	Groom	E-2837										
270	Clown Sitting on Ball	12270										
271	Boy Angel on Cloud	**12335**										
272	Mom & Dad w/Girl/ Adoption	100145										
273	Mom & Dad w/Boy/ Adoption	100153										
274	Boy with Football	100188				111120						
275	Boy Standing in Ink Spot	100269										
276	Pilgrim & Indian w/Turkey	**100544**										
277	Boy & Girl in Box				101702	102350 112399 520233						
278	Angel with Black Lamb	102261				102288						
279	Three Mini Animals	102296										
280	Girl with Muff	102342		102318		102326		102334				

BOLD = Suspended   *Italics* = Limited Edition   Shaded Area = Retired   Enclosed in a box = Annual

(265) My Guardian Angel	(264) Silent Night	(263) God Gave His Best	(262) Tell Me A Story	(261) The Story of God's Love
(270) Lord Keep Me On The Ball	(269) Groom	(268) Sharing Our Joy Together	(267) Baby's First Trip	(266) My Guardian Angel
(275) Help Lord, I'm In A Spot	(274) I'm A Possibility	(273) God Bless The Day We Found You	(272) God Bless The Day We Found You	(271) You Can Fly
(280) Wishing You A Cozy Christmas	(279) Mini Animal Figurines	(278) Shepherd Of Love	(277) Our First Christmas Together	(276) Brotherly Love

#	DESCRIPTIVE TITLE	FIG.	PLT.	BELL	MUSC.	ORN.	DOLL	THMBL.	FRAME	CNDL. CLMB.	BOX	NITE LITE
281	Fireman Holding Puppy	102393				102385						
282	Nurse with Potted Plant	102482				102407						
283	Rocking Horse					102474						
284	Husband/Wife/Puppy/ & Cookies	**102490**										
285	Baby Girl w/Candy Cane					102504						
286	Baby Boy w/Candy Cane					102512						
287	Clown on Elephant				102520							
288	Boy Angel w/B'day Cake	**102962**										
289	Boy Clown						100455					
290	Girl Clown						100463					
291	Doll w/Stand						102253					
292	Uncle Sam Holding Bible with Dog	102938										
293	Girl Holding Lamb	PM-851										
294	Boy with Lamb & Book	PM-852										
295	Girl with Embroidery Hoop/ Bird	E-0006 E-0106				PM-864						
296	Teddy/Caboose - For Baby	15938										
297	Lamb - Age 1	15946										
298	Seal - Age 2	15962										
299	Pig - Age 3	15954										
300	Elephant - Age 4	15970										

BOLD = Suspended   *Italics* = Limited Edition   Shaded Area = Retired   Enclosed in a box = Annual

(281) Love Rescued Me	(282) Angel Of Mercy	(283) Rocking Horse	(284) Sharing Our Christmas Together	(285) Baby's First Christmas
(286) Baby's First Christmas	(287) Let's Keep In Touch	(288) It's The Birthday Of A King	(289) Bong Bong	(290) Candy
(291) Connie	(292) God Bless America	(293) The Lord Is My Shepherd	(294) I Love To Tell The Story	(295) Birds Of A Feather Collect Together
(296) May Your Birthday Be Warm	(297) Happy Birthday Little Lamb	(298) God Bless You On Your Birthday	(299) Heaven Bless Your Special Day	(300) May Your Birthday Be Gigantic

#	DESCRIPTIVE TITLE	FIG.	PLT.	BELL	MUSC.	ORN.	DOLL	THMBL.	FRAME	CNDL. CLMB.	BOX	NITE LITE
301	Lion - Age 5	15989										
302	Giraffe - Age 6	15997										
303	Clown with Pull Rope	16004										
304	Clown with Drum	B-0001										
305	Praying Grandma	PM-861										
306	1986 Dated Reindeer					102466						
307	Nativity Set w/Cassette	104000										
308	Lamb & Bunny										**E-9266**	
	Lamb & Skunk											
309	Dog										**E-9283**	
	Cat											
310	Baby Boy								**12033**			
311	Baby Girl								12041			
312	Complete Wedding Party	E-2838										
313	Bride	E-2846						100633*				
314	Birthday Boy	12157										
315	Girl with Piano				12580							
316	Girl with Flowers & Deer	100048										
317	Girl/Boy Bandaging Heart	100080										
318	Girl Graduate	106208										
319	Girl/Crutches/Bible	107999										
320	Boy in Car	PM-862										

BOLD = Suspended   *Italics* = Limited Edition   Shaded Area = Retired   Enclosed in a box = Annual

301 — This Day Is Something To Roar About

302 — Keep Looking Up

303 — Bless The Days Of Our Youth

304 — Our Club Can't Be Beat

305 — Grandma's Prayer

306 — Reindeer

307 — Come Let Us Adore Him

308 — I'm Falling For Somebunny, Our Love Is Heaven-Scent

309 — Forever Friends

310 — God's Precious Gift

311 — God's Precious Gift

312 — This Is The Day Which The Lord Hath Made

313 — Bride *The Lord Bless You And Keep You

314 — This Is The Day The Lord Has Made

315 — Lord, Keep My Life In Tune

316 — To My Deer Friend

317 — He's The Healer Of Broken Hearts

318 — Congratulations, Princess

319 — He Walks With Me

320 — I'm Following Jesus

48

#	DESCRIPTIVE TITLE	FIG.	PLT.	BELL	MUSC.	ORN.	DOLL	THMBL.	FRAME	CNDL. CLMB.	BOX	NITE LITE
321	Boy Painting Valentine	PM-873										
322	Girl w/Crayon/Valentine	PM-874										
323	Girl with Sick Bear	100102										
324	Girl on Scale	·100196										
325	Parents of the Groom	100498										
326	Parents of the Bride	100501										
327	Girl with Skunk	100528										
328	Boy w/Gardening Mother	100536										
329	Girl at Gate to Heaven	101826										
330	Clown Balancing	101842				113964*						
331	Clowns on Unicycle	101850										
332	Bridal Arch	102369										
333	Boy with Hat & Fish	103497				114006						
334	Boy Graduate	106194										
335	Raccoon Holding Fish	BC-861										
336	Girl Sending Package to Friend	E-0007 E-0107										
337	Nativity w/Backdrop/Video	104523										
338	Shepherd and Lambs	103004										
339	Nurse Doll						12491					
340	Girl/Cat/Bird Cage	100226										

BOLD = Suspended   Italics = Limited Edition   Shaded Area = Retired   Enclosed in a box = Annual

(325) God Bless Our Family	(324) The Spirit Is Willing But The Flesh Is Weak	(323) Make Me A Blessing	(322) Loving You Dear Valentine	(321) Loving You Dear Valentine
(330) Smile Along The Way *without base & ball	(329) No Tears Past The Gate	(328) I Picked A Very Special Mom	(327) Scent From Above	(326) God Bless Our Family
(335) Fishing For Friends	(334) God Bless You Graduate	(333) My Love Will Never Let You Go	(332) Wedding Arch	(331) Lord Help Us Keep Our Act Together
(340) The Lord Giveth & The Lord Taketh Away	(339) Angie, The Angel Of Mercy	(338) We Belong To The Lord	(337) Dealer's Only Nativity	(336) Sharing Is Universal

#	DESCRIPTIVE TITLE	FIG.	PLT.	BELL	MUSC.	ORN.	DOLL	THMBL.	FRAME	CNDL. CLMB.	BOX	NITE LITE
341	Kids around Lamp Post		102954		109746*	523062*						
342	Baby Boy/Tub	102970										
343	Boy Giving Girl Ring	104019										
344	Boy Mending Hobby Horse	104027										
345	Girl Cheerleader	104035				113999						
346	Girl Clown with Books	104396										
347	Bear on a Sled					104515						
348	Baby Boy/Wood Tub	104817										
349	Girl Angel on Stool	104825										
350	Boy Reading Scroll	105635										
351	Dentist/Patient/Pull Tooth	105813										
352	Elephant Showering Mouse	105945										
353	Boy with Donkey	106151										
354	Schoolboy Clown	106216										
355	Baby Boy/Dog	109231										
356	Baby Girl/Rocking Horse					109401						
357	Baby Boy/Rocking Horse					109428						
358	Girl with Ice Cream	109754	523801*									
359	Family Thanksgiving Set	109762										
360	Girl with Present	110930		109835		109770		109843				

BOLD = Suspended   *Italics* = Limited Edition   Shaded Area = Retired   Enclosed in a box = Annual

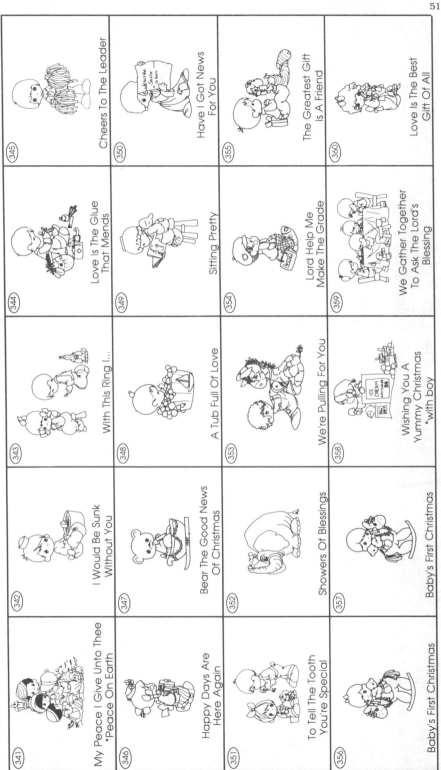

341

My Peace I Give Unto Thee
*Peace On Earth

342

I Would Be Sunk
Without You

343

With This Ring I....

344

Love Is The Glue
That Mends

345

Cheers To The Leader

346

Happy Days Are
Here Again

347

Bear The Good News
Of Christmas

348

A Tub Full Of Love

349

Sitting Pretty

350

Have I Got News
For You

351

To Tell The Tooth
You're Special

352

Showers Of Blessings

353

We're Pulling For You

354

Lord Help Me
Make The Grade

355

The Greatest Gift
Is A Friend

356

Baby's First Christmas

357

Baby's First Christmas

358

Wishing You A
Yummy Christmas
*with boy

359

We Gather Together
To Ask The Lord's
Blessing

360

Love Is The Best
Gift Of All

#	DESCRIPTIVE TITLE	FIG.	PLT.	BELL	MUSC.	ORN.	DOLL	THMBL.	FRAME	CNDL. CLMB.	BOX	NITE LITE
361	Grandma on a Sled	109819										
362	4 Piece Large Nativity	111333										
363	Baby Girl/Wood Tub	112313										
364	Clown with Cymbals	B-0102 B-0002										
365	'84 Giveaway Medallion		12246 (Medallion)									
366	Girl Feeding Lamb	PM-871										
367	Girl/Doll/Sleigh	109983				521574*						
368	Girl/Plant in Snow	109991										
369	Girl with Kite	110019										
370	Girl with Umbrella	110027										
371	Girl with Potted Plant	110035										
372	Girl/Dress Up as Bride	110043										
373	Girl With Pearl	102903										
374	Boy Holding Bluebird	E-7156R										
375	Boy Waiting /Seed/Grow	PM-872										
376	Brass Filigree Giveaway Ornament/Kids					PM-009						
377	Cowboy/Fence/Guitar	105821										
378	Groom/Trunk/Bride	106755										
379	Couple on Couch with Wedding Album	106763										
380	Anniversary Couple with Dog	106798										

BOLD = Suspended   *Italics* = Limited Edition   Shaded Area = Retired   Enclosed in a box = Annual

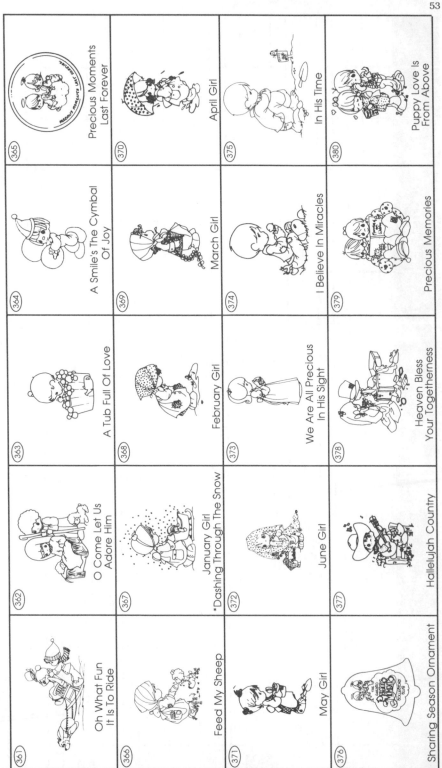

361 Oh What Fun It Is To Ride

362 O Come Let Us Adore Him

363 A Tub Full Of Love

364 A Smile's The Cymbal Of Joy

365 Precious Moments Last Forever

366 Feed My Sheep

367 January Girl *Dashing Through The Snow

368 February Girl

369 March Girl

370 April Girl

371 May Girl

372 June Girl

373 We Are All Precious In His Sight

374 I Believe In Miracles

375 In His Time

376 Sharing Season Ornament

377 Hallelujah Country

378 Heaven Bless Your Togetherness

379 Precious Memories

380 Puppy Love Is From Above

#	DESCRIPTIVE TITLE	FIG.	PLT.	BELL	MUSC.	ORN.	DOLL	THMBL.	FRAME	CNDL. CLMB.	BOX	NITE LITE
381	Girl Holding Poppy Plant	106836										
382	Girl Sewing Boy's Pants	106844										
383	Boy with Barbells	109487										
384	Clown Angel with Flowers	109584										
385	Boy/Basket/Chick	109924										
386	Girl with Hearts in Cloud	109967										
387	Boy with Flower	109975										
388	Girl Holding Bunny	109886										
389	Girl with Plunger	111155										
390	Girl with Flower	112143										
391	Boy with Broken Heart	114014										
392	Couple w/Dog & Puppies	114022										
393	Leopard - Age 7	109479										
394	Ostrich - Age 8	109460										
395	Skunk & Mouse	105953										
396	Boy with Braces & Dog	115479										
397	Girl/Balloons/Satchel	115231										
398	Mouse in Sugar Bowl	BC-871										
399	Girl/Flowerpot/Sunflower	E-0108				520349						
		E-0008										
400	Kitten Hanging on Wreath					520292						

BOLD = Suspended   *Italics* = Limited Edition   Shaded Area = Retired

* = Special Inspirational Title or piece derived from a portion of the line drawing

Enclosed in a box = Annual

381. Happy Birthday Poppy

382. Sew In Love

383. Believe The Impossible

384. Happiness Divine

385. Wishing You A Basket Full Of Blessings

386. Sending You My Love

387. Mommy, I Love You

388. Wishing You A Happy Easter

389. Faith Takes The Plunge

390. Mommy, I Love You

391. This Too Shall Pass

392. The Good Lord Has Blessed Us Tenfold

393. Wishing You Grrr-eatness

394. Isn't Eight Just Great

395. Brighten Someone's Day

396. Blessed Are They That Overcome

397. You Are My Main Event

398. Hi Sugar!

399. A Growing Love

400. Hang On For The Holly Days

#	DESCRIPTIVE TITLE	FIG.	PLT.	BELL	MUSC.	ORN.	DOLL	THMBL.	FRAME	CNDL. CLMB.	BOX	NITE LITE
401	Baby Boy Standing	E-2852A										
402	Baby Girl/Bow Hair	E-2852B										
403	Baby Boy Sitting	E-2852C										
404	Baby Girl Clapping Hands	E-2852D										
405	Baby Boy Crawling	E-2852E										
406	Baby Girl Lying Down	E-2852F										
407	Dog with Slippers	E-9267B										
408	Bunny with Carrot	E-9267C										
409	Lamb with Bird on Back	E-9267E										
410	Christmas Wreath					111465 (Wreath)						
411	Kids on Cloud under Dome	E-7350										
412	Pig with Patches	E-9267F										
413	Cat with Bow Tie	E-9267D										
414	Teddy Bear	E-9267A										
415	Retailer's Wreath Bell			112348								
416	Boy Balancing Ball	12238A										
417	Girl Holding Balloon	12238B										
418	Boy Bending over Ball	12238C										
419	Girl with Flower Pot	12238D										
420	Rhino with Bird	104418										

BOLD = Suspended   *Italics* = Limited Edition   Shaded Area = Retired   Enclosed in a box = Annual

* = Special Inspirational Title or piece derived from a portion of the line drawing

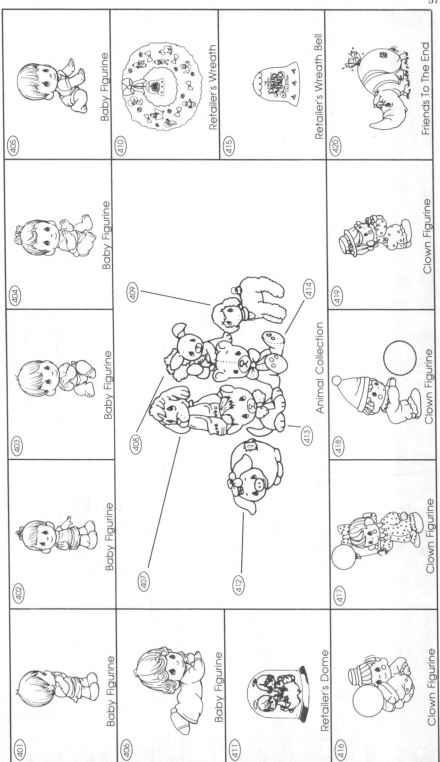

401

402 Baby Figurine

403 Baby Figurine

404 Baby Figurine

405 Baby Figurine

406 Baby Figurine

407

408

409

410 Retailer's Wreath

411 Retailer's Dome

412

413

414

415 Retailer's Wreath Bell

416 Clown Figurine

417 Clown Figurine

418 Clown Figurine

419 Clown Figurine

420 Friends To The End

Animal Collection

58

#	DESCRIPTIVE TITLE	FIG.	PLT.	BELL	MUSC.	ORN.	DOLL	THMBL.	FRAME	CNDL. CLMB.	BOX	NITE LITE
421	Girl Holding Doll with Dog	105643										
422	Wreath Contestant Orn.					PM-008						
423	Girl with Kitten	109800										
424	Girl with Puppy in Basket	110051										
425	Girl in Swimming Pool	110078										
426	Girl Balancing Books	110086										
427	Girl with Pumpkins	110094										
428	Girl in Pilgrim Suit	110108										
429	Girl with Christmas Candle	110116										
430	Girl Adding Seasoning	111163										
431	Bunnies	115274 522996*										
432	Baby Boy in Sleigh					115282 523194						
433	Couple with Gifts	115290										
434	Girl with Calendar & Clock	115339		115304		115320 520241 523208						
435	Baby Girl in Sleigh					520276		115312				
436	Puppy in Stocking											
437	Angel w/Newspaper/Dog	520357										
438	Girl Decorating Reindeer	522317	520284									
439	Girl Painting Butterfly	PM-881										
440	Pippin Popping out of a Birthday Cake	B-0003 B-0103										

BOLD = Suspended   *Italics* = Limited Edition   Shaded Area [box] = Retired

* = Special Inspirational Title or piece derived from a portion of the line drawing

Enclosed in a box = Annual

(421) Something's Missing When You're Not Around	(422) Wreath Contestant Ornament	(423) Meowie Christmas	(424) July Girl	(425) August Girl
(426) September Girl	(427) October Girl	(428) November Girl	(429) December Girl	(430) 'Tis The Season
(431) Some Bunny's Sleeping *Some Bunnies Sleeping	(432) Baby's First Christmas	(433) Our First Christmas Together	(434) Time To Wish You A Merry Christmas	(435) Baby's First Christmas
(436) You Are My Gift Come True	(437) Jesus The Savior Is Born	(438) Merry Christmas, Deer	(439) God Bless You For Touching My Life	(440) The Sweetest Club Around

60

#	DESCRIPTIVE TITLE	FIG.	PLT.	BELL	MUSC.	ORN.	DOLL	THMBL.	FRAME	CNDL. CLMB.	BOX	NITE LITE
441	Bunny with Stuffed Carrot	BC-881										
442	Boy/Dog/Trash Can	PM-882										
443	Girl with Lily	522376										
444	Girl/Puppies/Box	C-0109				522961						
		C-0009										
445	Boy Tangled in Lights	558125 (Art Plas Stocking Hanger)										
446	Bride Holding Up Dress	520799										
447	Angel with Butterfly Net	520640										
448	Girl Holding Trophy	520829										
449	Mouse Wiping Clown's Tear	520632										
450	Boy w/Newspaper over Head	520683										
451	Kangaroo/Baby in Pouch	521175										
452	Grandpa/Cane/Dog	520810										
453	Two Girls Having Tea Party	520748										
454	Boy Holding Girl up to Fountain	520675										
455	Girl with Hen & Easter Egg	520667										
456	Dog Pulling Boy's Fish'g Line	520721										
457	Indian Couple in Canoe	520772										
458	Nurse X-raying Boy's Heart	520624										
459	Boy Proposing to Girl	520845										
460	Bride & Groom in Car	520780					521558* 525324*					

BOLD = Suspended   *Italics* = Limited Edition   Shaded Area = Retired   Enclosed in a box = Annual

* = Special Inspirational Title or piece derived from a portion of the line drawing   ◆ = Two Year Collectible

(441) Somebunny Cares	(442) You Just Cannot Chuck A Good Friendship	(443) His Love Will Shine On You	(444) Always Room For One More	(445) Stocking Hanger
(446) Someday My Love	(447) I'm So Glad You Fluttered Into My Life	(448) You Are My Number One	(449) A Friend Is Someone Who Cares	(450) Sending You Showers Of Blessings
(451) Hello World!	(452) We Need A Good Friend Through The Ruff Times	(453) Friendship Hits The Spot	(454) Your Love Is So Uplifting	(455) Eggspecially For You
(456) Just A Line To Wish You A Happy Day	(457) Many Moons In Same Canoe, Blessum You	(458) My Heart Is Exposed With Love	(459) Wishing You A Perfect Choice	(460) Wishing You Roads Of Happiness *Our First Christmas Together

#	DESCRIPTIVE TITLE	FIG.	PLT.	BELL	MUSC.	ORN.	DOLL	THMBL.	FRAME	CNDL. CLMB.	BOX	NITE LITE
461	Boy w/Baby Feeding Dog	520705										
462	Girl w/Paint & Ladder	520802										
463	Orphan Girl	520853										
464	Boy at Crossroads	520756										
465	Two Puppies	520764										
466	Bridal Couple/Candle	520837										
467	Girl with Chalkboard	520861										
468	Angel w/ Baby Name Book	523097										
469	Teddy in Rocker	522856										
470	Puppy Resting on Elbow					520462						
471	Boy/Fallen Christmas Tree	522112				521590*						
472	Boy Dining with Turkey	522031										
473	Boy Playing Football/Dog	522023										
474	Boy & Girl on Motorcycle	522201										
475	Girl with Lamp Post				521507							
476	Girl on Telephone	521477										
477	Girl w/Snowball Tied with Ribbon					521302						
478	Boy/Pkg./Puppy & Bat	522120										
479	Family Christmas Scene		523003			523704						
480	Boy by Tree Stump	521949										

BOLD = Suspended   *Italics* = Limited Edition   Shaded Area = Retired   Enclosed in a box = Annual

* = Special Inspirational Title or piece derived from a portion of the line drawing

◆ = Two Year Collectible

63

465 Puppy Love	464 Jesus Is The Only Way	463 I Belong To The Lord	462 My Days Are Blue Without You	461 Baby's First Pet
470 Christmas Is Ruff Without You	469 Have A Beary Merry Christmas	468 Jesus Is The Sweetest Name I Know	467 Sharing Begins In The Heart	466 The Lord Is Your Light To Happiness
475 The Light Of The World Is Jesus	474 Bon Voyage!	473 May Your Life Be Blessed With Touchdowns	472 Thank You Lord For Everything	471 Don't Let The Holidays Get You Down *without axe
480 Wishing You A Cozy Season	479 May Your Christmas Be A Happy Home	478 Wishing You A Very Successful Season	477 May All Your Christmases Be White	476 Tell It To Jesus

#	DESCRIPTIVE TITLE	FIG.	PLT.	BELL	MUSC.	ORN.	DOLL	THMBL.	FRAME	CNDL. CLMB.	BOX	NITE LITE
481	Angel on Cloud w/Manger	522252										
482	Girl Playing Violin	522546		522821		522848						
483	Angel Holding Commandments	521868						522554				
484	Giraffe with Baby Bear	522260										
485	Girl with Ballot Box	PM-891										
486	Boy Pushing Lawn Mower	PM-892										
487	Teddy Bear with Balloon	B-0104										
		B-0004										
488	Teddy w/ Bee & Beehive	BC-891										
489	Girl at Table with Figurine	C-0110										
		C-0010										
490	Girl with Fan	523526										
491	Angel outside Chapel	523011										
492	Girls with Flower	521817										
		525049										
493	Ballerina	520551										
494	Girl on Hobby Horse	521205										
495	B&G Kiss'g under Mistletoe	523747										
496	Girl Wearing Boxing Gloves	521396										
497	Mom-To-Be w/Baby Book	523453										
498	Boy with Kite	521957										
499	Girl on Roller Skates	521280				521566*						
500	Boy & Girl in Garden	522090										

BOLD = Suspended   *Italics* = Limited Edition   Shaded Area = Retired   Enclosed in a box = Annual

* = Special Inspirational Title or piece derived from a portion of the line drawing   ◆ = Two Year Collectible

64

(481) He Is The Star Of The Morning

(482) Oh Holy Night

(483) The Greatest Of These Is Love

(484) To Be With You Is Uplifting

(485) You Will Always Be My Choice

(486) Mow Power To Ya

(487) Have A Beary Special Birthday

(488) Can't Bee Hive Myself Without You

(489) My Happiness

(490) I'm A Precious Moments Fan

(491) There's A Christian Welcome Here

(492) Good Friends Are Forever

(493) Lord, Turn My Life Around

(494) Hope You're Up And On The Trail Again

(495) Blessings From Above

(496) Faith Is A Victory

(497) The Good Lord Always Delivers

(498) High Hopes

(499) Happy Trip *Glide Through The Holidays

(500) There Shall Be Showers Of Blessings

#	DESCRIPTIVE TITLE	FIG.	PLT.	BELL	MUSC.	ORN.	DOLL	THMBL.	FRAME	CNDL. CLMB.	BOX	NITE LITE
501	Gorilla and Parrot	521043										
502	Girl Sweep Dust under Rug	521779										
503	Girl w/Account Bks & Glue	521450										
504	Kneeling Girl w/Bouquet	522287										
505	Girl with Apple	521310										
506	Girl Holding Bible & Cross	523496										
507	Girl/Sleep'g Chick in Egg	524522										
508	Boy Pull Wagon/Lily & Girl	521892										
509	Girl/Valentine behind Back	523518										
510	Boy Whispering to Girl	521841										
511	Girl w/Letters "Y" "O" "U"	521418										
512	Fireplace with Stockings	524883										
513	Teddy Bear in Package	524875										
514	Mouse on Cheese/Kitten	524484										
515	Girl and Melting Snowman	524913										
516	Baby Girl with Pie					523771						
517	Baby Boy with Pie					523798						
518	Nurse at Desk w/Clock	523739										
519	Girl with Book and Candle	523836		523828		523852		523844				
520	Crying Girls Hugging	521183										

BOLD = Suspended *Italics* = Limited Edition Shaded Area = Retired Enclosed in a box = Annual

* = Special Inspirational Title or piece derived from a portion of the line drawing

♦ = Two Year Collectible

(501)	(502)	(503)	(504)	(505)
To My Favorite Fan	Sweep All Your Worries Away	Lord, Help Me Stick To My Job	Thinking Of You Is What I Really Like To Do	Yield Not To Temptation
(506)	(507)	(508)	(509)	(510)
This Day Has Been Made In Heaven	Always In His Care	Easter's On Its Way	God Is Love Dear Valentine	Love Is From Above
(511)	(512)	(513)	(514)	(515)
I'll Never Stop Loving You	Christmas Fireplace	Happy Birthday Dear Jesus	Not A Creature Was Stirring	We're Going To Miss You
(516)	(517)	(518)	(519)	(520)
Baby's First Christmas	Baby's First Christmas	Time Heals	Once Upon A Holy Night	That's What Friends Are For

#	DESCRIPTIVE TITLE	FIG.	PLT.	BELL	MUSC.	ORN.	DOLL	THMBL.	FRAME	CNDL. CLMB.	BOX	NITE LITE
521	Kitten with Ornament					520497						

BOLD = Suspended   *Italics* = Limited Edition   Shaded Area = Retired   Enclosed in a box = Annual

* = Special Inspirational Title or piece derived from a portion of the line drawing

= Two Year Collectible

69

Wishing You A
Purr-fect Holiday

521

NOTES

GREENBOOK ALPHA-LOG

The GREENBOOK ALPHA-LOG lists PRECIOUS MOMENTS Inspirational Titles alphabetically, cross-referencing the Descriptive Title, GREENBOOK ART CHART Number, and Enesco Item Number for each figurine, plate, bell, musical, ornament, doll, thimble, frame, candle climber, box, and nite lite with that Inspirational Title. In addition, it is noted if each piece is an Annual, a Two-Year Collectible, a Limited Edition, Retired, or Suspended.

INSPIRATIONAL TITLE	DESCRIPTIVE TITLE	#	FIG.	PLT.	BELL	MUSC.	ORN.	DOLL	THMBL.	FRAME	CNDL. CLMB.	BOX	NITE LITE
A Friend Is Someone Who Cares	Mouse Wiping Tears	449	520632										
A Growing Love	Girl/Flowerpot/Sunflwr.	399	E-0108				520349						
			E-0008										
A Monarch Is Born	Boy/Butterfly/Manger	190	**E-5380**										
A Smile's The Cymbal Of Joy	Clown with Cymbals	364	B-0102										
			B-0002										
A Tub Full Of Love	Baby Girl/Wood Tub	363	112313										
A Tub Full Of Love	Baby Boy/Wood Tub	348	104817										
Aaron	Boy Angel	247						12424					
Always In His Care	Girl/Chick in Egg	507	524522										
Always Room For One More	Girl/Box/Puppies	444	C-0009				522961						
			C-0109										
Angel Of Mercy	Nurse w/Potted Plant	282	102482				102407						
Angie, The Angel Of Mercy	Nurse Doll	339						12491					
Animal Collection	Animals	147	E-9267 (For A-F see ART CHART Numbers 407, 408, 409, 412, 413, & 414.)										
April Girl	Girl with Umbrella	370	110027										
August Girl	Girl in Pool	425	110078										
Autumn's Praise	Girl/Hands Behind Her	228	12084	12122		408751♦		408808♦					
Baby Figurines		178	E-2852 (For A-F see ART CHART Numbers 401-406.)										
Baby's First Christmas	Baby Boy Hold Bottle	257	15539				15903						
Baby's First Christmas	Boy w/Candy Cane	286					102512						
Baby's First Christmas	Boy Holding Block	95					**E-2372**						
Baby's First Christmas	Baby Girl w/Bottle	258	15547				15911						
Baby's First Christmas	Baby/Chms. Stocking	89					**E-2362**						
Baby's First Christmas	Girl w/Candy Cane	285					102504						
Baby's First Christmas	Boy with Teddy	1					**E-5631**						
Baby's First Christmas	Girl with Bunny	2					**E-5632**						
Baby's First Christmas	Girl/Rocking Horse	356					109401						
Baby's First Christmas	Boy/Rocking Horse	357					109428						
Baby's First Christmas	Boy in Sleigh	432					115282						
							523194						
Baby's First Christmas	Girl in Sleigh	435					520241						
							523208						
Baby's First Christmas	Baby Girl wth Pie	516					523771						
Baby's First Christmas	Baby Boy with Pie	517					523798						

No.	Name	Figurine	Item No.	Other Nos.
	Baby's First Haircut	Angel Cut Baby's Hair	12211	
46	Baby's First Pet	Boy/Baby/Feed Dog	520705	
172	Baby's First Picture	Baby's First Photo	E-2841	
173	Baby's First Step	Angel Carrying Baby	**E-2840**	
267	Baby's First Trip	Angel Pushing Buggy	**16012**	
36	Be Not Weary In Well Doing	Girl Helper	E-3111	
347	Bear The Good News Of Christmas	Bear on Sled		104515
52	Bear Ye One Another's Burdens	Sad Boy w/Teddy	**E-5200**	
383	Believe The Impossible	Boy w/Barbells	109487	
248	Bethany	Girl Angel		**12432**, PM-864
225	Birds Of A Feather Collect Together	Girl w/Embroidery Hoop/Bird	E-0006	E-0106
303	Bless The Days Of Our Youth	Clown w/Pull Rope	16004	
113	Bless This House	Boy/Girl Paint Dog Hse	**E-7164**	
139	Bless You Two	Groom Carrying Bride	E-9255	
31	Blessed Are The Peacemakers	Boy Hold Cat & Dog	**E-3107**	E-0521
28	Blessed Are The Pure In Heart	Rocking Cradle	E-3104	E-0518, E-5392
396	Blessed Are They That Overcome	Boy w/Braces & Dog	115479	
495	Blessings From Above	B&G Kiss'g /Mistletoe	523747	
120	Blessings From My House To Yours	Girl Look'g Birdhouse	**E-0503**	
474	Bon Voyage!	B&G on Motorcycle	522201	100455
289	Bong Bong	Boy Clown		
313	Bride	Bride	E-2846	
170	Bridesmaid	Bridesmaid	E-2831	
395	Brighten Someone's Day	Skunk & Mouse	105953	
125	Bringing God's Blessing To You	Girl Angel Push Jesus	**E-0509**	
276	Brotherly Love	Pilgrim/Indian/Turkey	**100544**	
96	Bundles Of Joy	Girl with Presents	E-2374	
39	But Love Goes On Forever	B/G Angels on Cloud	E-3115, E-0001	E-0102, E-0202 } Plaques
56	But Love Goes On Forever	Boy Angel on Cloud	**E-5627**	E-6118
57	But Love Goes On Forever	Girl Angel on Cloud	**E-5628**	
90	Camel	Camel	E-2363	
100	Camel, Donkey, Cow	Camel, Donkey, Cow	**E-2386**	
290	Candy	Girl Clown	100463	

BOLD = Suspended   *Italics* = Limited Edition   Shaded Area = Retired   Enclosed in a box = Annual

◆ = Two Year Collectible

73

INSPIRATIONAL TITLE	DESCRIPTIVE TITLE	#	FIG.	PLT.	BELL	MUSC.	ORN.	DOLL	THMBL.	FRAME	CNDL. CLMB.	BOX	NITE LITE
Can't Bee Hive Myself W/O You	Teddy w/Bee & Hive	488	BC-891										
Cheers To The Leader	Girl Cheerleader	345	104035				113999						
Christmas Fireplace	Fireplace w/ Stockings	512	524883										
Christmas Is A Time To Share	Boy Giving Toy Lamb	24	E-2802			E-2806							
Christmas Is Ruff Without You	Puppy Rest'g on Elbow	470					520462						
Christmas Joy From Head To Toe	Girl with Stocking	88	E-2361										
Christmastime Is For Sharing	Boy Giving Teddy	121	E-0504	E-0505									
Clown Figurines/Thimbles	Mini Clowns	235	12238 (A-D) Also see ART CHART Numbers 416-419.						100668				
Collection Plaque		56	E-6901 (Plaque)										
Come Let Us Adore Him	Boy w/Manger Baby	21	E-2011										
Come Let Us Adore Him	Manger w/Child	62	E-5619										
Come Let Us Adore Him	Nativity Set/Cassette	307	104000										
Come Let Us Adore Him	Nativity	22	E-2800 / E-2395	E-5646		E-2810	E-5633						
Congratulations, Princess	Girl Graduate	318	106208										
Connie	Doll with Stand	29						102253					
Cow	Cow with Bell	69	E-5638										
Crown Him Lord Of All	Boy/Manger/Crown	25	E-2803			E-2807							
Cubby	Groom Doll	11						E-7267B					
Dashing Through The Snow	Girl/Doll/Sleigh (Jan.)	36					521574						
Dawn's Early Light	Girl Covering Kitten	160	PM-831										
"Dealers Only" Nativity	Nativity w/Backdrop	337	104523										
Debbie	Debbie Doll	76						E-6214G					
December Girl	Girl/Christmas Candle	429	110116										
Donkey	Donkey	63	E-5621										
Don't Let The Holidays Get You Down	Boy w/Christmas Tree	47	522112				521590						
Dropping In For Christmas	Boy Ice Skater/Cap	84	E-2350				E-2369						
Dropping Over For Christmas	Girl with Pie	97	E-2375				E-2376						
Easter's On Its Way	Boy/Wagon/Lily/Girl	508	521892										
Eggs Over Easy	Girl with Fry Pan	45	E-3118										
Eggspecially For You	Girl/Hen/Easter Egg	455	520667										

Title	Figurine	#	Item No.		
Faith Is A Victory	Girl/Boxing Gloves		521596		
Faith Takes The Plunge	Girl with Plunger	389	111155		
February Girl	Girl/Plant in Snow	368	109991		
Feed My Sheep	Girl Feeding Lamb	365	PM-871		
Fishing For Friends	Raccoon Holding Fish	335	BC-861		
Flower Girl	Flower Girl	202	E-2835		
For God So Loved The World	Deluxe Nativity	192	**E-5382**		
Forever Friends	Dog/Cat	305			**E-9283**
Forgiving Is Forgetting	B&G w/Bandage	136	**E-9252**		
Four Seasons	Four Seasons Thimbles	226 227 228 229			100641
Friends Never Drift Apart	Kids in Boat	219	100250	522937	
Friends To The End	Rhino with Bird	420	104418		
Friendship Hits The Spot	Two Girls/Tea Party	453	520748		
Get Into The Habit Of Prayer	Nun	233	12203		
Glide Through The Holidays	Girl on Roller Skates	492		521566	
Goat	Goat	91	E-2364		
God Bless America	Uncle Sam/Bible/Dog	292	102938		
God Bless Our Family	Parents of the Groom	325	100498		
God Bless Our Family	Parents of the Bride	326	100501		
God Bless Our Home	B&G/Sandcastle	239	12319		
God Bless Our Years Together	5th Anniversary Piece	249	12440		
God Bless The Bride	Bride w/Flower Girl	171	E-2832		
God Bless The Day We Found You	Mom/Dad/Girl w/Adoption	272	100145		
God Bless The Day We Found You	Mom/Dad/Boy w/Adoption	273	100153		
God Bless You For Touching My Life	Girl Painting Butterfly	439	PM-881		
God Bless You Graduate	Boy Graduate	334	106194		
God Bless You On Your Birthday	Seal - Age 2	298	15962		
God Bless You With Rainbows	Angel/Rainbow	199			16020
God Blessed Our Year Together With So Much Love And Happiness	1st Anniversary	180	E-2854		

BOLD = Suspended   *Italics* = Limited Edition   Shaded Area = Retired   Enclosed in a box = Annual   ◆ = Two Year Collectible

76

INSPIRATIONAL TITLE	DESCRIPTIVE TITLE	#	FIG.	PLT.	BELL	MUSC.	ORN.	DOLL	THMBL.	FRAME	CNDL. CLMB.	BOX	NITE LITE
God Blessed Our Years	Happy Anniversary	179	E-2853										
Together With So Much	5th Anniversary	181	E-2855										
Love And Happiness	10th Anniversary	182	E-2856										
	25th Anniversary	183	E-2857										
	40th Anniversary	184	E-2859										
	50th Anniversary	185	E-2860										
God Gave His Best	Girl with Ornament	263	15806										
God Is Love	Girl w/Goose in Lap	60	E-5213										
God Is Love, Dear Valentine	Boy Holding Heart	102	E-7153										
God Is Love, Dear Valentine	Girl Holding Heart	103	E-7154						100625				
God Is Love Dear Valentine	Girl w/Valentine	509	523518										
God Is Watching Over You	Boy w/Ice Bag/Head	112	E-7163										
God Loveth A Cheerful Giver	Girl with Puppies	20	E-1378										
God Sends The Gift Of His Love	Girl/Present/Kitten	204	E-6613										
God Sent His Love	Angel w/Holly Wreath	259	15881		15873		15768		15865				
God Sent His Son	Girl Look'g in Manger	123	E-0507										
God Sent You Just In Time	Clown/Jack-in-Box	256				15504	113972						
God Understands	Boy w/Report Card	12	E-1379B		E-5211								
God's Precious Gift	Baby Boy	310								12033			
God's Precious Gift	Baby Girl	311								12041			
God's Promises Are Sure	Angel Wind Rainbow	142	E-9260										
God's Ray Of Mercy	Boy Angel/Flashlight	200	PM-841										
God's Speed	Boy Jogging w/Dog	44	E-3112										
Good Friends Are Forever	Girls with Flower	492	521817										
			525049										
Grandma's Prayer	Praying Grandma	305	PM-861										
Groom	Groom	269	E-2837										
Groomsman	Groomsman w/Frog	172	E-2836										
Hallelujah Country	Cowboy/Guitar	377	105821										
Halo. & Merry Christmas	Angels/Snowman	241	12351										
Hang On For The Holly Days	Kitten Hang/Wreath	400					520292						
Happiness Divine	Clown Angel/Flowers	384	109584										
Happiness Is The Lord	Boy Playing Banjo	242	12378										
Happiness Is The Lord	Boy Clown w/Ball	235					15830						

Name	Number											
Happy Birthday Little Lamb	Lamb - Age 1											
Happy Birthday Poppy	15946											
Happy Birthday Poppy	106836											
Happy Days Are Here Again	104396											
Happy Trip	521280											
Have A Beary Merry Christmas	522856											
Have A Beary Special Birthday	B-0104											
	B-0004											
Have A Heavenly Christmas	Boy in Airplane					12416						
Have I Got News For You	105635											
He Careth For You	E-1377B											
He Cleansed My Soul	100277					112380						
He Is My Song	12394											
He Is The Star Of The Morning	522252											
He Leadeth Me	E-1377A											
He Upholdeth Those Who Call	E-0526											
He Walks With Me	107999											
He Watches Over Us All	E-3105											
Heaven Bless You	520934				100285							
Heaven Bless Your Special Day	15954											
Heaven Bless Your Togetherness	106755											
Hello, Lord, It's Me Again	PM-811											
Hello World!	521175											
Help Lord, I'm In A Spot	100269											
He's The Healer Of Broken Hearts	100080											
Hi Sugar!	BC-871											
High Hopes	521957											
His Burden Is Light	E-1380G											
His Eye Is On The Sparrow	E-0530											
His Love Will Shine On You	522376											
His Name Is Jesus	E-5381											
His Sheep Am I	E-7161											
Holy Smokes	E-2351											
Honk If You Love Jesus	15490					15857						
Hope You're Up And On The Trail Again	521205											
Houses And Palm Tree	E-2387											

BOLD = Suspended   *Italics* = Limited Edition   Shaded Area = Retired   Enclosed in a box = Annual   ◆ = Two Year Collectible

77

INSPIRATIONAL TITLE	DESCRIPTIVE TITLE	#	FIG.	PLT.	BELL	MUSC.	ORN.	DOLL	THMBL.	FRAME	CNDL. CLMB.	BOX	NITE LITE
How Can Two Walk Together Except They Agree	B/G Horse Costume	145	E-9263										
I Believe In Miracles	Boy Holding Chick	105	E-7156	E-9257									
I Believe In Miracles	Boy Holding Bluebird	374	E-7156R										
I Believe In The Old Rugged Cross	Girl Holding Cross	224	103632				522953						
I Belong To The Lord	Orphan Girl	463	520853										
I Get A Bang Out Of You	Clown Hold'g Balloons	236	12262										
I Get A Kick Out Of You	Girl w/Bucket on Head	167	E-2827										
I Love To Tell The Story	Boy w/Lamb & Book	294	PM-852										
I Picked A Very Special Mom	Boy w/Garden'g Mom	328	100536										
I Would Be Sunk Without You	Baby Boy/Tub	342	102970										
If God Be For Us, Who Can Be Against Us	Boy at Pulpit	154	E-9285										
I'll Never Stop Loving You	Girl w/Letters "Y" "O" "U"	511	521418										
I'll Play My Drum For Him	Drummer Boy/Manger	87	E-2356 E-2360 E-5384	E-2357	E-2358	E-2355	E-2359						
I'm A Possibility	Boy w/Football	274	100188				111120						
I'm A PRECIOUS MOMENTS Fan	Girl with Fan	490	523526									E-9266	
I'm Falling For Somebunny	Lamb and Bunny	308											
I'm Following Jesus	Boy in Car	320	PM-862										
I'm Sending You A White Christmas	Girl Mailing Snowball	169	E-2829	101834		112402	112372						
I'm So Glad You Fluttered Into My Life	Angel w/Butterfly Net	447	520640										
In His Time	Boy/Wait/Seed/Grow	375	PM-872										
Isn't Eight Just Great	Ostrich - Age 8	394	109460										
Isn't He Precious?	Girl with Broom	189	E-5379 522988										
Isn't He Wonderful	Boy Angel Pray'g/Harp	70	E-5639										
Isn't He Wonderful	Girl Angel/Pray'g/Harp	71	E-5640										
It Is Better To Give Than To Receive	Policeman Writing Tkt.	237	12297										

Name	Description	Ref	Item #					
It's What's Inside That Counts	Boy with Books	(42)	**E-3119**					
January Girl	Girl/Doll/Sleigh	(367)	109983					
Jesus Is Born	Angels in Chariot	(23)	**E-2801**					
Jesus Is Born	B&G Playing Angels	(17)	**E-2012**		E-2809			
Jesus Is Born	Shepherd	(64)					E-5623	
Jesus Is Coming Soon	Mary Knitting Booties	(240)	**12343**					
Jesus Is The Answer	Boy Patching World	(15)	**E-1381**					
Jesus Is The Light	Girl w/Doll & Candle	(4)	E-1373G					
Jesus Is The Light That Shines	Boy/Candle/Mouse	(119)	**E-0502**			E-0537		
Jesus Is The Only Way	Boy at Crossroads	(464)	520756					
Jesus Is The Sweetest Name I Know	Angel w/Baby Book	(468)	523097					
Jesus Loves Me	Boy with Teddy	(1)	E-1372B / E-9278	**E-9275**	E-5208			E-7170	E-9280
Jesus Loves Me	Girl with Bunny	(2)	E-1372G / E-9279 / 104531	**E-9276**	E-5209			E-7171	E-9281
Jesus The Savior Is Born	Angel/Newspaper	(437)	520357					
Join In On The Blessings	Girl w/Dues Bank	(205)	E-0104 / E-0404					
Joy To The World	Boy Angel/Trumpet	(79)				E-2343		
Joy To The World	Boy Playing Harp	(188)	**E-5378**			E-5388		E-2344
July Girl	Girl w/Puppy/Basket	(424)	110051					
June Girl	Girl Dress Up/Bride	(372)	110043					
Junior Bridesmaid	Junior Bridesmaid	(210)	E-2845					
Just A Line To Wish You A Happy Day	Dog Pulling Boy's Fishing Line	(456)	520721					
Katie Lynne	Baby Collector's Doll	(134)				E-0539		
Keep Looking Up	Giraffe - Age 6	(302)	15997					
Kristy	Baby Collector's Doll	(177)				E-2851		
Let Heaven & Nature Sing	Angel/Friends Caroll'g	(81)	*E-2347*		E-2346			
Let Love Reign	Girl/Chicks/Umbrella	(149)	**E-9273**			E-0532		
Let Not The Sun Go Down Upon Your Wrath	Boy w/Dog on Stairs	(55)	**E-5203**					

BOLD = Suspended   *Italics* = Limited Edition   Shaded Area = Retired   Enclosed in a box = Annual   ◆ = Two Year Collectible

INSPIRATIONAL TITLE	DESCRIPTIVE TITLE	#	FIG.	PLT.	BELL	MUSC.	ORN.	DOLL	THMBL.	FRAME	CNDL. CLMB.	BOX	NITE LITE
Let The Heavens Rejoice	Praying Angel	77			E-5622		E-5629						
Let The Whole World Know	B/G Baptism Bucket	114	E-7165			E-7186							
Let Us Call The Club To Order	Club Meeting	158	E-0103										
			E-0303										
Let's Keep In Touch	Clown on Elephant	287				102520							
Lord Give Me A Song	Girl Play'g Harmonica	245	12386										
Lord Give Me Patience	Bandaged Boy/Sign	108	E-7159										
Lord, Help Me Make The Grade	Schoolboy Clown	354	106216										
Lord, Help Me Stick To My Job	Girl w/Account Bks.	503	521450										
Lord, Help Us Keep Our Act Together	Clowns on Unicycle	331	101850										
Lord I'm Coming Home	Baseball Player/Bat	215	100110										
Lord Keep Me On My Toes	Ballerina	216	100129				102423						
Lord Keep Me On The Ball	Clown Sitting on Ball	270	12270										
Lord, Keep My Life In Tune	Boy Playing Piano	231				12165							
Lord, Keep My Life In Tune	Girl with Piano	315				12580							
Lord, Turn My Life Around	Ballerina	493	520551										
Love Beareth All Things	Nurse Give Shot/Bear	102	E-7158										
Love Cannot Break A True Friendship	Girl w/Piggy Bank	48	E-4722										
Love Covers All	Girl/Heart Quilt	225	12009						12254				
Love Is From Above	Boy Whisper'g to Girl	510	521841										
Love Is Kind	Boy w/Turtle	11	E-1379A										
Love Is Kind	Girl with Gift	198					E-5391						
Love Is Kind	Girl with Mouse	187	E-5377										
Love Is Kind	B/G on Swing	175		E-2847									
Love Is Patient	B/G Chalkboard	135	E-9251										
Love Is Patient	Girl with Slate	133					E-0536						
Love Is Patient	Boy with Slate	132					E-0535						
Love Is Sharing	Girl at School Desk	111	E-7162		109835	E-7185							
Love Is The Best Gift Of All	Girl with Present	360	110930				109770		109843				
Love Is The Glue That Mends	Boy Mending Horse	344	104027										
Love Lifted Me	Boy Helping Friend	53	E-5201										
Love Lifted Me	B/G on Seesaw	6	E-1375A										
Love Never Fails	Teacher/Report Card	238	12300										

Title	Description	No.	Item No.			
Love Rescued Me	Fireman Hold Puppy	28	102393		102385	
Loving Is Sharing	Boy Sharing w/Puppy	34	E-3110B			
Loving Is Sharing	Girl Sharing w/Puppy	35	E-3110G			
Loving Thy Neighbor	Mother Wrap Bread	176		*E-2848*		
Loving You	Boy Holding Heart	102				**12017**
Loving You	Girl Holding Heart	103				**12025**
Loving You Dear Valentine	Boy Paint'g Valentine	321	PM-873			
Loving You Dear Valentine	Girl/Valentine	322	PM-874			
Make A Joyful Noise	Girl with Goose	5	E-1374G / 520322	*E-7174*	522910	
Make Me A Blessing	Girl w/Sick Bear	323	100102			
Many Moons In Same Canoe, Blessum You	Indians in Canoe	457	520772			
March Girl	Girl with Kite	369	110019			
May All Your Christmases Be White	Girl/Snowball	477			521302	
May Girl	Girl/Potted Plant	371	110035			
May God Bless You With A Perfect Holiday Season	Girl In Scarf/Cap	197			**E-5390**	
May You Have The Sweetest Christmas	Mother w/Cookie Sheet	260	15776			
May Your Birthday Be A Blessing	Girl at Table with Dolls	166	**E-2826**			
May Your Birthday Be Gigantic	Elephant - Age 4	300	15970			
May Your Birthday Be Warm	Teddy/Caboose	296	15938			
May Your Christmas Be A Happy Home	Family Christmas Scene	479	523003		523704	
May Your Christmas Be Blessed	Girl with Bible	186	**E-5376**			
May Your Christmas Be Cozy	Boy/PJ's/Teddy	80	**E-2345**			
May Your Christmas Be Delightful	Boy Tangled in Christmas Lights	254	15482		15849	
May Your Christmas Be Happy	Girl Clown/Balloon	235				
May Your Christmas Be Warm	Boy/Pot Belly Stove	82	**E-2348**		**15822**	
May Your Life Be Blessed With Touchdowns	Boy Playing Football	473	522023			

BOLD = Suspended   *Italics* = Limited Edition   Shaded Area = Retired   Enclosed in a box = Annual   ◆ = Two Year Collectible

82

INSPIRATIONAL TITLE	DESCRIPTIVE TITLE	#	FIG.	PLT.	BELL	MUSC.	ORN.	DOLL	THMBL.	FRAME	CNDL. CLMB.	BOX	NITE LITE
Meowie Christmas	Girl with Kitten	423	109800										
Merry Christmas, Deer	Girl/Reindeer	438	522317	520284									
Mikey	Mikey	75						E-6214B					
Mini Animal Figurines	3 Mini Animals	279	102296										
Mommy, I Love You	Girl with Flower	390	112143										
Mommy, I Love You	Boy with Flower	387	109975										
Mother Sew Dear	Mother Needlepoint'g	30	E-3106	E-5217	E-7181	E-7182	E-0514	E-2850	13293	E-7241			
Mouse With Cheese	Mouse with Cheese	99					E-2381						
Mow Power To Ya	Boy Push Lawn Mower	486	PM-892										
My Days Are Blue Without You	Girl/Paint/Ladder	462	520802										
My Guardian Angel	Boy Angel on Cloud	56				E-5205							
My Guardian Angel	Girl Angel on Cloud	57				E-5206							
My Guardian Angel	Boy Angel	265								E-7168			
My Guardian Angel	Girl Angel	266								E-7169			
My Guardian Angels	B/G Angels/Cloud	39											E-5207
My Happiness	Girl @ Table w/Figurine	482	C-0110 C-0010										
My Heart Is Exposed With Love	Nurse/Xray/Heart	458	520624										
My Love Will Never Let You Go	Boy w/Hat & Fish	333	103497				114006						
My Peace I Give Unto Thee	Kids/ Lamp Post	341		102954									
No Tears Past The Gate	Girl/Gate to Heaven	329	101826										
Nobody's Perfect	Boy w/Dunce Cap	148	E-9268										
Not A Creature Was Stirring	Mouse/Cheese/Kitten	514	524484										
November Girl	Girl in Pilgrim Suit	428	110108										
O Come All Ye Faithful	Boy Carolling	86	E-2353			E-2352	E-0531						
O Come Let Us Adore Him	4 Piece Nativity	362	111333										
O, How I Love Jesus	Indian Boy	13	E-1380B										
October Girl	Girl with Pumpkins	427	110094										
Oh Holy Night	Girl Playing Violin	482	522546		522821		522848		522554				
Oh What Fun It Is To Ride	Grandma on a Sled	361	109819										
Oh Worship The Lord	Boy Angel/Candle	194	E-5385										
Oh Worship The Lord	Girl Angel Praying	195	E-5386										
Once Upon A Holy Night	Girl w/Bk & Candle	519	523836		523828		523852		523844				

Title	Figure Description	No.							
Our Club Can't Be Beat	Clown with Drum	(304)				B-0001			
Our First Christmas Together	B & G in Box	(277)				101702	102350 112399 520233		
Our First Christmas Together	Girl Knitting Tie	(98)	E-2377	E-2378					
Our First Christmas Together	Bride 'N Groom	(38)				E-2385			
Our First Christmas Together	Couple with Gifts	(433)		115290					
Our First Christmas Together	Bride/Groom in Car	(460)				521558 525324			
Our Love Is Heaven Scent	Lamb and Skunk	(308)							E-9266
P.D.	Baby Boy	(252)						12475	
Part Of Me Wants To Be Good	Boy Angel/Devil Suit	(230)	12149						
Peace Amid The Storm	Boy Reading Bible	(49)	E-4723			E-5389			
Peace On Earth	Boy in Choir	(196)							
Peace On Earth	Boy/Globe/Teddy	(26)	E-2804						
Peace On Earth	Choir Boys/Bandages	(51)	E-4725		E-4726				
Peace On Earth	Girl w/Lion & Lamb	(155)	E-9287						
Peace On Earth	Kids around Lamp Post	(341)	E-1374B			109746	523062		
Praise The Lord Anyhow	Boy with Dog	(19)	E-9254						
Praise The Lord Anyhow	Girl at Typewriter	(138)	E-5214						
Prayer Changes Things	B & G Praying @ Table	(61)	E-1375B						
Prayer Changes Things	B & G with Bluebirds	(7)		E-5210					
Prayer Changes Things	Girl Praying in Field	(58)	E-2828						
Precious Memories	Girl/Trunk/Wedding	(168)	106763						
Precious Memories	Couple/Couch/Album	(379)	12246						
Precious Moments	Giveaway Medallion	(365)							
Prepare Ye The Way Of The Lord	B/G Prep Manger	(124)	E-0508						
Press On	Girl Ironing Clothes	(146)	E-9265						
Puppy Love	Two Puppies	(465)	520764						
Puppy Love Is From Above	Anniversary Couple	(380)	106798						
Put On A Happy Face	Boy Clown/Mask	(159)	PM-822						

BOLD = Suspended *Italics* = Limited Edition Shaded Area = Retired Enclosed in a box = Annual ◆ = Two Year Collectible

83

INSPIRATIONAL TITLE	DESCRIPTIVE TITLE	#	FIG.	PLT.	BELL	MUSC.	ORN.	DOLL	THMBL.	FRAME	CNDL. CLMB.	BOX	NITE LITE
Reindeer	Reindeer	306					102466						
Rejoice O Earth	Angel with Trumpet	67	E-5636 520268			E-5645	113980						
Rejoicing With You	Christening	50	E-4724	E-7172									
Retailer's Dome	Kids on Cloud/Dome	411	E-7350										
Retailer's Wreath	'87 Christmas Wreath	410					111465 (Wreath)						
Retailer's Wreath Bell	Retailer's Wreath Bell	415			112348								
Ringbearer	Ringbearer	208	E-2833										
Rocking Horse	Rocking Horse	283					102474						
Scent From Above	Girl with Skunk	327	100528										
Seek And Ye Shall Find	Girl/Shopping Bag	104	E-0005 E-0105										
Seek Ye The Lord	Boy Grad/Scroll	143	E-9261										
Seek Ye The Lord	Girl Grad/Scroll	144	E-9262										
Sending My Love	Boy/Bow & Arrow	212	100056										
Sending You A Rainbow	Girl Angel/Sprnkl Can	150	E-9288										
Sending You My Love	Girl w/Hearts/Cloud	386	109967										
Sending You Showers Of Blessings	Boy/Newspapers over Head	450	520683										
September Girl	Girl Balancing Books	424	110086										
Serve With A Smile	Tennis Boy	222					102431						
Serve With A Smile	Tennis Girl	218					102458						
Serving The Lord	Tennis Boy	222	100293										
Serving The Lord	Tennis Girl	218	100161										
Sew In Love	Girl Sewing Pants	382	106844										
Sharing Begins In The Heart	Girl with Chalkboard	467	520861										
Sharing Is Universal	Girl/Package/Friend	336	E-0007 E-0107										
Sharing Our Christmas Together	Husband/Wife/Puppy and Cookies	284	102490										
Sharing Our Joy Together	Bridesmaid w/Kitten	268	E-2834										
Sharing Our Season Together	Boy & Girl/Sled	118	E-0501			E-0519							
Sharing Season Ornament	Brass Filagree/Kids	370					PM-009						
Shepherd Of Love	Angel w/Black Lamb	278	102261				102288						

Name	Description	#				
Showers Of Blessings	Elephant /Mouse	(352) 105945				
Silent Knight	Boy Angel/Knight	(73)		**E-5642**		
Silent Night	Christmas Tree	(264)		15814		
Sitting Pretty	Girl Angel/Stool	(345) 104825				
Smile Along The Way	Clown Balancing	(330) 101842			113964	
Smile, God Loves You	Boy w/Black Eye	(3) **E-1373B**				
Smile, God Loves You	Girl with Curlers	(117) PM-821				
Some Bunnies Sleeping	Bunnies	(43) 522996				
Some Bunny's Sleeping	Bunnies	(43) 115274				
Somebunny Cares	Bunny/Stuffed Carrot	(44) BC-881				
Someday My Love	Bride with Dress	(446) 520799				
Something's Missing When You're Not Around	Girl Holding Doll with Dog	(421) 105643			105643	
Stocking Hanger	Boy Tangl'd Lights	(445) 558125				
Summer's Joy	Girl w/Crossed Arms	(22) 12076	12114	408743◆		408794◆
Surround Us With Joy	Boy with Wreath	(22)				
Surrounded With Joy	Boy with Wreath	(22) **E-0506**	E-0522	E-0513		
Sweep All Your Worries Away	Girl/Dust under Rug	(502) 521779				

Name	Description	#				
Tammy	Bride Doll	(116)				*E-7267G*
Taste And See That The Lord Is Good	Girl Angel Making Food	(150) **E-9274**				
Tell It To Jesus	Girl on Telephone	(476) 521477				
Tell Me A Story	Boy Sit Listen/Story	(262) 15792				
Tell Me The Story Of Jesus	Girl/Doll/Book	(83) **E-2349**	15237			
Thank You For Coming To My Ade	Lemonade Stand	(54) **E-5202**		**E-0533**		
Thank You Lord For Everything	Boy/Turkey/Dine	(472) 522031				
Thanking Him For You	Girl Praying in Field	(58) **E-7155**				
That's What Friends Are For	Crying Girls Hugging	(520) 521183				
The End Is In Sight	Dog Rip g Boy's Pants	(137) **E-9253**				
The First Noel	Boy Angel/Candle	(92) **E-2365**		**E-2367**		
The First Noel	Girl Angel Praying	(93) **E-2366**		E-2368		
The Good Lord Always Delivers	Mom-To-Be w/Baby Bk	(497) 523453				
The Good Lord Has Blessed Us Ten Fold		(392) 114022				
The Greatest Gift Is A Friend	Baby Boy/Dog	(355) 109231				

BOLD = Suspended   *Italics* = Limited Edition   Shaded Area = Retired   Enclosed in a box = Annual   ◆ = Two Year Collectible

85

INSPIRATIONAL TITLE	DESCRIPTIVE TITLE	#	FIG.	PLT.	BELL	MUSC.	ORN.	DOLL	THMBL.	FRAME	CNDL. CLMB.	BOX	NITE LITE
The Greatest Of These Is Love	Commandments	483	521868										
The Hand That Rocks The Future	Girl Rocking Cradle	32	E-3108	E-9256		E-5204							
The Heavenly Light	Angel with Flashlight	68	E-5637										
The Joy Of The Lord Is My Strength	Mother w/Babies	217	100137										
The Light Of The World Is Jesus	Girl w/Lamp Post	475				521507							
The Lord Bless You And Keep You	Boy Graduate	46	E-4720		E-7175					E-7177			
The Lord Bless You And Keep You	Bride 'N Groom	38	E-3114	E-5216	E-7179	E-7180				E-7166		E-7167	
The Lord Bless You And Keep You	Girl Graduate	47	E-4721		E-7176					E-7178			
The Lord Bless You And Keep You	Bride	313							100633				
The Lord Giveth & The Lord Taketh Away	Girl with Cat & Birdcage	340	100226										
The Lord Is My Shepherd	Girl Holding Lamb	293	PM-851										
The Lord Is Your Light To Happiness	Bridal Couple Light'g Candle	466	520837										
The Lord Will Carry You Through	Clown w/Dog/Mud	251	12467										
The Perfect Grandpa	Grandpa in Rocker	109	E-7160				E-0517						
The Purr-fect Grandma	Grandma in Rocker	33	E-3109	E-7173		E-7184	E-0516						
The Spirit Is Willing But The Flesh Is Weak	Girl/Candy/Scale	324	100196		E-7183				13307	E-7242			
The Story Of God's Love	Father Reading Bible	261	15784										
The Sweetest Club Around	Pippin/Pop/Cake	440	B-0003 & B-0103										
The Voice Of Spring	Girl by Fence	220	12068	12106									
The Wonder Of Christmas	Boy/Sled/Girl/Tree	202	E-5396			408735◆		408786◆					
Thee I Love	Boy Carving Tree	40	E-3116										
There Is Joy In Serving Jesus	Waitress Carry Food	108	E-7157										
There Shall Be Showers Of Blessings	B&G in Garden	500	522090										
There's A Christian Welcome Here	Angel outside Chapel	491	523011										
There's A Song In My Heart	Girl Playing Triangle	232	12173										
They Followed The Star	Angel/3 Kings	72	E-5641										

Item	Description	No.	Stock No.			
They Followed The Star	3 Kings/Camels		108243			
Thinking Of You Is What I Really Like To Do	Kneel'g Girl/Bouquet	504	522287			
This Day Has Been Made In Heaven	Girl/Bible/Cross	506	523496			
This Day Is Something To Roar About	Lion - Age 5	301	15989			
This Is The Day Which The Lord Has Made	Birthday Boy	314	12157			
This Is The Day Which The Lord Hath Made	Complete Wedding Party	312	E-2838			
This Is Your Day To Shine	Girl Polishing Table	192	E-2822			
This Too Shall Pass	Boy w/Broken Heart	391	114014			
Thou Art Mine	Boy Writing in Sand	37	E-3113			
Time Heals	Nurse at Desk w/Clock	518	523739			
Time To Wish You A Merry Christmas	Girl/Calendar/Clock	434	115339	115304	115320	115312
Timmy	Boy Jogger	203				E-5397
'Tis The Season	Girl Adding Seasoning	430	111163			
To A Special Dad	Boy in Dad's Duds	59	E-5212		**E-0515**	
To A Very Special Mom	Girl w/Floppy Hat	164	E-2824			
To A Very Special Sister	Bows/Sister's Hair	165	E-2825			
To Be With You Is Uplifting	Giraffe/Baby Bear	484	522260			
To God Be The Glory	Boy Holding Frame	163	**E-2823**			
To My Deer Friend	Girl w/Flowers/Deer	316	100048			
To My Favorite Fan	Gorilla and Parrot	501	521043			
To My Favorite Paw	Boy Sitting w/Teddy	211	**100021**			
To My Forever Friend	Two Girls w/Flowers	214	100072		113956	
To Somebunny Special	Bunny	152	E-9282 (A)			
To Tell The Tooth You're Special	Dentist/Patient Pulled Tooth	35	105813			
To Thee With Love	Girl w/Box/Kittens	43	**E-3120**		E-0534	**12483**
Trish	Baby Girl	253				
Trust And Obey	Policeman Writing Tkt.	237			102377	
Trust In The Lord	Angel/Fly Lessons	157	**E-9289**			
Trust In The Lord To The Finish	Boy w/Racing Cup	207	PM-842			

BOLD = Suspended   *Italics* = Limited Edition   Shaded Area = Retired   Enclosed in a box = Annual   ◆ = Two Year Collectible

INSPIRATIONAL TITLE	DESCRIPTIVE TITLE	#	FIG.	PLT.	BELL	MUSC.	ORN.	DOLL	THMBL.	FRAME	CNDL. CLMB.	BOX	NITE LITE
Tubby's First Christmas	Rooster & Bird on Pig	126	E-0511										
Two Section Wall	Two Section Wall	74	E-5644										
Unicorn	Unicorn	94					E-2371						
Unto Us A Child Is Born	B/G Reading Book	18	E-2013			E-2808							
Unto Us A Child Is Born	Nativity Scene	201		E-5395									
Unto Us A Child Is Born	Shepherd	64					E-5630						
Waddle I Do Without You	Clown/Bskt./Goose	250	12459				112364						
Walking By Faith	Boy Pulling Wagon	41	E-3117										
We Are All Precious In His Sight	Girl with Pearl	373	102903										
We Are God's Workmanship	Bonnet Girl/Butterfly	140	E-9258										
We Belong To The Lord	Damien-Dutton	338	103004										
We Gather Together To Ask The Lord's Blessing	Thanksgiving Set	350	109762										
We Have Seen His Star	Boy Holding Lamb	16	E-2010		E-5620								
We Need A Good Friend Through The Ruff Times	Grandpa/Cane/Dog	452	520810										
We Saw A Star	2 Angels Sawing Star	245				12408							
Wedding Arch	Bridal Arch	332	102369										
Wee Three Kings	Three Kings	66	E-5635	E-0538		E-0520	E-5634						
We're Going To Miss You	Girl/Melting Snowman	513	524913										
We're In It Together	Boy with Piggy	141	E-9259										
We're Pulling For You	Boy with Donkey	353	106151										
Winter's Song	Girl Feeding Birds	229	12092	12130		408778◆		408816◆					
Wishing You A Basket Full Of Blessings	Boy/Basket/Chick	385	109924										
Wishing You A Cozy Christmas	Girl with Muff	280	102342		102318		102326		102334				
Wishing You A Cozy Season	Boy by Stump	480	521949										
Wishing You A Happy Easter	Girl Holding Bunny	385	109886										
Wishing You A Merry Christmas	Carollers w/Puppy	200				E-5394							
Wishing You A Merry Christmas	Girl in Choir	193	E-5383		E-5393		E-5387						
Wishing You A Perfect Choice	Boy Propose to Girl	459	520845										
Wishing You A Purr-fect Holiday	Kitten with Ornament	521					520497						

Title	Description				
Wishing You A Season Filled With Joy	Boy/Santa Cap/Dog	(27) E-2805			
Wishing You A Very Successful Season	Boy/Package/Puppy	(478) 522120			
Wishing You A Yummy Christmas	Girl with Ice Cream	(358) 109754	523801		
Wishing You Grr-eatness	Leopard - Age 7	(393) 109479			
Wishing You Roads Of Happiness	Bride & Groom in Car	(460) 520780			
With This Ring I.....	Boy Giving Girl Ring	(343) 104019			
Worship The Lord	Boy Kneeling/Church	(223) 102229			
Worship The Lord	Girl Kneeling /Church	(218) 100064			
Wreath Contestant Ornament	Boy/Girl/Cloud	(422) PM-008			

Title	Description				
Yield Not To Temptation	Girl with Apple	(505) 521310			
You Are My Gift Come True	Puppy in Stocking	(436)	520276		
You Are My Main Event	Girl/Balloons/Satchel	(397) 115231			
You Are My Number One	Girl Holding Trophy	(448) 520829			
You Can Fly	Boy Angel on Cloud	(271) **12335**			
You Can't Run Away From God	Boy & Dog Run Away	(129) E-0525			
You Have Touched So Many Hearts	Girl with Hearts	(161) E-2821 / 523283	112577	112356	
You Just Cannot Chuck A Good Friendship	Boy/Dog/Trash	(442) PM-882			
You Will Always Be My Choice	Girl with Ballot Box	(485) PM-891			
Your Love Is So Uplifting	Boy Hold Girl/Fountain	(454) 520675			
You're Worth Your Weight In Gold	Pig	(151) E-9282 (B)			

BOLD = Suspended   *Italics* = Limited Edition   Shaded Area = Retired   Enclosed in a box = Annual   ♦ = Two Year Collectible

QUICK REFERENCE • Item Number Order

Many times certain pieces become important as part of a group. PRECIOUS MOMENTS groups that have become important are included in this QUICK REFERENCE SECTION. Groups included are The "Original 21," Limited Editions, Two-Year Collectibles, the Re-introduced piece, Retired pieces, Suspended pieces, Dated Annuals, Annuals, The Enesco PRECIOUS MOMENTS Birthday Club pieces, and The Enesco PRECIOUS MOMENTS Collectors' Club pieces.

In addition, the OUTLINE OF ANNUALS Section groups annual collectibles by series and product type. The OUTLINE OF THE SERIES Section itemizes the individual pieces that comprise each series.

There's a QUICK REFERENCE CALENDAR as well. It's a summary, by year, of Retired, Suspended, and Annual pieces.

THE "ORIGINAL 21"

E-1372B	Jesus Loves Me
E-1372G	Jesus Loves Me
E-1373B	Smile, God Loves You
E-1373G	Jesus Is The Light
E-1374B	Praise The Lord Anyhow
E-1374G	Make A Joyful Noise
E-1375A	Love Lifted Me
E-1375B	Prayer Changes Things
E-1376	Love One Another
E-1377A	Love Leadeth Me
E-1377B	He Careth For You
E-1378	God Loveth A Cheerful Giver
E-1379A	Love Is Kind
E-1379B	God Understands
E-1380B	O, How I Love Jesus
E-1380G	His Burden Is Light
E-1381	Jesus Is The Answer
E-2010	We Have Seen His Star
E-2011	Come Let Us Adore Him
E-2012	Jesus Is Born
E-2013	Unto Us A Child Is Born

LIMITED EDITIONS

E-0538	15,000	Wee Three Kings
E-2347	15,000	Let Heaven And Nature Sing
E-2847	15,000	Love Is Kind
E-2848	15,000	Loving Thy Neighbor
E-5215	15,000	Love One Another
E-5217	15,000	Mother Sew Dear
E-5395	15,000	Unto Us A Child Is Born
E-5646	15,000	Come Let Us Adore Him
E-7173	15,000	Purr-fect Grandma
E-7174	15,000	Make A Joyful Noise
E-7267B	5,000	Tammy
E-7267G	5,000	Cubby
E-9256	15,000	The Hand That Rocks The Future
E-9257	15,000	I Believe In Miracles
12491	12,500	Angie, The Angel Of Mercy
100455	12,000	Bong Bong
100463	12,000	Candy
102253	7,500	Connie
104531	1,000	Jesus Loves Me
520322	1,500	Make A Joyful Noise
523283	2,000	You Have Touched So Many Hearts

TWO-YEAR COLLECTIBLES

408735	1990, 1991	The Voice Of Spring
408743	1990, 1991	Summer's Joy
408751	1990, 1991	Autumn's Praise
408778	1990, 1991	Winter's Song
408786	1990, 1991	The Voice Of Spring
408794	1990, 1991	Summer's Joy
408808	1990, 1991	Autumn's Praise
408816	1990, 1991	Winter's Song

RE-INTRODUCED

E-7156R   1987   I Believe In Miracles

RETIRED

E-0506	1989	Surrounded With Joy
E-0519	1986	Sharing Our Season Together
E-0525	1989	You Can't Run Away From God
E-0530	1987	His Eye Is On The Sparrow
E-0532	1986	Let Heaven And Nature Sing
E-0534	1989	To Thee With Love
E-1373B	1984	Smile God Loves You
E-1373G	1988	Jesus Is The Light
E-1374B	1982	Praise The Lord Anyhow
E-1378	1981	God Loveth A Cheerful Giver
E-1380G	1984	His Burden Is Light
E-1380B	1984	O, How I Love Jesus
E-2011	1981	Come Let Us Adore Him
E-2351	1987	Holy Smokes
E-2353	1986	O Come All Ye Faithful
E-2368	1984	The First Noel
E-2369	1986	Dropping In For Christmas
E-2371	1988	Unicorn
E-2376	1985	Dropping Over For Christmas
E-2805	1985	Wishing You A Season Filled With Joy
E-2806	1984	Christmas Is A Time To Share
E-2822	1988	This Is Your Day To Shine
E-2841	1986	Baby's First Picture
E-2850	1985	Mother Sew Dear
E-3107	1985	Blessed Are The Peacemakers
E-3111	1985	Be Not Weary In Well Doing
E-3112	1983	God's Speed
E-3118	1983	Eggs Over Easy
E-5211	1984	God Understands
E-5377	1987	Love Is Kind
E-5388	1987	Joy To The World
E-5645	1988	Rejoice O Earth
E-6120	1984	We Have Seen His Star
E-7157	1986	There Is Joy In Serving Jesus
E-7185	1985	Love Is Sharing
E-9273	1987	Let Love Reign
E-9274	1986	Taste And See That The Lord Is Good
12459	1989	Waddle I Do Without You
12467	1988	The Lord Will Carry You Through
15504	1989	God Sent You Just In Time
100129	1988	Lord Keep Me On My Toes
100269	1989	Help Lord, I'm In A Spot

SUSPENDED

E-0501	1986	Sharing Our Season Together
E-0502	1986	Jesus Is The Light That Shines
E-0503	1986	Blessings From My House To Yours
E-0507	1987	God Sent His Son
E-0508	1986	Prepare Ye The Way Of The Lord
E-0509	1987	Bringing God's Blessing To You
E-0515	1988	To A Special Dad
E-0520	1986	Wee Three Kings
E-0521	1987	Blessed Are The Pure In Heart
E-0526	1985	He Upholdeth Those Who Call
E-0531	1986	O Come All Ye Faithful
E-0533	1988	Tell Me The Story Of Jesus
E-0535	1986	Love Is Patient
E-0536	1986	Love Is Patient
E-0537	1985	Jesus Is The Light
E-0539	1988	Katie Lynne
E-1375B	1984	Prayer Changes Things
E-1377A	1984	He Leadeth Me
E-1377B	1984	He Careth For You
E-1379A	1984	Love Is Kind
E-1379B	1984	God Understands
E-1381	1984	Jesus Is The Answer
E-2010	1984	We Have Seen His Star
E-2012	1984	Jesus Is Born
E-2013	1984	Unto Us A Child Is Born
E-2343	1988	Joy To The World
E-2344	1985	Joy To The World
E-2345	1984	May Your Christmas Be Cozy
E-2346	1989	Let Heaven And Nature Sing
E-2348	1988	May Your Christmas Be Warm
E-2349	1985	Tell Me The Story Of Jesus
E-2350	1984	Dropping In For Christmas
E-2352	1984	O Come All Ye Faithful
E-2355	1984	I'll Play My Drum For Him
E-2356	1985	I'll Play My Drum For Him
E-2361	1986	Christmas Joy From Head To Toe
E-2362	1988	Baby's First Christmas
E-2364	1989	Goat
E-2365	1984	The First Noel
E-2366	1984	The First Noel
E-2367	1984	The First Noel
E-2372	1985	Baby's First Christmas
E-2377	1985	Our First Christmas Together
E-2378	1985	Our First Christmas Together
E-2381	1984	Mouse With Cheese
E-2386	1984	Camel, Donkey, Cow
E-2801	1984	Jesus Is Born
E-2802	1984	Christmas Is The Time To Share
E-2803	1984	Crown Him Lord Of All
E-2804	1984	Peace On Earth
E-2807	1984	Crown Him Lord Of All
E-2808	1984	Unto Us A Child Is Born
E-2809	1985	Jesus Is Born
E-2823	1987	To God Be The Glory
E-2826	1986	May Your Birthday Be A Blessing

SUSPENDED CONTINUED

E-2827	1986	I Get A Kick Out Of You
E-2840	1988	Baby's First Step
E-2851	1989	Kristy Doll
E-3105	1984	He Watches Over Us All
E-3108	1984	The Hand That Rocks The Future
E-3119	1984	It's What's Inside That Counts
E-3120	1986	To Thee With Love
E-4720	1987	The Lord Bless You And Keep You
E-4722	1985	Love Cannot Break A True Friendship
E-4723	1984	Peace Amid The Storm
E-4725	1984	Peace On Earth
E-4726	1984	Peace On Earth
E-5200	1984	Bear Ye One Another's Burdens
E-5201	1984	Love Lifted Me
E-5202	1984	Thank You For Coming To My Ade
E-5203	1984	Let Not The Sun Go Down Upon Your Wrath
E-5205	1985	My Guardian Angel
E-5206	1988	My Guardian Angel
E-5207	1984	My Guardian Angel
E-5208	1985	Jesus Loves Me
E-5209	1985	Jesus Loves Me
E-5210	1984	Prayer Changes Things
E-5213	1989	God Is Love
E-5214	1984	Prayer Changes Things
E-5216	1987	The Lord Bless You And Keep You
E-5376	1986	May Your Christmas Be Blessed
E-5378	1989	Joy To The World
E-5380	1986	A Monarch Is Born
E-5381	1987	His Name Is Jesus
E-5382	1986	For God So Loved The World
E-5385	1986	Oh Worship The Lord
E-5386	1986	Oh Worship The Lord
E-5389	1986	Peace On Earth
E-5390	1989	May God Bless You With A Perfect Holiday Season
E-5391	1989	Love Is Kind
E-5394	1986	Wishing You A Merry Christmas
E-5619	1985	Come Let Us Adore Him
E-5620	1985	We Have Seen His Star
E-5623	1984	Jesus Is Born
E-5627	1985	But Love Goes On Forever
E-5628	1985	But Love Goes On Forever
E-5630	1985	Unto Us A Child Is Born
E-5631	1985	Baby's First Christmas
E-5632	1985	Baby's First Christmas
E-5633	1984	Come Let Us Adore Him
E-5634	1984	Wee Three Kings
E-5639	1985	Isn't He Wonderful
E-5640	1985	Isn't He Wonderful
E-5641	1985	They Followed The Star
E-5642	1985	Silent Knight
E-6118	1988	But Love Goes On Forever
E-6214B	1985	Mikey
E-6214G	1985	Debbie
E-6613	1987	God Sends The Gift Of His Love
E-6901	1986	Collection Plaque

SUSPENDED CONTINUED

E-7153	1986	God Is Love, Dear Valentine
E-7154	1986	God Is Love, Dear Valentine
E-7155	1984	Thanking Him For You
E-7156	1985	I Believe In Miracles
E-7159	1985	Lord Give Me Patience
E-7160	1986	The Perfect Grandpa
E-7161	1984	His Sheep Am I
E-7162	1984	Love Is Sharing
E-7163	1984	God Is Watching Over You
E-7164	1984	Bless This House
E-7165	1987	Let The Whole World Know
E-7167	1985	The Lord Bless You And Keep You
E-7168	1984	My Guardian Angel
E-7169	1984	My Guardian Angel
E-7170	1985	Jesus Loves Me
E-7171	1985	Jesus Loves Me
E-7172	1985	Rejoicing With You
E-7175	1985	The Lord Bless You And Keep You
E-7176	1985	The Lord Bless You And Keep You
E-7177	1987	The Lord Bless You And Keep You
E-7178	1987	The Lord Bless You And Keep You
E-7181	1988	Mother Sew Dear
E-7183	1988	The Purr-fect Grandma
E-7186	1986	Let The Whole World Know
E-7241	1986	Mother Sew Dear
E-7242	1988	The Purr-fect Grandma
E-9251	1985	Love Is Patient
E-9252	1989	Forgiving Is Forgetting
E-9253	1985	The End Is In Sight
E-9260	1987	God's Promises Are Sure
E-9261	1986	Seek Ye The Lord
E-9262	1986	Seek Ye The Lord
E-9263	1985	How Can Two Walk Together Except They Agree
E-9266	1988	I'm Falling For Somebunny & Our Love Is Heaven-Scent
E-9275	1984	Jesus Loves Me
E-9276	1984	Jesus Loves Me
E-9280	1985	Jesus Loves Me
E-9281	1985	Jesus Loves Me
E-9283A	1984	Forever Friends - Dog
E-9283B	1984	Forever Friends - Cat
E-9285	1985	If God Be For Us, Who Can Be Against Us
E-9287	1986	Peace On Earth
E-9288	1986	Sending You A Rainbow
E-9289	1987	Trust In The Lord
12017	1987	Loving You
12025	1987	Loving You
12033	1987	God's Precious Gift
12149	1989	Part Of Me Wants To Be Good
12165	1989	Lord, Keep My Life In Tune
12203	1986	Get Into The Habit Of Prayer
12211	1987	Baby's First Haircut
12297	1987	It Is Better To Give Than To Receive
12335	1988	You Can Fly
12343	1986	Jesus Is Coming Soon
12351	1988	Halo, And Merry Christmas

SUSPENDED CONTINUED

12408	1987	We Saw A Star
12424	1986	Aaron
12432	1986	Bethany
12475	1986	P.D.
12483	1986	Trish
15822	1989	May Your Christmas Be Happy
15830	1989	Happiness Is The Lord
16012	1989	Baby's First Trip
16020	1989	God Bless You With Rainbows
100021	1988	To My Favorite Paw
100544	1989	Brotherly Love
100625	1989	God Is Love, Dear Valentine
100668	1988	Clown Thimbles
102415	1989	It's A Perfect Boy
102431	1988	Serve With A Smile
102458	1988	Serve With A Smile
102490	1988	Sharing Our Christmas Together
102962	1989	It's The Birthday Of A King

QUICK REFERENCE • Item Number Order

DATED ANNUALS

E-0505	1983	Christmastime Is For Sharing
E-0513	1983	Surround Us With Joy
E-0518	1983	Blessed Are The Pure In Heart
E-0522	1983	Surrounded With Joy
E-2357	1982	I'll Play My Drum For Him
E-2358	1982	I'll Play My Drum For Him*
E-2359	1982	I'll Play My Drum For Him
E-5383	1984	Wishing You A Merry Christmas
E-5387	1984	Wishing You A Merry Christmas
E-5392	1984	Blessed Are The Pure In Heart
E-5393	1984	Wishing You A Merry Christmas
E-5396	1984	The Wonder Of Christmas
E-5622	1981	Let The Heavens Rejoice
E-5629	1981	Let The Heavens Rejoice
15237	1985	Tell Me The Story Of Jesus
15539	1985	Baby's First Christmas
15547	1985	Baby's First Christmas
15768	1985	God Sent His Love
15865	1985	God Sent His Love
15873	1985	God Sent His Love
15881	1985	God Sent His Love
15903	1985	Baby's First Christmas
15911	1985	Baby's First Christmas
101834	1986	I'm Sending You A White Christmas
102318	1986	Wishing You A Cozy Christmas
102326	1986	Wishing You A Cozy Christmas
102334	1986	Wishing You A Cozy Christmas
102342	1986	Wishing You A Cozy Christmas
102350	1986	Our First Christmas Together
102466	1986	Reindeer Ornament
102504	1986	Baby's First Christmas
102512	1986	Baby's First Christmas
102954	1987	My Peace I Give Unto Thee
104515	1987	Bear The Good News Of Christmas
109401	1987	Baby's First Christmas
109428	1987	Baby's First Christmas
109770	1987	Love Is The Best Gift Of All
109835	1987	Love Is The Best Gift Of All
109843	1987	Love Is The Best Gift Of All
110930	1987	Love Is The Best Gift Of All
112399	1987	Our First Christmas Together
115282	1988	Baby's First Christmas
115304	1988	Time To Wish You A Merry Christmas
115312	1988	Time To Wish You A Merry Christmas
115320	1988	Time To Wish You A Merry Christmas
115339	1988	Time To Wish You A Merry Christmas
520233	1988	Our First Christmas Together
520241	1988	Baby's First Christmas

* Prototypes were dated, it appears actual production wasn't.

DATED ANNUALS CONTINUED

520276	1988	You Are My Gift Come True
520284	1988	Merry Christmas, Deer
520292	1988	Hang On For The Holly Days
520462	1989	Christmas Is Ruff Without You
520497	1990	Wishing You A Purr-fect Holiday
521558	1989	Our First Christmas Together
522546	1989	Oh Holy Night
522554	1989	Oh Holy Night
522821	1989	Oh Holy Night
522848	1989	Oh Holy Night
523003	1989	May Your Christmas Be A Happy Home
523062	1989	Peace On Earth
523194	1989	Baby's First Christmas
523208	1989	Baby's First Christmas
523704	1990	May Your Christmas Be A Happy Home
523771	1990	Baby's First Christmas
523798	1990	Baby's First Christmas
523801	1990	Wishing You A Yummy Christmas
523828	1990	Once Upon A Holy Night
523836	1990	Once Upon A Holy Night
523844	1990	Once Upon A Holy Night
523852	1990	Once Upon A Holy Night
525324	1990	Our First Christmas Together

ANNUALS

E-2838	1987	This Is The Day Which The Lord Hath Made
12068	1985	The Voice Of Spring
12076	1985	Summer's Joy
12084	1986	Autumn's Praise
12092	1986	Winter's Song
12106	1985	The Voice Of Spring
12114	1985	Summer's Joy
12122	1986	Autumn's Praise
12130	1986	Winter's Song
100536	1987	I Picked A Very Special Mom
100641	1986	Four Seasons Thimbles
102903	1987	We Are All Precious In His Sight
102938	1986	God Bless America
107999	1987	He Walks With Me
114022	1988	The Good Lord Has Blessed Us Tenfold
115231	1988	You Are My Main Event
115479	1988	Blessed Are They That Overcome
520861	1989	Sharing Begins In The Heart
522376	1989	His Love Will Shine On You
523526	1990	I'm A PRECIOUS MOMENTS Fan
524522	1990	Always In His Care
525049	1990	Good Friends Are Forever

THE CLUBS

"Symbols of Membership" are received with enrollment in the Club. Charter members who renew receive "Symbols of Charter Membership." All members have the option to purchase "Membership Pieces" that are crafted exclusively for Club Members.

The Enesco PRECIOUS MOMENTS Collectors' Club is on a calendar year basis. Collectors renewing or joining by December 31 receive that year's Symbol of Membership. Order forms for the Membership Pieces must be taken to an authorized Enesco PRECIOUS MOMENTS Retailer by March 31 of the following year.

The Enesco PRECIOUS MOMENTS Birthday Club's year runs from July 1 to June 30. Order forms for the Membership Pieces must be redeemed by September 30.

Currently The Enesco PRECIOUS MOMENTS Collectors' Club membership fee is $21.00 for new members, $19.50 for renewals. The Enesco PRECIOUS MOMENTS Birthday Club membership fee is $11.50 for new members, $10.00 for renewals.

THE ENESCO PRECIOUS MOMENTS BIRTHDAY CLUB

SYMBOLS OF CHARTER MEMBERSHIP

B-0001	1986	Our Club Can't Be Beat
B-0102	1987	A Smile's The Cymbal Of Joy
B-0103	1988	The Sweetest Club Around
B-0104	1989	Have A Beary Special Birthday

SYMBOLS OF MEMBERSHIP

B-0002	1987	A Smile's The Cymbal Of Joy
B-0003	1988	The Sweetest Club Around
B-0004	1989	Have A Beary Special Birthday

MEMBERSHIP PIECES

BC-861	Fishing For Friends
BC-871	Hi Sugar!
BC-881	Somebunny Cares
BC-891	Can't Bee Hive Myself Without You

THE ENESCO PRECIOUS MOMENTS COLLECTORS' CLUB

SYMBOLS OF CHARTER MEMBERSHIP

E-0001	1981	But Love Goes On Forever
E-0102	1982	But Love Goes On Forever
E-0103	1983	Let Us Call The Club To Order
E-0104	1984	Join In On The Blessings
E-0105	1985	Seek And Ye Shall Find
E-0106	1986	Birds Of A Feather Collect Together
E-0107	1987	Sharing Is Universal
E-0108	1988	A Growing Love
C-0109	1989	Always Room For One More
C-0110	1990	My Happiness

SYMBOLS OF MEMBERSHIP

E-0202	1982	But Love Goes On Forever
E-0303	1983	Let Us Call The Club To Order
E-0404	1984	Join In On The Blessings
E-0005	1985	Seek And Ye Shall Find
E-0006	1986	Birds Of A Feather Collect Together
E-0007	1987	Sharing Is Universal
E-0008	1988	A Growing Love
C-0009	1989	Always Room For One More
C-0010	1990	My Happiness

MEMBERSHIP PIECES

PM-811	Hello Lord, It's Me Again
PM-821	Smile, God Loves You
PM-822	Put On A Happy Face
PM-831	Dawn's Early Light
PM-841	God's Ray Of Mercy
PM-842	Trust In The Lord To The Finish
PM-851	The Lord Is My Shepherd
PM-852	I Love To Tell The Story
PM-861	Grandma's Prayer
12440	God Bless Our Years Together
PM-862	I'm Following Jesus
PM-871	Feed My Sheep
PM-872	In His Time
PM-873	Loving You Dear Valentine
PM-874	Loving You Dear Valentine
PM-881	God Bless You For Touching My Life
PM-882	You Just Cannot Chuck A Good Friendship
PM-891	You Will Always Be My Choice
PM-892	Mow Power To Ya

SHARING SEASON ORNAMENTS

PM-864	1986	Birds Of A Feather Collect Together
PM-009	1987	Sharing Season Ornament
520349	1988	A Growing Love
522961	1989	Always Room For One More

QUICK REFERENCE • Outline of Annuals

JOY OF CHRISTMAS PLATE SERIES   (Series of 4, Dated)
E-2357	1982	Il Play My Drum For Him
E-0505	1983	Christmastime Is For Sharing
E-5396	1984	The Wonder Of Christmas
15237	1985	Tell Me The Story Of Jesus

THE FOUR SEASONS PLATES   (Set of 4, Unnumbered Certificate)
12106	1985	The Voice Of Spring
12114	1985	Summer's Joy
12122	1986	Autumn's Praise
12130	1986	Winter's Song

THE FOUR SEASONS FIGURINES   (Set of 4, Unnumbered Certificate)
12068	1985	The Voice Of Spring
12076	1985	Summer's Joy
12084	1986	Autumn's Praise
12092	1986	Winter's Song

THE FOUR SEASONS THIMBLES   (Set of 4)
100641	1986	Four Seasons Thimbles

CHRISTMAS LOVE PLATE SERIES   (Series of 4, Dated)
101834	1986	I'm Sending You A White Christmas
102954	1987	My Peace I Give To Thee
520284	1988	Merry Christmas, Deer
523003	1989	May Your Christmas Be A Happy Home

SPECIAL EASTER SEAL FIGURINES
107999	1987	He Walks With Me
115479	1988	Blessed Are They That Overcome
522376	1989	His Love Will Shine On You
524522	1990	Always In His Care

SPECIAL EVENTS PIECES
115231	1988	You Are My Main Event
520861	1989	Sharing Begins In The Heart
523526	1990	I'm A PRECIOUS MOMENTS Fan
525049	1990	Good Friends Are Forever

ANNUAL FIGURINES   (Dated)
E-5383	1984	Wishing You A Merry Christmas
15539	1985	Baby's First Christmas (Boy)
15547	1985	Baby's First Christmas (Girl)
15881	1985	God Sent His Love
102342	1986	Wishing You A Cozy Christmas
110930	1987	Love Is The Best Gift Of All
115339	1988	Time To Wish You A Merry Christmas
522546	1989	Oh Holy Night
523836	1990	Once Upon A Holy Night

ANNUAL BELLS (Dated)

E-5622	1981	Let The Heavens Rejoice
E-2358	1982	I'll Play My Drum For Him
E-0522	1983	Surrounded With Joy
E-5393	1984	Wishing You A Merry Christmas
15873	1985	God Sent His Love
102318	1986	Wishing You A Cozy Christmas
109835	1987	Love Is The Best Gift Of All
115304	1988	Time To Wish You A Merry Christmas
522821	1989	Oh Holy Night
523828	1990	Once Upon A Holy Night

ANNUAL ORNAMENTS (Dated)

E-5629	1981	Let The Heavens Rejoice
E-2359	1982	I'll Play My Drum For Him
E-0513	1983	Surround Us With Joy
E-0518	1983	Blessed Are The Pure In Heart
E-5387	1984	Wishing You A Merry Christmas
E-5392	1984	Blessed Are The Pure In Heart
15768	1985	God Sent His Love
15903	1985	Baby's First Christmas (Boy)
15911	1985	Baby's First Christmas (Girl)
102326	1986	Wishing You A Cozy Christmas
102350	1986	Our First Christmas Together
102504	1986	Baby's First Christmas (Girl)
102512	1986	Baby's First Christmas (Boy)
109401	1987	Baby's First Christmas (Girl)
109428	1987	Baby's First Christmas (Boy)
109770	1987	Love Is The Best Gift Of All
112399	1987	Our First Christmas Together
115282	1988	Baby's First Christmas (Boy)
115320	1988	Time To Wish You A Merry Christmas
520233	1988	Our First Christmas Together
520241	1988	Baby's First Christmas (Girl)
520276	1988	You Are My Gift Come True
521558	1989	Our First Christmas Together
522848	1989	Oh Holy Night
523062	1989	Peace On Earth
523194	1989	Baby's First Christmas (Boy)
523208	1989	Baby's First Christmas (Girl)
523704	1990	May Your Christmas Be A Happy Home
523771	1990	Baby's First Christmas (Girl)
523798	1990	Baby's First Christmas (Boy)
523852	1990	Once Upon A Holy Night
525324	1990	Our First Christmas Together

ANNUAL THIMBLES (Dated)

15865	1985	God Sent His Love
102334	1986	Wishing You A Cozy Christmas
109843	1987	Love Is The Best Gift Of All
115312	1988	Time To Wish You A Merry Christmas
522554	1989	Oh Holy Night
523844	1990	Once Upon A Holy Night

OUTLINE OF ANNUALS CONTINUED

BIRTHDAY COLLECTION ANNUAL ORNAMENTS   (Dated)

102466	1986	Reindeer
104515	1987	Bear The Good News Of Christmas
520292	1988	Hang On For The Holly Days
520462	1989	Christmas Is Ruff Without You
520497	1990	Wishing You A Purr-fect Holiday

CHRISTMAS BLESSINGS PLATE SERIES   (Dated)

| 523801 | 1990 | Wishing You A Yummy Christmas |

OUTLINE OF THE SERIES

MOTHER'S LOVE PLATE SERIES   (Series of 4, Individually Numbered)

E-5217	Mother Sew Dear
E-7173	The Purr-Fect Grandma
E-9256	The Hand That Rocks The Future
E-2848	Loving Thy Neighbor

INSPIRED THOUGHTS PLATE SERIES   (Series of 4, Individually Numbered)

E-5215	Love One Another
E-7174	Make A Joyful Noise
E-9257	I Believe In Miracles
E-2847	Love Is Kind

CHRISTMAS COLLECTION PLATE SERIES   (Series of 4, Individually Numbered)

E-5646	Come Let Us Adore Him
E-2347	Let Heaven And Nature Sing
E-0538	Wee Three Kings
E-5395	Unto Us A Child Is Born

BRIDAL SERIES   (Series of 8)

E-2831	Bridesmaid
E-2836	Groomsman
E-2835	Flower Girl
E-2833	Ringbearer
E-2845	Junior Bridesmaid
E-2837	Groom
E-2846	Bride
E-2838	This Is The Day Which The Lord Hath Made

"BABY'S FIRST" SERIES   (Series of 5)

E-2840	Baby's First Step
E-2841	Baby's First Picture
12211	Baby's First Haircut
16012	Baby's First Trip
520705	Baby's First Pet

OUTLINE OF THE SERIES CONTINUED

CLOWN SERIES   (Series of 4)
12262	I Get A Bang Out Of You
12459	Waddle I Do Without You
12467	The Lord Will Carry You Through
12270	Lord Keep Me On The Ball

REJOICE IN THE LORD BAND SERIES   (Series of 6)
12165	Lord, Keep My Life In Tune
12173	There's A Song In My Heart
12378	Happiness Is The Lord
12386	Lord Give Me A Song
12394	He Is My Song
12580	Lord, Keep My Life In Tune

CALENDAR GIRL SERIES   (Series of 12)
109983	January Girl
109991	February Girl
110019	March Girl
110027	April Girl
110035	May Girl
110043	June Girl
110051	July Girl
110078	August Girl
110086	September Girl
110094	October Girl
110108	November Girl
110116	December Girl

THE FAMILY CHRISTMAS SCENE SERIES   (Series of 7)
15776	May You Have The Sweetest Christmas
15784	The Story Of God's Love
15792	Tell Me A Story
15806	God Gave His Best
15814	Silent Night
522856	Have A Beary Merry Christmas
524883	Christmas Fireplace

THE BIRTHDAY CIRCUS TRAIN SERIES   (Series of 10)
15938	May Your Birthday Be Warm
15946	Happy Birthday Little Lamb
15962	God Bless You On Your Birthday
15954	Heaven Bless Your Special Day
15970	May Your Birthday Be Gigantic
15989	This Day Is Something To Roar About
15997	Keep Looking Up
109479	Wishing You Grrr-eatness
109460	Isn't Eight Just Great
16004	Bless The Days Of Our Youth

	1981	1982
RETIRED	E-1378 God Loveth A Cheerful Giver E-2011 Come Let Us Adore Him	E-1374B Praise The Lord Anyhow
SUSPENDED		
ANNUALS	E-5622 Let The Heavens Rejoice E-5629 Let The Heavens Rejoice	E-2357 I'll Play My Drum For Him E-2358 I'll Play My Drum For Him E-2359 I'll Play My Drum For Him

	1983	1984
R E T I R E D	E-3112 God's Speed E-3118 Eggs Over Easy	E-1373B Smile, God Loves You E-1380G His Burden Is Light E-1380B O, How I Love Jesus E-2368 The First Noel E-2806 Christmas Is A Time To Share E-5211 God Understands E-6120 We Have Seen His Star
S U S P E N D E D		E-1375B Prayer Changes Things E-1377A He Leadeth Me E-1377B He Careth For You E-1379A Love Is Kind E-1379B God Understands E-1381 Jesus Is The Answer E-2010 We Have Seen His Star E-2012 Jesus Is Born E-2013 Unto Us A Child Is Born E-2345 May Your Christmas Be Cozy E-2350 Dropping In For Christmas E-2352 O Come All Ye Faithful E-2355 I'll Play My Drum For Him E-2365 The First Noel E-2366 The First Noel E-2367 The First Noel E-2381 Mouse with Cheese E-2386 Camel, Donkey, Cow Ornaments E-2801 Jesus Is Born E-2802 Christmas Is The Time To Share E-2803 Crown Him Lord Of All E-2804 Peace On Earth E-2807 Crown Him Lord Of All E-2808 Unto Us A Child Is Born E-3105 He Watches Over Us All E-3108 The Hand That Rocks The Future E-3119 It's What's Inside That Counts E-4723 Peace Amid The Storm E-4725 Peace On Earth E-4726 Peace On Earth E-5200 Bear Ye One Another's Burdens E-5201 Love Lifted Me E-5202 Thank You For Coming To My Ade E-5203 Let Not The Sun Go Down Upon Your Wrath E-5207 My Guardian Angel E-5210 Prayer Changes Things E-5214 Prayer Changes Things E-5623 Jesus Is Born E-5633 Come Let Us Adore Him E-5634 Wee Three Kings E-7155 Thanking Him For You E-7161 His Sheep Am I E-7162 Love Is Sharing E-7163 God Is Watching Over You E-7164 Bless This House E-7168 My Guardian Angel E-7169 My Guardian Angel E-9275 Jesus Loves Me E-9276 Jesus Loves Me E-9283A Forever Friends - Dog E-9283B Forever Friends - Cat
A N N U A L S	E-0505 Christmastime Is For Sharing E-0513 Surround Us With Joy E-0518 Blessed Are The Pure In Heart E-0522 Surrounded With Joy	E-5383 Wishing You A Merry Christmas E-5387 Wishing You A Merry Christmas E-5392 Baby's First Christmas E-5393 Wishing You A Merry Christmas E-5396 The Wonder Of Christmas

1985

RETIRED	E-2376	Dropping Over For Christmas
	E-2805	Wishing You A Season Filled With Joy
	E-2850	Mother Sew Dear
	E-3107	Blessed Are The Peacemakers
	E-3111	Be Not Weary In Well Doing
	E-7185	Love Is Sharing

SUSPENDED	E-0526	He Upholdeth Those Who Call
	E-0537	Jesus Is The Light
	E-2344	Joy To The World
	E-2349	Tell Me The Story Of Jesus
	E-2356	I'll Play My Drum For Him
	E-2372	Baby's First Christmas
	E-2377	Our First Christmas Together
	E-2378	Our First Christmas Together
	E-2809	Jesus Is Born
	E-4722	Love Cannot Break A True Friendship
	E-5205	My Guardian Angel
	E-5208	Jesus Loves Me
	E-5209	Jesus Loves Me
	E-5619	Come Let Us Adore Him
	E-5620	We Have Seen His Star
	E-5627	But Love Goes On Forever
	E-5628	But Love Goes On Forever
	E-5630	Unto Us A Child Is Born
	E-5631	Baby's First Christmas
	E-5632	Baby's First Christmas
	E-5639	Isn't He Wonderful
	E-5640	Isn't He Wonderful
	E-5641	They Followed The Star
	E-5642	Silent Knight
	E-6214B	Mikey
	E-6214G	Debbie
	E-7156	I Believe In Miracles
	E-7159	Lord Give Me Patience
	E-7167	The Lord Bless You And Keep You
	E-7170	Jesus Loves Me
	E-7171	Jesus Loves Me
	E-7172	Rejoicing With You
	E-7175	The Lord Bless You And Keep You
	E-7176	The Lord Bless You And Keep You
	E-9251	Love Is Patient
	E-9253	The End Is In Sight
	E-9263	How Can Two Walk Together Except They Agree
	E-9280	Jesus Loves Me
	E-9281	Jesus Loves Me
	E-9285	If God Be For Us, Who Can Be Against Us

ANNUALS	12068	The Voice Of Spring*
	12076	Summer's Joy*
	12106	The Voice Of Spring*
	12114	Summer's Joy*
	15237	Tell Me The Story Of Jesus
	15539	Baby's First Christmas
	15547	Baby's First Christmas
	15768	God Sent His Love
	15865	God Sent His Love
	15873	God Sent His Love
	15881	God Sent His Love
	15903	Baby's First Christmas
	15911	Baby's First Christmas

*Not Dated

1986

RETIRED	E-0519	Sharing Our Season Together
	E-0532	Let Heaven And Nature Sing
	E-2353	O Come All Ye Faithful
	E-2369	Dropping In For Christmas
	E-2841	Baby's First Picture
	E-7157	There Is Joy In Serving Jesus
	E-9274	Taste And See That The Lord Is Good

SUSPENDED	E-0501	Sharing Our Season Together
	E-0502	Jesus Is The Light That Shines
	E-0503	Blessings From My House To Yours
	E-0508	Prepare Ye The Way Of The Lord
	E-0520	Wee Three Kings
	E-0531	O Come All Ye Faithful
	E-0535	Love Is Patient
	E-0536	Love Is Patient
	E-2361	Christmas Joy From Head To Toe
	E-2826	May Your Birthday Be A Blessing
	E-2827	I Get A Kick Out Of You
	E-3120	To Thee With Love
	E-5376	May Your Christmas Be Blessed
	E-5380	A Monarch Is Born
	E-5382	For God So Loved The World
	E-5385	Oh Worship The Lord
	E-5386	Oh Worship The Lord
	E-5389	Peace On Earth
	E-5394	Wishing You A Merry Christmas
	E-6901	Collection Plaque
	E-7153	God Is Love, Dear Valentine
	E-7154	God Is Love, Dear Valentine
	E-7160	The Perfect Grandpa
	E-7186	Let The Whole World Know
	E-7241	Mother Sew Dear
	E-9261	Seek Ye The Lord
	E-9262	Seek Ye The Lord
	E-9287	Peace On Earth
	E-9288	Sending You A Rainbow
	12203	Get Into The Habit Of Prayer
	12343	Jesus Is Coming Soon
	12424	Aaron
	12432	Bethany
	12475	P.D.
	12483	Trish

ANNUALS	12084	Autumn's Praise*
	12092	Winter's Song*
	12122	Autumn's Praise*
	12130	Winter's Song*
	100641	Four Seasons Thimbles*
	102938	God Bless America*
	101834	I'm Sending You A White Christmas
	102318	Wishing You A Cozy Christmas
	102326	Wishing You A Cozy Christmas
	102334	Wishing You A Cozy Christmas
	102342	Wishing You A Cozy Christmas
	102350	Our First Christmas Together
	102466	Reindeer Ornament
	102504	Baby's First Christmas
	102512	Baby's First Christmas

*Not Dated

	1987		1988	
R	E-0530	His Eye Is On The Sparrow	E-1373G	Jesus Is The Light
E	E-2351	Holy Smokes	E-2371	Unicorn
T	E-5377	Love Is Kind	E-2822	This Is Your Day To Shine
I	E-5388	Joy To The World	E-5645	Rejoice O Earth
R	E-9273	Let Love Reign	12467	The Lord Will Carry You Through
E			100129	Lord Keep Me On My Toes
D				
	E-0507	God Sent His Son	E-0515	To A Special Dad
	E-0509	Bringing God's Blessing To You	E-0533	Tell Me The Story Of Jesus
	E-0521	Blessed Are The Pure In Heart	E-0539	Katie Lynne
	E-2823	To God Be The Glory	E-2343	Joy To The World
	E-4720	The Lord Bless You And Keep You	E-2348	May Your Christmas Be Warm
	E-5216	The Lord Bless You And Keep You	E-2362	Baby's First Christmas
	E-5381	His Name Is Jesus	E-2840	Baby's First Step
S	E-6613	God Sends The Gift Of His Love	E-5206	My Guardian Angel
U	E-7165	Let The Whole World Know	E-6118	But Love Goes On Forever
S	E-7177	The Lord Bless You And Keep You	E-7181	Mother Sew Dear
P	E-7178	The Lord Bless You And Keep You	E-7183	The Purr-fect Grandma
E	E-9260	God's Promises Are Sure	E-7242	The Purr-fect Grandma
N	E-9289	Trust In The Lord	E-9266	I'm Falling For Somebunny &
D	12017	Loving You		Our Love Is Heaven-Scent
E	12025	Loving You	12335	You Can Fly
D	12033	God's Precious Gift	12351	Halo, And Merry Christmas
	12211	Baby's First Haircut	100021	To My Favorite Paw
	12297	It Is Better To Give Than To Receive	100668	Clown Thimbles
	12408	We Saw A Star	102431	Serve With A Smile
			102458	Serve With A Smile
			102490	Sharing Our Christmas Together
	E-2838	This Is The Day Which The Lord Hath Made*	114022	The Good Lord Blessed Us Tenfold*
	100536	I Picked A Very Special Mom*	115231	You Are My Main Event*
A	102903	We Are All Precious In His Sight*	115479	Blessed Are They That Overcome*
N	107999	He Walks With Me*		
N			115282	Baby's First Christmas
U	102954	My Peace I Give Unto Thee	115304	Time To Wish You A Merry Christmas
A	104515	Bear The Good News Of Christmas	115312	Time To Wish You A Merry Christmas
L	109401	Baby's First Christmas	115320	Time To Wish You A Merry Christmas
S	109428	Baby's First Christmas	115339	Time To Wish You A Merry Christmas
	109770	Love Is The Best Gift Of All	520233	Our First Christmas Together
	109835	Love Is The Best Gift Of All	520241	Baby's First Christmas
	109843	Love Is The Best Gift Of All	520276	You Are My Gift Come True
	110930	Love Is The Best Gift Of All	520284	Merry Christmas Deer
	112399	Our First Christmas Together	520292	Hang On For The Holly Days
	*Not Dated		*Not Dated	

1989

RETIRED

E-0506	Surrounded With Joy
E-0525	You Can't Run Away From God
E-0534	To Thee With Love
12459	Waddie I Do Without You
15504	God Sent You Just In Time
100269	Help Lord, I'm In A Spot

SUSPENDED

E-2346	Let Heaven And Nature Sing
E-2364	Goat
E-2851	Kristy
E-5213	God Is Love
E-5378	Joy To The World
E-5390	May God Bless You With A Perfect Holiday Season
E-5391	Love Is Kind
E-9252	Forgiving Is Forgetting
12149	Part Of Me Wants To Be Good
12165	Lord, Keep My Life In Tune
15822	May Your Christmas Be Happy
15830	Happiness Is The Lord
16012	Baby's First Trip
16020	God Bless You With Rainbows
100544	Brotherly Love
100625	God Is Love, Dear Valentine
102415	It's A Perfect Boy
102962	It's The Birthday Of A King

ANNUALS

520861	Sharing Begins In The Heart*
522376	His Love Will Shine On You*
520462	Christmas Is Ruff Without You
521558	Our First Christmas Together
522546	Oh Holy Night
522554	Oh Holy Night
522821	Oh Holy Night
522848	Oh Holy Night
523003	May Your Christmas Be A Happy Home
523062	Peace On Earth
523194	Baby's First Christmas
523208	Baby's First Christmas

*Not Dated

1990

RETIRED and SUSPENDED Pieces for 1990 not announced at Press Time.

ANNUALS

523526	I'm A PRECIOUS MOMENTS Fan*
524522	Always In His Care*
525049	Good Friends Are Forever*
520497	Wishing You A Purr-fect Holiday
520704	May Your Christmas Be A Happy Home
523771	Baby's First Christmas
523798	Baby's First Christmas
523801	Wishing You A Yummy Christmas
523828	Once Upon A Holy Night
523836	Once Upon A Holy Night
523844	Once Upon A Holy Night
523852	Once Upon A Holy Night
525324	Our First Christmas Together

*Not Dated

INSURING YOUR PRECIOUS MOMENTS COLLECTIBLES

Every day we receive phone calls from collectors who have experienced a loss. Basically, they can be divided into two groups — those who had their collection insured and are coping with the emotional aspect of the loss and those who have the same emotional trauma but must deal with a financial loss as well because they were not properly insured.

As an educated collector, you must be aware your homeowner's or renter's policy may not automatically cover the loss of your collectibles. We suggest you contact your insurance agent and ask what coverage your policy provides. You might also want to inquire about a "Scheduled Personal Property Endorsement for Fine Arts" to determine if the comprehensive coverage this special policy provides is worth the additional premium dollars in your individual case.

In addition, for your protection, we suggest you do the following:

- Maintain a complete up-to-date inventory listing of your PRECIOUS MOMENTS collectibles including the title of each piece, the Enesco Item Number, a brief description, the annual symbol and current value (GREENBOOK Market Price). If you have a one-of-a-kind piece and need a Market Price, write to us. Keep the original bill of sale, or, if it was a gift, record the name of the person who gave it to you as well as the occasion or date.

- Take photos of your collection in its normal setting to document ownership if and when you have a loss.

- Keep the inventory listing and photos in a safe place, not on the same premises as your collection.

By addressing the insurance issue now, you can eliminate surprises if and when you have a loss.

HOW TO READ A GREENBOOK LISTING

GREENBOOK Listings are in Enesco Item Number order.

Enesco PRECIOUS MOMENTS Collectors' Club and Enesco PRECIOUS MOMENTS Birthday Club pieces are in separate sections at the end of the Listings.

Enesco Item Numbers can be found on the understamp of most pieces produced from 1982 to the present.

If you don't know the Enesco Item Number, but you do know the Inspirational Title, use the ALPHA-LOG to obtain the Enesco Item Number. If you don't know the Enesco Item Number or the Inspirational Title, use the ART CHART to obtain the Enesco Item Number.

The following is a step-by-step explanation of how to read a GREENBOOK listing using the figurine E-1374B, *Praise The Lord Anyhow,* as an example:

PRAISE THE LORD ANYHOW		Figurine	See "Nobody's Perfect!" Section					
E-1374B	79	Boy with Dog and	UPP	$ 8.00	5.00"	NM	Retired/Sec	$105.00
(19)	81	Ice Cream Cone	UPP	8.00		TRI	Retired/Sec	95.00
	82		UPP	17.00		HRG	Retired/Sec	95.00

This portion of a listing is the **INSPIRATIONAL TITLE**.

PRAISE THE LORD ANYHOW		Figurine	See "Nobody's Perfect!" Section					
E-1374B	79	Boy with Dog and	UPP	$ 8.00	5.00"	NM	Retired/Sec	$105.00
(19)	81	Ice Cream Cone	UPP	8.00		TRI	Retired/Sec	95.00
	82		UPP	17.00		HRG	Retired/Sec	95.00

This portion of a listing is the **TYPE OF PRODUCT**.

PRAISE THE LORD ANYHOW		Figurine	See "Nobody's Perfect!" Section					
E-1374B	79	Boy with Dog and	UPP	$ 8.00	5.00"	NM	Retired/Sec	$105.00
(19)	81	Ice Cream Cone	UPP	8.00		TRI	Retired/Sec	95.00
	82		UPP	17.00		HRG	Retired/Sec	95.00

This portion of a listing is reserved for **MISCELLANEOUS INFORMATION**. For example, if the piece is listed in the NOBODY'S PERFECT! Section of the Guide that will be noted here. Other information appearing here includes series or set information, if a piece is dated, the tune if it's a musical, if it has a certificate, if it's individually numbered, or if the piece is a Nativity Addition.

PRAISE THE LORD ANYHOW		Figurine	See "Nobody's Perfect!" Section					
E-1374B	79	Boy with Dog and	UPP	$ 8.00	5.00"	NM	Retired/Sec	$105.00
(19)	81	Ice Cream Cone	UPP	8.00		TRI	Retired/Sec	95.00
	82		UPP	17.00		HRG	Retired/Sec	95.00

This portion of a listing is the **ENESCO ITEM NUMBER**. It appears in brochures, catalogs, ads, and on the understamp of most pieces produced from 1982 to the present. It is a quick and absolute means of identification.

PRAISE THE LORD ANYHOW		Figurine	See "Nobody's Perfect!" Section					
E-1374B	79	Boy with Dog and	UPP	$ 8.00	5.00"	NM	Retired/Sec	$105.00
(19)	81	Ice Cream Cone	UPP	8.00		TRI	Retired/Sec	95.00
	82		UPP	17.00		HRG	Retired/Sec	95.00

This portion of a listing is the **GREENBOOK ART CHART NUMBER**.

PRAISE THE LORD ANYHOW		Figurine	See "Nobody's Perfect!" Section					
E-1374B	79	Boy with Dog and	UPP	$ 8.00	5.00"	NM	Retired/Sec	$105.00
(19)	81	Ice Cream Cone	UPP	8.00		TRI	Retired/Sec	95.00
	82		UPP	17.00		HRG	Retired/Sec	95.00

This portion of a listing is the **YEAR OF ISSUE**. The GREENBOOK lists the year of issue for each change in annual symbol. A very common error made by collectors is to mistake the copyright date for the year of issue because the copyright date appears on the understamp written out as © 19XX. In other words, in order to determine what year your piece was produced, you must refer to the annual symbol, not the © date.

PRAISE THE LORD ANYHOW		Figurine	See "Nobody's Perfect!" Section					
E-1374B	79	Boy with Dog and	UPP	$ 8.00	5.00"	NM	Retired/Sec	$105.00
(19)	81	Ice Cream Cone	UPP	8.00		TRI	Retired/Sec	95.00
	82		UPP	17.00		HRG	Retired/Sec	95.00

This portion of a listing is the **DESCRIPTIVE TITLE**.

PRAISE THE LORD ANYHOW		Figurine	See "Nobody's Perfect!" Section					
E-1374B	79	Boy with Dog and	UPP	$ 8.00	5.00"	NM	Retired/Sec	$105.00
(19)	81	Ice Cream Cone	UPP	8.00		TRI	Retired/Sec	95.00
	82		UPP	17.00		HRG	Retired/Sec	95.00

This portion of a listing is the **EDITION SIZE**. Editions are either limited or open (unlimited). The GREENBOOK identifies editions that are limited in one of five ways. They are: 1) A Specific Number - i.e. 15,000, 2) By Year (Annual), 3) Two-Year Collectible (2yr), 4) Available to Club Members Only (MemOnly), or 5) An Unspecified Production Period (UPP).

.....continued on next page

HOW TO READ A GREENBOOK LISTING CONTINUED

PRAISE THE LORD ANYHOW		Figurine	See "Nobody's Perfect!" Section				
E-1374B	79	Boy with Dog and	UPP	$ 8.00	5.00"	NM	Retired/Sec $105.00
(19)	81	Ice Cream Cone	UPP	8.00		TRI	Retired/Sec 95.00
	82		UPP	17.00		HRG	Retired/Sec 95.00

This portion of a listing is the **ISSUE PRICE** (Suggested Retail). GREENBOOK Listings include issue prices for each piece when it was first introduced and for each year the annual symbol is/was changed.

PRAISE THE LORD ANYHOW		Figurine	See "Nobody's Perfect!" Section				
E-1374B	79	Boy with Dog and	UPP	$ 8.00	5.00"	NM	Retired/Sec $105.00
(19)	81	Ice Cream Cone	UPP	8.00		TRI	Retired/Sec 95.00
	82		UPP	17.00		HRG	Retired/Sec 95.00

This portion of a listing is the **SIZE** in inches; diameter for plates and plaques, height for figurines, bells.....

PRAISE THE LORD ANYHOW		Figurine	See "Nobody's Perfect!" Section				
E-1374B	79	Boy with Dog and	UPP	$ 8.00	5.00"	NM	Retired/Sec $105.00
(19)	81	Ice Cream Cone	UPP	8.00		TRI	Retired/Sec 95.00
	82		UPP	17.00		HRG	Retired/Sec 95.00

This portion of a listing is the **ANNUAL SYMBOL**. Since mid-1981 Enesco has indicated when PRECIOUS MOMENTS collectibles were produced by including an annual symbol as part of the understamp. Pieces crafted prior to 1981 have no annual symbol and have become known as "No Marks."

The GREENBOOK defines "No Mark" as prior to mid-1981.

There are also "Unmarked" PRECIOUS MOMENTS collectibles. It was not until 1984 that some product types such as plates and ornaments were marked with an annual symbol. The GREENBOOK defines 1981, 1982, and 1983 pieces that fall into this category as "Unmarked."

An "Unmarked" piece can also be a production error. Some pieces simply miss getting marked.

The facing page illustrates the different symbols and their meanings.

"Unmarked " pieces are designated as "UM" in the listings.

ANNUAL SYMBOLS:

Prior to 1981	"No Mark" (NM)		
1981	Triangle (TRI)	△	Symbol of the Triune - God, the Father, Son and Holy Spirit
1982	Hourglass (HRG)	⧗	Symbol of Time
1983	Fish (FSH)	🐟	Earliest symbol used by believers of the early apostolic church
1984	Cross (CRS)	✝	Symbol of Christianity recognized worldwide
1985	Dove (DVE)	🕊	Symbol of love and peace
1986	Olive Branch (OLB)	🌿	Symbol of peace and understanding
1987	Cedar Tree (CED)	🌲	Symbol of strength, beauty, and preservation
1988	Flower (FLW)	⚘	Represents God's love toward His children
1989	Bow & Arrow (B&A)	➴	Represents the power of the Bible
1990	Flame (FLM)	🕯	Designed for those who have found comfort through PRECIOUS MOMENTS

SPECIAL SYMBOLS:

Diamond (DIA)	◇
Easter Lily	Easter Seals
Rosebud	🌹

.....continued on next page

HOW TO READ A GREENBOOK LISTING CONTINUED

PRAISE THE LORD ANYHOW		Figurine	See "Nobody's Perfect!" Section					
E-1374B	79	Boy with Dog and	UPP	$ 8.00	5.00"	NM	Retired/Sec	$105.00
(19)	81	Ice Cream Cone	UPP	8.00		TRI	Retired/Sec	95.00
	82		UPP	17.00		HRG	Retired/Sec	95.00

This portion of a listing is the **MARKET STATUS**. Enesco periodically retires and suspends individual pieces. As a result, GREENBOOK uses eight different classifications of availability or market status. They are Primary, Secondary, Retired/Primary, Retired/Secondary, Suspended/Primary, Suspended/Secondary, Discontinued/Primary, and Discontinued/Secondary. Definitions of the eight different market status classifications are as follows:

PRIMARY   Piece available from retailers at issue price.

SECONDARY   Piece *not* generally available from retailers at issue price.

RETIRED/PRIMARY   Piece with specific Enesco Item Number will never be produced again. Piece still available from retailers at issue price.

RETIRED/SECONDARY   Piece with specific Enesco Item Number will never be produced again. Piece *not* generally available from retailers at issue price.

SUSPENDED/PRIMARY   Piece with specific Enesco Item Number not currently being produced but may be produced in the future. Piece still available from retailers at issue price.

SUSPENDED/SECONDARY   Piece with specific Enesco Item Number not currently being produced but may be produced in the future. Piece *not* generally available from retailers at issue price.

DISCONTINUED/PRIMARY   Production ceased on piece with specific Enesco Item Number. Piece still available from retailers at issue price.

DISCONTINUED/SECONDARY   Production ceased on piece with specific Enesco Item Number. Piece *not* generally available from retailers at issue

PRAISE THE LORD ANYHOW		Figurine	See "Nobody's Perfect!" Section					
E-1374B	79	Boy with Dog and	UPP	$ 8.00	5.00"	NM	Retired/Sec	$105.00
(19)	81	Ice Cream Cone	UPP	8.00		TRI	Retired/Sec	95.00
	82		UPP	17.00		HRG	Retired/Sec	95.00

This portion of a listing is the **GREENBOOK MARKET PRICE**. It reflects the current primary and secondary market prices for each piece. The prices reported *are not absolute* but are a reliable guide based on extensive experience in gathering information about market prices and how they are affected by market status as well as edition limits, year of issue, and popularity of the piece.

CHEAT SHEET

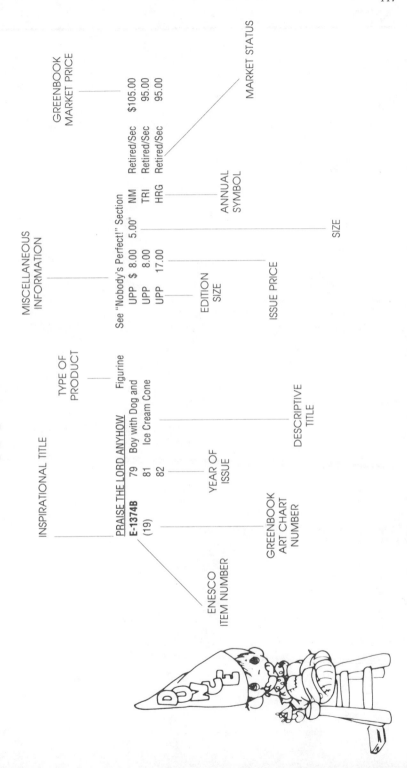

INSPIRATIONAL TITLE

TYPE OF PRODUCT

MISCELLANEOUS INFORMATION

GREENBOOK MARKET PRICE

MARKET STATUS

PRAISE THE LORD ANYHOW

E-1374B	79	Boy with Dog and	Figurine	See "Nobody's Perfect!" Section			
(19)	81	Ice Cream Cone		UPP	$ 8.00	5.00"	NM	Retired/Sec	$105.00
	82			UPP	8.00		TRI	Retired/Sec	95.00
				UPP	17.00		HRG	Retired/Sec	95.00

ENESCO ITEM NUMBER

GREENBOOK ART CHART NUMBER

YEAR OF ISSUE

DESCRIPTIVE TITLE

EDITION SIZE

ISSUE PRICE

SIZE

ANNUAL SYMBOL

NOTES

GREENBOOK LISTINGS

The GREENBOOK LISTINGS are where specific factual information as well as Secondary Market Prices for each collectible can be found. GREENBOOK Listings are in Enesco Item Number order. The Enesco PRECIOUS MOMENTS Collectors' Club and The Enesco PRECIOUS MOMENTS Birthday Club pieces are in separate sections at the end of the Listings. Enesco Item Numbers can be found on the understamp of most pieces produced from 1982 to the present. If you don't know the Enesco Item Number, but you do know the Inspirational Title, use the ALPHA-LOG to obtain the Enesco Item Number. If you don't know the Enesco Item Number or the Inspirational Title, use the ART CHART to obtain the Enesco Item Number.

SHARING OUR SEASON TOGETHER   Figurine

E-0501	83	Boy Pushing Girl on Sled	UPP	$50.00	4.90"	FSH	Susp/Sec	$115.00
(118)	84		UPP	50.00		CRS	Susp/Sec	105.00
	85		UPP	50.00		DVE	Susp/Sec	100.00
	86		UPP	50.00		OLB	Susp/Sec	95.00

JESUS IS THE LIGHT THAT SHINES   Figurine

E-0502	83	Boy with Candle & Mouse	UPP	$22.50	5.25"	FSH	Susp/Sec	$60.00
(119)	84		UPP	23.00		CRS	Susp/Sec	50.00
	85		UPP	23.00		DVE	Susp/Sec	45.00
	86		UPP	23.00		OLB	Susp/Sec	45.00

BLESSINGS FROM MY HOUSE TO YOURS   Figurine

E-0503	83	Girl in Snow Looking at	UPP	$27.00	5.80"	FSH	Susp/Sec	$70.00
(120)	84	Birdhouse	UPP	27.00		CRS	Susp/Sec	55.00
	85		UPP	27.00		DVE	Susp/Sec	50.00
	86		UPP	27.00		OLB	Susp/Sec	50.00

CHRISTMASTIME IS FOR SHARING   Figurine

E-0504	83	Boy Giving Teddy to	UPP	$37.00	5.25"	FSH	Secondary	$60.00
(121)	84	a Poor Boy	UPP	37.00		CRS	Secondary	50.00
	85		UPP	37.00		DVE	Secondary	47.50
	86		UPP	37.00		OLB	Secondary	47.50
	87		UPP	37.00		CED	Secondary	47.50
	88		UPP	40.00		FLW	Secondary	47.50
	89		UPP	47.50		B&A	Primary	47.50
	90		OPEN	47.50		FLM	Primary	47.50

CHRISTMASTIME IS FOR SHARING   Plate, Dated   Second Issue "Joy Of Christmas" Series

E-0505	83	Boy Giving Teddy to	Annual	$40.00	8.50"	UM	Secondary	$90.00
(121)		a Poor Boy						

SURROUNDED WITH JOY   Figurine

E-0506	83	Boy with Wreath	UPP	$21.00	4.15"	FSH	Retired/Sec	$75.00
(122)	84		UPP	21.00		CRS	Retired/Sec	60.00
	85		UPP	21.00		DVE	Retired/Sec	60.00
	86		UPP	21.00		OLB	Retired/Sec	55.00
	87		UPP	21.00		CED	Retired/Sec	55.00
	88		UPP	23.00		FLW	Retired/Sec	55.00
	89		UPP	27.50		B&A	Retired/Sec	50.00

GOD SENT HIS SON   Figurine

E-0507	83	Girl Looking into Manger	UPP	$32.50	5.50"	FSH	Susp/Sec	$70.00
(123)	84		UPP	32.50		CRS	Susp/Sec	55.00
	85		UPP	32.50		DVE	Susp/Sec	50.00
	86		UPP	32.50		OLB	Susp/Sec	50.00
	87		UPP	32.50		CED	Susp/Sec	50.00

PREPARE YE THE WAY OF THE LORD   Figurine   6 Piece Set

E-0508	83	Angels Preparing Manger	UPP	$75.00	5.75"	FSH	Susp/Sec	$110.00
(124)	84		UPP	75.00		CRS	Susp/Sec	100.00
	85		UPP	75.00		DVE	Susp/Sec	95.00
	86		UPP	75.00		OLB	Susp/Sec	95.00

BRINGING GOD'S BLESSING TO YOU   Figurine

E-0509	83	Girl Angel Pushing Jesus	UPP	$35.00	5.50"	FSH	Susp/Sec	$70.00
(125)	84	in Buggy	UPP	35.00		CRS	Susp/Sec	60.00
	85		UPP	35.00		DVE	Susp/Sec	60.00
	86		UPP	35.00		OLB	Susp/Sec	55.00
	87		UPP	35.00		CED	Susp/Sec	55.00

TUBBY'S FIRST CHRISTMAS   Figurine   Nativity Addition

E-0511	83	Rooster & Bird on Pig	UPP	$12.00	3.25"	FSH	Secondary	$20.00
(126)	84		UPP	12.00		CRS	Secondary	15.00
	85		UPP	12.00		DVE	Secondary	15.00
	86		UPP	12.00		OLB	Secondary	15.00
	87		UPP	12.00		CED	Secondary	15.00
	88		UPP	13.50		FLW	Secondary	15.00
	89		UPP	15.00		B&A	Primary	15.00
	90		OPEN	15.00		FLM	Primary	15.00

IT'S A PERFECT BOY   Figurine   Nativity Addition

E-0512	83	Boy Angel with Red Cross	UPP	$18.50	4.75"	FSH	Secondary	$30.00
(127)	84	Bag	UPP	18.50		CRS	Secondary	25.00
	85		UPP	18.50		DVE	Secondary	25.00
	86		UPP	18.50		OLB	Secondary	25.00
	87		UPP	18.50		CED	Secondary	25.00
	88		UPP	21.00		FLW	Secondary	25.00
	89		UPP	25.00		B&A	Primary	25.00
	90		OPEN	25.00		FLM	Primary	25.00

SURROUND US WITH JOY   Ornament, Dated

E-0513	83	Boy with Wreath	Annual	$ 9.00	3.00"	FSH	Secondary	$60.00
(122)								

MOTHER SEW DEAR   Ornament

E-0514	83	Mother Needlepointing	UPP	$ 9.00	3.00"	FSH	Secondary	$22.00
(30)	84		UPP	10.00		CRS	Secondary	18.00
	85		UPP	10.00		DVE	Secondary	13.50
	86		UPP	10.00		OLB	Secondary	13.50
	87		UPP	10.00		CED	Secondary	13.50
	88		UPP	11.00		FLW	Secondary	13.50
	89		UPP	13.50		B&A	Primary	13.50
	90		OPEN	13.50		FLM	Primary	13.50

TO A SPECIAL DAD   Ornament

E-0515	83	Boy in Dad's Duds	UPP	$ 9.00	3.00"	FSH	Susp/Sec	$35.00
(59)	84		UPP	10.00		CRS	Susp/Sec	30.00
	85		UPP	10.00		DVE	Susp/Sec	30.00
	86		UPP	10.00		OLB	Susp/Sec	30.00
	87		UPP	10.00		CED	Susp/Sec	25.00
	88		UPP	11.00		FLW	Susp/Sec	25.00

THE PURR-FECT GRANDMA   Ornament

E-0516	83	Grandma in Rocker	UPP	$ 9.00	3.00"	FSH	Secondary	$22.00
(33)	84		UPP	10.00		CRS	Secondary	18.00
	85		UPP	10.00		DVE	Secondary	13.50
	86		UPP	10.00		OLB	Secondary	13.50
	87		UPP	10.00		CED	Secondary	13.50
	88		UPP	11.00		FLW	Secondary	13.50
	89		UPP	13.50		B&A	Primary	13.50
	90		OPEN	13.50		FLM	Primary	13.50

THE PURR-FECT GRANDPA   Ornament

E-0517	83	Grandpa in Rocking Chair	UPP	$ 9.00	3.00"	FSH	Secondary	$22.00
(109)	84		UPP	10.00		CRS	Secondary	18.00
	85		UPP	10.00		DVE	Secondary	13.50
	86		UPP	10.00		OLB	Secondary	13.50
	87		UPP	10.00		CED	Secondary	13.50
	88		UPP	11.00		FLW	Secondary	13.50
	89		UPP	13.50		B&A	Primary	13.50
	90		OPEN	13.50		FLM	Primary	13.50

BLESSED ARE THE PURE IN HEART   Ornament, Dated

E-0518 (28)	83	Baby in Cradle	Annual	$ 9.00	2.00"	FSH	Secondary	$40.00

SHARING OUR SEASON TOGETHER   Musical   TUNE: Winter Wonderland

E-0519 (118)	83	Boy Pushing Girl on Sled	UPP	$70.00	6.00"	FSH	Retired/Sec	$125.00
	84		UPP	70.00		CRS	Retired/Sec	105.00
	85		UPP	70.00		DVE	Retired/Sec	100.00
	86		UPP	70.00		OLB	Retired/Sec	100.00

WEE THREE KINGS   Musical   TUNE: We Three Kings

E-0520 (66)	83	Three Kings	UPP	$60.00	7.00"	FSH	Susp/Sec	$90.00
	84		UPP	60.00		CRS	Susp/Sec	75.00
	85		UPP	60.00		DVE	Susp/Sec	75.00
	86		UPP	60.00		OLB	Susp/Sec	70.00

BLESSED ARE THE PURE IN HEART   Frame

E-0521 (28)	83	Baby in Cradle	UPP	$18.00	4.50"	FSH	Susp/Sec	$35.00
	84		UPP	19.00		CRS	Susp/Sec	30.00
	85		UPP	19.00		DVE	Susp/Sec	30.00
	86		UPP	19.00		OLB	Susp/Sec	30.00
	87		UPP	19.00		CED	Susp/Sec	30.00

SURROUNDED WITH JOY   Bell, Dated

E-0522 (122)	83	Boy with Wreath	Annual	$18.00	5.15"	UM	Secondary	$65.00

ONWARD CHRISTIAN SOLDIERS   Figurine

E-0523 (128)	*	Knight in Armor	UPP	$24.00	6.25"	UM	Secondary	$75.00
	83		UPP	24.00		FSH	Secondary	50.00
	84		UPP	24.00		CRS	Secondary	35.00
	85		UPP	24.00		DVE	Secondary	33.00
	86		UPP	24.00		OLB	Secondary	33.00
	87		UPP	24.00		CED	Secondary	33.00
	88		UPP	30.00		FLW	Secondary	33.00
	89		UPP	33.00		B&A	Primary	33.00
	90		OPEN	33.00		FLM	Primary	33.00

[NOTE: Also exists with a DECAL FISH.]
* UNMARKED (UM) pieces could have been produced in any of the years of production.

YOU CAN'T RUN AWAY FROM GOD   Figurine

E-0525 (129)	83	Boy and Dog Running Away	UPP	$28.50	5.15"	HRG	Retired/Sec	$115.00
	83		UPP	28.50		FSH	Retired/Sec	85.00
	84		UPP	28.50		CRS	Retired/Sec	75.00
	85		UPP	28.50		DVE	Retired/Sec	75.00
	86		UPP	28.50		OLB	Retired/Sec	70.00
	87		UPP	28.50		CED	Retired/Sec	70.00
	88		UPP	35.00		FLW	Retired/Sec	65.00
	89		UPP	38.50		B&A	Retired/Sec	65.00

[NOTE: Also exists with a DECAL FISH.]

HE UPHOLDETH THOSE WHO CALL   Figurine

E-0526 (130)	*	Angel Catching Skater	UPP	$35.00	5.15"	UM	Susp/Sec	$95.00
	83		UPP	35.00		FSH	Susp/Sec	65.00
	84		UPP	35.00		CRS	Susp/Sec	60.00
	85		UPP	35.00		DVE	Susp/Sec	60.00

[NOTE: Also exists with a removable INKED FISH.]
* UNMARKED (UM) pieces could have been produced in any of the years of production.

HIS EYE IS ON THE SPARROW   Figurine

E-0530	83	Girl with Bird in Hand	UPP	$28.50	5.25"	FSH	Retired/Sec	$90.00
(131)	84		UPP	28.50		CRS	Retired/Sec	75.00
	85		UPP	28.50		DVE	Retired/Sec	70.00
	86		UPP	28.50		OLB	Retired/Sec	70.00
	87		UPP	28.50		CED	Retired/Sec	70.00

O COME ALL YE FAITHFUL   Ornament

E-0531	83	Boy Caroller	UPP	$10.00	3.25"	FSH	Susp/Sec	$35.00
(86)	84		UPP	10.00		CRS	Susp/Sec	30.00
	85		UPP	10.00		DVE	Susp/Sec	25.00
	86		UPP	10.00		OLB	Susp/Sec	25.00

LET HEAVEN AND NATURE SING   Ornament

E-0532	83	Angel with Book and Songbird	UPP	$ 9.00	3.10"	FSH	Retired/Sec	$45.00
(81)	84		UPP	10.00		CRS	Retired/Sec	35.00
	85		UPP	10.00		DVE	Retired/Sec	30.00
	86		UPP	10.00		OLB	Retired/Sec	30.00

TELL ME THE STORY OF JESUS   Ornament

E-0533	83	Girl with Doll Reading Book	UPP	$ 9.00	3.00"	FSH	Susp/Sec	$40.00
(83)	84		UPP	10.00		CRS	Susp/Sec	35.00
	85		UPP	10.00		DVE	Susp/Sec	30.00
	86		UPP	10.00		OLB	Susp/Sec	30.00
	87		UPP	10.00		CED	Susp/Sec	30.00
	88		UPP	11.00		FLW	Susp/Sec	30.00

TO THEE WITH LOVE   Ornament

E-0534	83	Girl with Box of Kittens	UPP	$ 9.00	3.25"	FSH	Retired/Sec	$45.00
(43)	84		UPP	10.00		CRS	Retired/Sec	40.00
	85		UPP	10.00		DVE	Retired/Sec	35.00
	86		UPP	10.00		OLB	Retired/Sec	30.00
	87		UPP	10.00		CED	Retired/Sec	30.00
	88		UPP	11.00		FLW	Retired/Sec	30.00
	89		UPP	13.50		B&A	Retired/Sec	30.00

LOVE IS PATIENT   Ornament

E-0535	83	Boy with Slate	UPP	$ 9.00	2.75"	FSH	Susp/Sec	$40.00
(132)	84		UPP	10.00		CRS	Susp/Sec	35.00
	85		UPP	10.00		DVE	Susp/Sec	35.00
	86		UPP	10.00		OLB	Susp/Sec	30.00

LOVE IS PATIENT   Ornament

E-0536	83	Girl with Slate	UPP	$ 9.00	3.10"	FSH	Susp/Sec	$45.00
(133)	84		UPP	10.00		CRS	Susp/Sec	40.00
	85		UPP	10.00		DVE	Susp/Sec	35.00
	86		UPP	10.00		OLB	Susp/Sec	35.00

JESUS IS THE LIGHT THAT SHINES   Ornament

E-0537	83	Boy in Night Cap with Candle	UPP	$ 9.00	3.00"	FSH	Susp/Sec	$45.00
(119)	84		UPP	10.00		CRS	Susp/Sec	40.00
	85		UPP	10.00		DVE	Susp/Sec	40.00

WEE THREE KINGS   Plate   Third Issue "Christmas Collection" Series   Individually Numbered

E-0538	83	Three Kings	15,000	$40.00	8.50"	UM	Secondary	$40.00
(66)								

KATIE LYNNE   Doll

E-0539	83	Baby Collector's Doll	UPP	$150.00	16.00"	FSH	Susp/Sec	$175.00
(134)	84		UPP	165.00		CRS	Susp/Sec	175.00
	85		UPP	165.00		DVE	Susp/Sec	175.00
	86		UPP	165.00		OLB	Susp/Sec	175.00
	87		UPP	165.00		CED	Susp/Sec	175.00
	88		UPP	175.00		FLW	Susp/Prim	175.00

JESUS LOVES ME Figurine

E-1372B	79	Boy with Teddy	UPP	$ 7.00	4.50"	NM	Secondary	$85.00
(1)	81		UPP	10.00		TRI	Secondary	75.00
	82		UPP	15.00		HRG	Secondary	50.00
	83		UPP	15.00		FSH	Secondary	35.00
	84		UPP	17.00		CRS	Secondary	25.00
	85		UPP	17.00		DVE	Secondary	23.00
	86		UPP	17.00		OLB	Secondary	23.00
	87		UPP	17.00		CED	Secondary	23.00
	88		UPP	21.00		FLW	Secondary	23.00
	89		UPP	23.00		B&A	Primary	23.00
	90		OPEN	23.00		FLM	Primary	23.00

JESUS LOVES ME Figurine

E-1372G	79	Girl with Bunny	UPP	$ 7.00	4.50"	NM	Secondary	$100.00
(2)	81		UPP	10.00		TRI	Secondary	95.00
	82		UPP	15.00		HRG	Secondary	65.00
	83		UPP	15.00		FSH	Secondary	35.00
	84		UPP	17.00		CRS	Secondary	25.00
	85		UPP	17.00		DVE	Secondary	23.00
	86		UPP	17.00		OLB	Secondary	23.00
	87		UPP	17.00		CED	Secondary	23.00
	88		UPP	21.00		FLW	Secondary	23.00
	89		UPP	23.00		B&A	Primary	23.00
	90		OPEN	23.00		FLM	Primary	23.00

SMILE, GOD LOVES YOU Figurine

E-1373B	79	Boy with Black Eye	UPP	$ 7.00	4.50"	NM	Retired/Sec	$95.00
(3)	81		UPP	12.00		TRI	Retired/Sec	85.00
	82		UPP	15.00		HRG	Retired/Sec	70.00
	83		UPP	15.00		FSH	Retired/Sec	65.00
	84		UPP	17.00		CRS	Retired/Sec	65.00

JESUS IS THE LIGHT Figurine

E-1373G	79	Girl with Doll and Candle	UPP	$ 7.00	4.50"	NM	Retired/Sec	$115.00
(4)	81		UPP	10.00		TRI	Retired/Sec	85.00
	82		UPP	15.00		HRG	Retired/Sec	75.00
	83		UPP	15.00		FSH	Retired/Sec	65.00
	84		UPP	17.00		CRS	Retired/Sec	55.00
	85		UPP	17.00		DVE	Retired/Sec	55.00
	86		UPP	17.00		OLB	Retired/Sec	55.00
	87		UPP	17.00		CED	Retired/Sec	50.00
	88		UPP	21.00		FLW	Retired/Sec	50.00

PRAISE THE LORD ANYHOW Figurine   See "Nobody's Perfect!" Section

E-1374B	79	Boy with Dog	UPP	$ 8.00	5.00"	NM	Retired/Sec	$105.00
(19)	81	and Ice Cream Cone	UPP	8.00		TRI	Retired/Sec	95.00
	82		UPP	17.00		HRG	Retired/Sec	95.00

MAKE A JOYFUL NOISE Figurine   See "Nobody's Perfect!" Section

E-1374G	79	Girl with Goose	UPP	$ 8.00	4.75"	NM	Secondary	$110.00
(5)	81		UPP	13.00		TRI	Secondary	95.00
	82		UPP	17.00		HRG	Secondary	65.00
	83		UPP	17.00		FSH	Secondary	35.00
	84		UPP	19.00		CRS	Secondary	25.00
	85		UPP	19.00		DVE	Secondary	25.00
	86		UPP	19.00		OLB	Secondary	25.00
	87		UPP	19.00		CED	Secondary	25.00
	88		UPP	23.00		FLW	Secondary	25.00
	89		UPP	25.00		B&A	Primary	25.00
	90		OPEN	25.00		FLM	Primary	25.00

LOVE LIFTED ME   Figurine

E-1375A	79	Boy & Girl on Seesaw	UPP	$11.00	5.00"	NM	Secondary	$100.00
(6)	81		UPP	17.00		TRI	Secondary	80.00
	82		UPP	21.00		HRG	Secondary	60.00
	83		UPP	21.00		FSH	Secondary	40.00
	84		UPP	22.50		CRS	Secondary	33.00
	85		UPP	22.50		DVE	Secondary	33.00
	86		UPP	22.50		OLB	Secondary	33.00
	87		UPP	22.50		CED	Secondary	33.00
	88		UPP	30.00		FLW	Secondary	33.00
	89		UPP	33.00		B&A	Primary	33.00
	90		OPEN	33.00		FLM	Primary	33.00

PRAYER CHANGES THINGS   Figurine

E-1375B	79	Boy & Girl with Bluebirds	UPP	$11.00	5.00"	NM	Susp/Sec	$190.00
(7)	81	on Shovel	UPP	17.00		TRI	Susp/Sec	130.00
	82		UPP	21.00		HRG	Susp/Sec	110.00
	83		UPP	21.00		FSH	Susp/Sec	100.00
	84		UPP	22.50		CRS	Susp/Sec	100.00

LOVE ONE ANOTHER   Figurine

E-1376	79	Boy & Girl Sitting on Stump	UPP	$10.00	4.75"	NM	Secondary	$105.00
(8)	81		UPP	16.00		TRI	Secondary	95.00
	82		UPP	21.00		HRG	Secondary	65.00
	83		UPP	21.00		FSH	Secondary	40.00
	84		UPP	22.50		CRS	Secondary	33.00
	85		UPP	22.50		DVE	Secondary	33.00
	86		UPP	22.50		OLB	Secondary	33.00
	87		UPP	22.50		CED	Secondary	33.00
	88		UPP	30.00		FLW	Secondary	33.00
	89		UPP	33.00		B&A	Primary	33.00
	90		OPEN	33.00		FLM	Primary	33.00

HE LEADETH ME   Figurine   See "Nobody's Perfect!"

E-1377A	79	Boy Leading Lamb	UPP	$ 9.00	4.75"	NM	Susp/Sec	$105.00
(9)	81		UPP	15.00		TRI	Susp/Sec	95.00
	82		UPP	19.00		HRG	Susp/Sec	80.00
	83		UPP	19.00		FSH	Susp/Sec	75.00
	84		UPP	19.00		CRS	Susp/Sec	75.00

HE CARETH FOR YOU   Figurine

E-1377B	79	Boy Helping Lamb	UPP	$ 9.00	4.00"	NM	Susp/Sec	$105.00
(10)	81		UPP	15.00		TRI	Susp/Sec	95.00
	82		UPP	19.00		HRG	Susp/Sec	85.00
	83		UPP	19.00		FSH	Susp/Sec	80.00
	84		UPP	19.00		CRS	Susp/Sec	80.00

GOD LOVETH A CHEERFUL GIVER   Figurine   First Retirement — May 1981

E-1378	79	Girl with Puppies	UPP	$11.00	5.15"	NM	Retired/Sec	$845.00
(20)								

LOVE IS KIND   Figurine

E-1379A	79	Boy with Turtle	UPP	$ 8.00	4.50"	NM	Susp/Sec	$115.00
(11)	81		UPP	13.00		TRI	Susp/Sec	95.00
	82		UPP	17.00		HRG	Susp/Sec	90.00
	83		UPP	17.00		FSH	Susp/Sec	85.00
	84		UPP	19.00		CRS	Susp/Sec	80.00

GOD UNDERSTANDS   Figurine

E-1379B	79	Boy with Report Card	UPP	$ 8.00	5.00"	NM	Susp/Sec	$115.00
(12)	81		UPP	13.00		TRI	Susp/Sec	95.00
	82		UPP	17.00		HRG	Susp/Sec	85.00
	83		UPP	17.00		FSH	Susp/Sec	80.00
	84		UPP	19.00		CRS	Susp/Sec	80.00

O, HOW I LOVE JESUS   Figurine

E-1380B	79	Indian Boy	UPP	$ 8.00	4.75"	NM	Retired/Sec	$110.00
(13)	81		UPP	13.00		TRI	Retired/Sec	85.00
	82		UPP	17.00		HRG	Retired/Sec	75.00
	83		UPP	17.00		FSH	Retired/Sec	70.00
	84		UPP	19.00		CRS	Retired/Sec	70.00

HIS BURDEN IS LIGHT   Figurine

E-1380G	79	Indian Girl	UPP	$ 8.00	4.75"	NM	Retired/Sec	$120.00
(14)	81		UPP	13.00		TRI	Retired/Sec	95.00
	82		UPP	17.00		HRG	Retired/Sec	75.00
	83		UPP	17.00		FSH	Retired/Sec	70.00
	84		UPP	19.00		CRS	Retired/Sec	70.00

JESUS IS THE ANSWER   Figurine

E-1381	79	Boy Patching World	UPP	$11.50	4.50"	NM	Susp/Sec	$140.00
(15)	81		UPP	19.00		TRI	Susp/Sec	100.00
	82		UPP	21.00		HRG	Susp/Sec	90.00
	83		UPP	21.00		FSH	Susp/Sec	80.00
	84		UPP	22.50		CRS	Susp/Sec	75.00

WE HAVE SEEN HIS STAR   Figurine

E-2010	79	Boy Holding Lamb	UPP	$ 8.00	5.50"	NM	Susp/Sec	$90.00
(16)	82		UPP	17.00		HRG	Susp/Sec	80.00
	83		UPP	17.00		FSH	Susp/Sec	70.00
	84		UPP	17.00		CRS	Susp/Sec	70.00

COME LET US ADORE HIM   Figurine   First Retirement — May 1981

E-2011	79	Boy with Manger Baby	UPP	$ 5.00	5.00"	NM	Retired/Sec	$325.00
(21)								

JESUS IS BORN   Figurine

E-2012	79	Boy & Girl Playing Angels	UPP	$12.00	6.25"	NM	Susp/Sec	$110.00
(17)	82		UPP	22.50		HRG	Susp/Sec	85.00
	83		UPP	22.50		FSH	Susp/Sec	80.00
	84		UPP	22.50		CRS	Susp/Sec	80.00

UNTO US A CHILD IS BORN   Figurine   See "Nobody's Perfect!" Section

E-2013	79	Boy & Girl Reading Book	UPP	$12.00	4.75"	NM	Susp/Sec	$105.00
(18)	82		UPP	22.50		HRG	Susp/Sec	85.00
	83		UPP	22.50		FSH	Susp/Sec	75.00
	84		UPP	22.50		CRS	Susp/Sec	75.00

JOY TO THE WORLD   Ornament

E-2343	82	Boy Angel Playing Trumpet	UPP	$ 9.00	2.00"	UM	Susp/Sec	$45.00
(79)	84		UPP	10.00		CRS	Susp/Sec	40.00
	85		UPP	10.00		DVE	Susp/Sec	35.00
	86		UPP	10.00		OLB	Susp/Sec	35.00
	87		UPP	10.00		CED	Susp/Sec	35.00
	88		UPP	11.00		FLW	Susp/Sec	35.00

JOY TO THE WORLD   Candle Climbers   Set of 2

E-2344	82	Boy Angel Playing Trumpet	UPP	$20.00	2.50"	UM	Susp/Sec	$50.00
(79)	84		UPP	20.00		CRS	Susp/Sec	45.00
	85		UPP	20.00		DVE	Susp/Sec	45.00

MAY YOUR CHRISTMAS BE COZY   Figurine

E-2345	82	Boy in Pajamas with Teddy	UPP	$23.00	4.25"	HRG	Susp/Sec	$65.00
(80)	83		UPP	23.00		FSH	Susp/Sec	55.00
	84		UPP	25.00		CRS	Susp/Sec	55.00

LET HEAVEN AND NATURE SING   Musical   TUNE: Joy To The World

E-2346	*	Angel with Friends Carolling	UPP	$50.00	6.00"	UM	Susp/Sec	$100.00
(81)	82		UPP	50.00		HRG	Susp/Sec	100.00
	83		UPP	55.00		FSH	Susp/Sec	85.00
	84		UPP	60.00		CRS	Susp/Sec	80.00
	85		UPP	60.00		DVE	Susp/Sec	80.00
	86		UPP	60.00		OLB	Susp/Sec	75.00
	87		UPP	60.00		CED	Susp/Sec	75.00
	88		UPP	65.00		FLW	Susp/Sec	75.00
	89		UPP	75.00		B&A	Susp/Prim	75.00

* UNMARKED (UM) pieces could have been produced in any of the years of production.

LET HEAVEN AND NATURE SING   Plate   Second Issue "Christmas Collection" Series
Individually Numbered

E-2347	82	Angel with Friends Carolling	15,000	$40.00	8.50"	UM	Secondary	$40.00
(81)								

MAY YOUR CHRISTMAS BE WARM   Figurine

E-2348	82	Boy Next to a Pot Belly Stove	UPP	$30.00	4.75"	HRG	Susp/Sec	$85.00
(82)	83		UPP	30.00		FSH	Susp/Sec	75.00
	84		UPP	33.00		CRS	Susp/Sec	70.00
	85		UPP	33.00		DVE	Susp/Sec	65.00
	86		UPP	33.00		OLB	Susp/Sec	65.00
	87		UPP	33.00		CED	Susp/Sec	65.00
	88		UPP	37.00		FLW	Susp/Sec	65.00

TELL ME THE STORY OF JESUS   Figurine

E-2349	82	Girl with Doll Reading Book	UPP	$30.00	5.00"	HRG	Susp/Sec	$80.00
(83)	83		UPP	30.00		FSH	Susp/Sec	75.00
	84		UPP	33.00		CRS	Susp/Sec	75.00
	85		UPP	33.00		DVE	Susp/Sec	70.00

DROPPING IN FOR CHRISTMAS   Figurine

E-2350	82	Boy Ice Skater in Santa Cap	UPP	$18.00	5.15"	HRG	Susp/Sec	$70.00
(84)	83		UPP	18.00		FSH	Susp/Sec	60.00
	84		UPP	18.00		CRS	Susp/Sec	60.00

HOLY SMOKES   Figurine

E-2351	82	Two Angels with Candles	UPP	$27.00	5.75"	HRG	Retired/Sec	$95.00
(85)	83		UPP	27.00		FSH	Retired/Sec	80.00
	84		UPP	30.00		CRS	Retired/Sec	80.00
	85		UPP	30.00		DVE	Retired/Sec	80.00
	86		UPP	30.00		OLB	Retired/Sec	75.00
	87		UPP	30.00		CED	Retired/Sec	75.00

O COME ALL YE FAITHFUL   Musical   TUNE: O Come All Ye Faithful

E-2352	*	Boy Carolling by Lamp Post	UPP	$45.00	7.25"	UM	Susp/Sec	$80.00
(86)	82		UPP	45.00		HRG	Susp/Sec	85.00
	83		UPP	45.00		FSH	Susp/Sec	70.00
	84		UPP	50.00		CRS	Susp/Sec	70.00

* UNMARKED (UM) pieces could have been produced in any of the years of production.

O COME ALL YE FAITHFUL   Figurine

E-2353	82	Boy Carolling by Lamp Post	UPP	$27.50	6.25"	HRG	Retired/Sec	$80.00
(86)	83		UPP	27.50		FSH	Retired/Sec	75.00
	84		UPP	30.00		CRS	Retired/Sec	70.00
	85		UPP	30.00		DVE	Retired/Sec	70.00
	86		UPP	30.00		OLB	Retired/Sec	70.00

I'LL PLAY MY DRUM FOR HIM   Musical   TUNE: Little Drummer Boy

E-2355	82	Drummer Boy at Manger	UPP	$45.00	6.75"	HRG	Susp/Sec	$90.00
(87)	83		UPP	45.00		FSH	Susp/Sec	80.00
	84		UPP	50.00		CRS	Susp/Sec	80.00

I'LL PLAY MY DRUM FOR HIM — Figurine

E-2356	82	Drummer Boy at Manger	UPP	$30.00	5.50"	HRG	Susp/Sec	$110.00
(87)	83		UPP	30.00		FSH	Susp/Sec	65.00
	84		UPP	33.00		CRS	Susp/Sec	60.00
	85		UPP	33.00		DVE	Susp/Sec	60.00

I'LL PLAY MY DRUM FOR HIM — Plate, Dated — First Issue "Joy of Christmas" Series

E-2357	82	Drummer Boy at Manger	Annual	$40.00	8.50"	UM	Secondary	$100.00
(87)								

I'LL PLAY MY DRUM FOR HIM — Bell, Dated?*

E-2358	82	Drummer Boy	Annual	$17.00	5.75"	UM	Secondary	$65.00
(87)								

  * Prototypes were dated, it appears actual production wasn't.

I'LL PLAY MY DRUM FOR HIM — Ornament, Dated

E-2359	82	Drummer Boy	Annual	$9.00	3.25"	HRG	Secondary	$100.00
(87)								

I'LL PLAY MY DRUM FOR HIM — Figurine — Nativity Addition

E-2360	82	Drummer Boy	UPP	$16.00	5.00"	HRG	Secondary	$35.00
(87)	83		UPP	16.00		FSH	Secondary	30.00
	84		UPP	17.00		CRS	Secondary	25.00
	85		UPP	17.00		DVE	Secondary	23.00
	86		UPP	17.00		OLB	Secondary	23.00
	87		UPP	17.00		CED	Secondary	23.00
	88		UPP	19.00		FLW	Secondary	23.00
	89		UPP	23.00		B&A	Primary	23.00
	90		OPEN	23.00		FLM	Primary	23.00

CHRISTMAS JOY FROM HEAD TO TOE — Figurine

E-2361	82	Girl with Stocking	UPP	$25.00	5.50"	HRG	Susp/Sec	$70.00
(88)	83		UPP	25.00		FSH	Susp/Sec	60.00
	84		UPP	27.50		CRS	Susp/Sec	55.00
	85		UPP	27.50		DVE	Susp/Sec	50.00
	86		UPP	27.50		OLB	Susp/Sec	50.00

BABY'S FIRST CHRISTMAS — Ornament — *See "Nobody's Perfect!" Section

E-2362	82	Baby Girl in Christmas	UPP	$ 9.00	3.50"	UM*	Susp/Sec	$45.00
(89)	84	Stocking	UPP	10.00		CRS	Susp/Sec	30.00
	85		UPP	10.00		DVE	Susp/Sec	30.00
	86		UPP	10.00		OLB	Susp/Sec	25.00
	87		UPP	10.00		CED	Susp/Sec	25.00
	88		UPP	11.00		FLW	Susp/Sec	25.00

CAMEL — Figurine — Nativity Addition

E-2363	82	Camel	UPP	$20.00	4.00"	HRG	Secondary	$40.00
(90)	83		UPP	20.00		FSH	Secondary	35.00
	84		UPP	22.50		CRS	Secondary	32.00
	85		UPP	22.50		DVE	Secondary	30.00
	86		UPP	22.50		OLB	Secondary	30.00
	87		UPP	22.50		CED	Secondary	30.00
	88		UPP	25.00		FLW	Primary	30.00
	89		UPP	30.00		B&A	Primary	30.00
	90		OPEN	30.00		FLM	Primary	30.00

GOAT — Figurine — Nativity Addition

E-2364	82	Goat	UPP	$10.00	3.00"	UM	Susp/Sec	$35.00
(91)	83		UPP	10.00		FSH	Susp/Sec	30.00
	84		UPP	11.00		CRS	Susp/Sec	30.00
	85		UPP	11.00		DVE	Susp/Sec	25.00
	86		UPP	11.00		OLB	Susp/Sec	25.00
	87		UPP	11.00		CED	Susp/Sec	25.00
	88		UPP	12.00		FLW	Susp/Sec	25.00
	89		UPP	15.00		B&A	Susp/Sec	25.00

THE FIRST NOEL   Figurine   Nativity Addition

E-2365	*	Boy Angel with Candle	UPP	$16.00	4.50"	UM	Susp/Sec	$45.00
(92)	82		UPP	16.00		HRG	Susp/Sec	45.00
	83		UPP	16.00		FSH	Susp/Sec	40.00
	84		UPP	16.00		CRS	Susp/Sec	40.00

* UNMARKED (UM) pieces could have been produced in any of the years of production.

THE FIRST NOEL   Figurine   Nativity Addition

E-2366	*	Girl Angel Praying	UPP	$16.00	4.50"	UM	Susp/Sec	$50.00
(93)	82		UPP	16.00		HRG	Susp/Sec	50.00
	83		UPP	16.00		FSH	Susp/Sec	45.00
	84		UPP	16.00		CRS	Susp/Sec	45.00

* UNMARKED (UM) pieces could have been produced in any of the years of production.

THE FIRST NOEL   Ornament

E-2367	82	Boy Angel with Candle	UPP	$ 9.00	3.10"	HRG	Susp/Sec	$45.00
(92)	83		UPP	9.00		FSH	Susp/Sec	35.00
	84		UPP	10.00		CRS	Susp/Sec	35.00

THE FIRST NOEL   Ornament

E-2368	82	Girl Angel Praying	UPP	$ 9.00	3.00"	HRG	Retired/Sec	$60.00
(93)	83		UPP	9.00		FSH	Retired/Sec	45.00
	84		UPP	10.00		CRS	Retired/Sec	45.00

DROPPING IN FOR CHRISTMAS   Ornament

E-2369	*	Boy Ice Skater in Santa Cap	UPP	$ 9.00	3.50"	UM	Retired/Sec	$50.00
(84)	82		UPP	9.00		HRG	Retired/Sec	45.00
	83		UPP	9.00		FSH	Retired/Sec	45.00
	84		UPP	10.00		CRS	Retired/Sec	35.00
	85		UPP	10.00		DVE	Retired/Sec	35.00
	86		UPP	10.00		OLB	Retired/Sec	35.00

* UNMARKED (UM) pieces could have been produced in any of the years of production.

UNICORN   Ornament

E-2371	82	Unicorn	UPP	$10.00	3.00"	UM	Retired/Sec	$55.00
(94)	84		UPP	10.00		CRS	Retired/Sec	45.00
	85		UPP	11.00		DVE	Retired/Sec	40.00
	86		UPP	11.00		OLB	Retired/Sec	40.00
	87		UPP	11.00		CED	Retired/Sec	40.00
	88		UPP	12.00		FLW	Retired/Sec	40.00

BABY'S FIRST CHRISTMAS   Ornament

E-2372	82	Boy Holding Block	UPP	$ 9.00	2.75"	UM	Susp/Sec	$45.00
(95)	84		UPP	10.00		CRS	Susp/Sec	35.00
	85		UPP	10.00		DVE	Susp/Sec	35.00

[NOTE: Exists with and without title in UM version.]

BUNDLES OF JOY   Figurine

E-2374	82	Girl with Presents	UPP	$27.50	6.75"	HRG	Secondary	$70.00
(96)	83		UPP	27.50		FSH	Secondary	45.00
	84		UPP	30.00		CRS	Secondary	40.00
	85		UPP	30.00		DVE	Secondary	40.00
	86		UPP	30.00		OLB	Secondary	40.00
	87		UPP	30.00		CED	Secondary	40.00
	88		UPP	33.50		FLW	Secondary	40.00
	89		UPP	40.00		B&A	Primary	40.00
	90		OPEN	40.00		FLM	Primary	40.00

DROPPING OVER FOR CHRISTMAS Figurine

E-2375	82	Girl with Pie	UPP	$30.00	5.15"	HRG	Secondary	$65.00
(97)	83		UPP	30.00		FSH	Secondary	45.00
	84		UPP	33.00		CRS	Secondary	42.50
	85		UPP	33.00		DVE	Secondary	42.50
	86		UPP	33.00		OLB	Secondary	42.50
	87		UPP	33.00		CED	Secondary	42.50
	88		UPP	37.00		FLW	Secondary	42.50
	89		UPP	42.50		B&A	Primary	42.50
	90		OPEN	42.50		FLM	Primary	42.50

DROPPING OVER FOR CHRISTMAS Ornament

E-2376	82	Girl with Pie	UPP	$ 9.00	3.00"	HRG	Retired/Sec	$50.00
(97)	83		UPP	9.00		FSH	Retired/Sec	45.00
	84		UPP	10.00		CRS	Retired/Sec	40.00
	85		UPP	10.00		DVE	Retired/Sec	40.00

OUR FIRST CHRISTMAS TOGETHER Figurine

E-2377	82	Girl Knitting Tie for Boy	UPP	$35.00	5.15"	HRG	Susp/Sec	$75.00
(98)	83		UPP	35.00		FSH	Susp/Sec	65.00
	84		UPP	37.50		CRS	Susp/Sec	60.00
	85		UPP	37.50		DVE	Susp/Sec	60.00

OUR FIRST CHRISTMAS TOGETHER Plate

E-2378	82	Girl Knitting Tie for Boy	UPP	$30.00	7.00"	UM	Susp/Sec	$55.00
(98)	84		UPP	30.00		CRS	Susp/Sec	45.00
	85		UPP	30.00		DVE	Susp/Sec	45.00

MOUSE WITH CHEESE Ornament

E-2381	82	Mouse with Cheese	UPP	$ 9.00	2.50"	HRG	Susp/Sec	$85.00
(99)	83		UPP	9.00		FSH	Susp/Sec	80.00
	84		UPP	10.00		CRS	Susp/Sec	85.00

OUR FIRST CHRISTMAS TOGETHER Ornament

E-2385	82	Bride and Groom	UPP	$10.00	4.00"	HRG	Secondary	$25.00
(38)	83		UPP	10.00		FSH	Secondary	20.00
	84		UPP	10.00		CRS	Secondary	18.00
	85		UPP	11.00		DVE	Secondary	15.00
	86		UPP	11.00		OLB	Secondary	15.00
	87		UPP	11.00		CED	Secondary	15.00
	88		UPP	12.00		FLW	Secondary	15.00
	89		UPP	15.00		B&A	Primary	15.00
	90		OPEN	15.00		FLM	Primary	15.00

CAMEL, DONKEY, AND COW Ornaments Set of 3

E-2386	*	Camel, Donkey, Cow	UPP	$25.00	2.25"	UM	Susp/Sec	$50.00
(100)	82		UPP	25.00		HRG	Susp/Sec	55.00
	83		UPP	25.00		FSH	Susp/Sec	50.00
	84		UPP	27.50		CRS	Susp/Sec	50.00

* UNMARKED (UM) pieces could have been produced in any of the years of production.

HOUSE SET AND PALM TREE Figurines Set of 3 Mini Nativity Addition

E-2387	82	Mini Houses and Palm Tree	UPP	$45.00	3.00"	HRG	Secondary	$80.00
(101)	83		UPP	45.00		FSH	Secondary	70.00
	84		UPP	50.00		CRS	Secondary	65.00
	85		UPP	50.00		DVE	Secondary	65.00
	86		UPP	50.00		OLB	Secondary	65.00
	87		UPP	50.00		CED	Secondary	65.00
	88		UPP	55.00		FLW	Primary	65.00
	89		UPP	65.00		B&A	Primary	65.00
	90		OPEN	65.00		FLM	Primary	65.00

COME LET US ADORE HIM   Figurines   Set of 11   *See "Nobody's Perfect!" Section

E-2395	82	Mini Nativity Set	UPP	$80.00	3.50"	HRG*	Secondary	$135.00
(22)	83		UPP	80.00		FSH	Secondary	120.00
	84		UPP	90.00		CRS	Secondary	115.00
	85		UPP	90.00		DVE	Secondary	110.00
	86		UPP	90.00		OLB	Secondary	110.00
	87		UPP	90.00		CED	Secondary	110.00
	88		UPP	95.00		FLW	Primary	110.00
	89		UPP	110.00		B&A	Primary	110.00
	90		OPEN	110.00		FLM	Primary	110.00

COME LET US ADORE HIM   Figurines   Set of 8

E-2800	80	Nativity Set	UPP	$70.00	4.75"	NM	Disc/Sec	$175.00
(22)	81		UPP	70.00		TRI	Disc/Sec	160.00
	82		UPP	80.00		HRG	Disc/Sec	155.00
	83		UPP	80.00		FSH	Disc/Sec	150.00
	84		UPP	90.00		CRS	Disc/Sec	145.00
	85		UPP	90.00		DVE	Disc/Sec	145.00
		Re-sculpted - See #104000						

JESUS IS BORN   Figurine

E-2801	80	Angels in Chariot	UPP	$37.00	5.75"	NM	Susp/Sec	$250.00
(23)	81		UPP	45.00		TRI	Susp/Sec	200.00
	82		UPP	50.00		HRG	Susp/Sec	195.00
	83		UPP	50.00		FSH	Susp/Sec	180.00
	84		UPP	50.00		CRS	Susp/Sec	165.00

CHRISTMAS IS A TIME TO SHARE   Figurine

E-2802	80	Boy Giving Toy Lamb	UPP	$20.00	5.00"	NM	Susp/Sec	$85.00
(24)	81		UPP	22.50		TRI	Susp/Sec	70.00
	82		UPP	25.00		HRG	Susp/Sec	60.00
	83		UPP	25.00		FSH	Susp/Sec	55.00
	84		UPP	27.50		CRS	Susp/Sec	55.00

CROWN HIM LORD OF ALL   Figurine

E-2803	80	Boy Holding Crown at Manger	UPP	$20.00	4.50"	NM	Susp/Sec	$70.00
(25)	81		UPP	22.50		TRI	Susp/Sec	65.00
	82		UPP	25.00		HRG	Susp/Sec	60.00
	83		UPP	25.00		FSH	Susp/Sec	60.00
	84		UPP	27.50		CRS	Susp/Sec	60.00

PEACE ON EARTH   Figurine

E-2804	80	Boy on Globe with Teddy	UPP	$20.00	6.00"	NM	Susp/Sec	$100.00
(26)	81		UPP	22.50		TRI	Susp/Sec	90.00
	82		UPP	25.00		HRG	Susp/Sec	80.00
	83		UPP	25.00		FSH	Susp/Sec	75.00
	84		UPP	27.50		CRS	Susp/Sec	70.00

WISHING YOU A SEASON FILLED WITH JOY   Figurine

E-2805	80	Boy in Santa Cap with Dog	UPP	$20.00	4.25"	NM	Retired/Sec	$115.00
(27)	81		UPP	22.50		TRI	Retired/Sec	105.00
	82		UPP	25.00		HRG	Retired/Sec	100.00
	83		UPP	25.00		FSH	Retired/Sec	90.00
	84		UPP	27.50		CRS	Retired/Sec	90.00
	85		UPP	27.50		DVE	Retired/Sec	90.00
		[NOTE: Exists in a double mark HRG & FSH.]						

CHRISTMAS IS A TIME TO SHARE   Musical   TUNE: Away in a Manger

E-2806	80	Boy Giving Toy Lamb	UPP	$35.00	6.00"	NM	Retired/Sec	$145.00
(24)	81	to Baby Jesus	UPP	35.00		TRI	Retired/Sec	145.00
	82		UPP	40.00		HRG	Retired/Sec	145.00
	83		UPP	45.00		FSH	Retired/Sec	125.00
	84		UPP	50.00		CRS	Retired/Sec	125.00

CROWN HIM LORD OF ALL — Musical — TUNE: O Come All Ye Faithful

E-2807	80	Boy Kneeling at Manger	UPP	$35.00	5.50"	NM	Susp/Sec	$85.00
(25)	81	with Crown	UPP	40.00		TRI	Susp/Sec	70.00
	82		UPP	45.00		HRG	Susp/Sec	65.00
	83		UPP	45.00		FSH	Susp/Sec	65.00
	84		UPP	45.00		CRS	Susp/Sec	65.00

UNTO US A CHILD IS BORN — Musical — TUNE: Jesus Loves Me

E-2808	80	Boy and Girl Reading Book	UPP	$35.00	5.75"	NM	Susp/Sec	$85.00
(18)	81		UPP	40.00		TRI	Susp/Sec	85.00
	82		UPP	45.00		HRG	Susp/Sec	65.00
	83		UPP	45.00		FSH	Susp/Sec	65.00
	84		UPP	50.00		CRS	Susp/Sec	65.00

JESUS IS BORN — Musical — TUNE: Hark! The Herald Angels Sing

E-2809	80	Boy and Girl Playing Angels	UPP	$35.00	7.00"	NM	Susp/Sec	$80.00
(17)	81		UPP	45.00		TRI	Susp/Sec	75.00
	82		UPP	45.00		HRG	Susp/Sec	75.00
	83		UPP	45.00		FSH	Susp/Sec	75.00
	84		UPP	50.00		CRS	Susp/Sec	75.00
	85		UPP	50.00		DVE	Susp/Sec	75.00

COME LET US ADORE HIM — Musical — TUNE: Joy To The World

E-2810	80	Nativity Scene	UPP	$45.00	6.50"	NM	Secondary	$105.00
(22)	81		UPP	45.00		TRI	Secondary	90.00
	82		UPP	60.00		HRG	Secondary	80.00
	83		UPP	60.00		FSH	Secondary	80.00
	84		UPP	65.00		CRS	Secondary	80.00
	85		UPP	65.00		DVE	Secondary	80.00
	86		UPP	65.00		OLB	Secondary	80.00
	87		UPP	65.00		CED	Secondary	80.00
	88		UPP	70.00		FLW	Primary	80.00
	89		UPP	80.00		B&A	Primary	80.00
	90		OPEN	80.00		FLM	Primary	80.00

YOU HAVE TOUCHED SO MANY HEARTS — Figurine

E-2821	84	Girl with Hearts	UPP	$25.00	5.50"	FSH	Secondary	$40.00
(161)	84		UPP	25.00		CRS	Secondary	35.00
	85		UPP	25.00		DVE	Secondary	33.00
	86		UPP	25.00		OLB	Secondary	33.00
	87		UPP	25.00		CED	Secondary	33.00
	88		UPP	30.00		FLW	Secondary	33.00
	89		UPP	33.00		B&A	Primary	33.00
	90		OPEN	33.00		FLM	Primary	33.00

THIS IS YOUR DAY TO SHINE — Figurine

E-2822	84	Girl Polishing Table	UPP	$37.50	6.00"	FSH	Retired/Sec	$85.00
(162)	84		UPP	37.50		CRS	Retired/Sec	80.00
	85		UPP	37.50		DVE	Retired/Sec	75.00
	86		UPP	37.50		OLB	Retired/Sec	70.00
	87		UPP	37.50		CED	Retired/Sec	70.00
	88		UPP	40.00		FLW	Retired/Sec	70.00

TO GOD BE THE GLORY — Figurine

E-2823	84	Boy Holding Picture Frame	UPP	$40.00	5.50"	FSH	Susp/Sec	$65.00
(163)	84		UPP	40.00		CRS	Susp/Sec	60.00
	85		UPP	40.00		DVE	Susp/Sec	55.00
	86		UPP	40.00		OLB	Susp/Sec	55.00
	87		UPP	40.00		CED	Susp/Sec	55.00

TO A VERY SPECIAL MOM — Figurine

E-2824	84	Girl with Floppy Hat	UPP	$27.50	5.75"	CRS	Secondary	$40.00
(164)	85		UPP	27.50		DVE	Secondary	35.00
	86		UPP	27.50		OLB	Secondary	35.00
	87		UPP	27.50		CED	Secondary	35.00
	88		UPP	32.50		FLW	Secondary	35.00
	89		UPP	35.00		B&A	Primary	35.00
	90		OPEN	35.00		FLM	Primary	35.00

TO A VERY SPECIAL SISTER — Figurine

E-2825	84	Girl Putting Bows in	UPP	$37.50	5.50"	CRS	Secondary	$50.00
(165)	85	Sister's Hair	UPP	37.50		DVE	Secondary	45.00
	86		UPP	37.50		OLB	Secondary	45.00
	87		UPP	37.50		CED	Secondary	45.00
	88		UPP	40.00		FLW	Secondary	45.00
	89		UPP	45.00		B&A	Primary	45.00
	90		OPEN	45.00		FLM	Primary	45.00

MAY YOUR BIRTHDAY BE A BLESSING — Figurine

E-2826	84	Girl at Table with Dolls	UPP	$37.50	5.25"	CRS	Susp/Sec	$60.00
(166)	85		UPP	37.50		DVE	Susp/Sec	55.00
	86		UPP	37.50		OLB	Susp/Sec	50.00

I GET A KICK OUT OF YOU — Figurine

E-2827	84	Girl with Bucket on Head	UPP	$50.00	4.75"	FSH	Susp/Sec	$85.00
(167)	84		UPP	50.00		CRS	Susp/Sec	80.00
	85		UPP	50.00		DVE	Susp/Sec	75.00
	86		UPP	50.00		OLB	Susp/Sec	70.00

PRECIOUS MEMORIES — Figurine

E-2828	84	Girl at Trunk with	UPP	$45.00	5.50"	CRS	Secondary	$65.00
(168)	85	Wedding Gown	UPP	45.00		DVE	Secondary	55.00
	86		UPP	45.00		OLB	Secondary	55.00
	87		UPP	45.00		CED	Secondary	55.00
	88		UPP	50.00		FLW	Secondary	55.00
	89		UPP	55.00		B&A	Primary	55.00
	90		OPEN	55.00		FLM	Primary	55.00

I'M SENDING YOU A WHITE CHRISTMAS — Figurine

E-2829	84	Girl Mailing Snowball	UPP	$37.50	5.00"	CRS	Secondary	$60.00
(169)	85		UPP	37.50		DVE	Secondary	47.50
	86		UPP	37.50		OLB	Secondary	47.50
	87		UPP	37.50		CED	Secondary	47.50
	88		UPP	40.00		FLW	Secondary	47.50
	89		UPP	47.50		B&A	Primary	47.50
	90		OPEN	47.50		FLM	Primary	47.50

BRIDESMAID — Figurine — First Issue "Bridal" Series

E-2831	84	Bridesmaid	UPP	$13.50	4.25"	CRS	Secondary	$20.00
(170)	85		UPP	13.50		DVE	Secondary	17.50
	86		UPP	13.50		OLB	Secondary	17.50
	87		UPP	13.50		CED	Secondary	17.50
	88		UPP	16.00		FLW	Secondary	17.50
	89		UPP	17.50		B&A	Primary	17.50
	90		OPEN	17.50		FLM	Primary	17.50

GOD BLESS THE BRIDE — Figurine

E-2832	84	Bride with Flower Girl	UPP	$35.00	5.50"	CRS	Secondary	$50.00
(171)	85		UPP	35.00		DVE	Secondary	45.00
	86		UPP	35.00		OLB	Secondary	45.00
	87		UPP	35.00		CED	Secondary	45.00
	88		UPP	40.00		FLW	Secondary	45.00
	89		UPP	45.00		B&A	Primary	45.00
	90		OPEN	45.00		FLM	Primary	45.00

RINGBEARER   Figurine   Fourth Issue "Bridal" Series

E-2833	85	Ringbearer	UPP	$11.00	3.00"	DVE	Secondary	$20.00
(208)	86		UPP	11.00		OLB	Secondary	15.00
	87		UPP	11.00		CED	Secondary	15.00
	88		UPP	13.00		FLW	Secondary	15.00
	89		UPP	15.00		B&A	Primary	15.00
	90		OPEN	15.00		FLM	Primary	15.00

SHARING OUR JOY TOGETHER   Figurine

E-2834	86	Bridesmaid with Kitten	UPP	$31.00	5.50"	OLB	Secondary	$45.00
(268)	87		UPP	31.00		CED	Secondary	38.50
	88		UPP	36.00		FLW	Secondary	38.50
	89		UPP	38.50		B&A	Primary	38.50
	90		OPEN	38.50		FLM	Primary	38.50

FLOWER GIRL   Figurine   Third Issue "Bridal" Series

E-2835	85	Flower Girl	UPP	$11.00	3.00"	DVE	Secondary	$20.00
(209)	86		UPP	11.00		OLB	Secondary	15.00
	87		UPP	11.00		CED	Secondary	15.00
	88		UPP	13.00		FLW	Secondary	15.00
	89		UPP	15.00		B&A	Primary	15.00
	90		OPEN	15.00		FLM	Primary	15.00

GROOMSMAN   Figurine   Second Issue "Bridal" Series

E-2836	84	Groomsman with Frog	UPP	$13.50	4.25"	CRS	Secondary	$20.00
(172)	85		UPP	13.50		DVE	Secondary	17.50
	86		UPP	13.50		OLB	Secondary	17.50
	87		UPP	13.50		CED	Secondary	17.50
	88		UPP	16.00		FLW	Secondary	17.50
	89		UPP	17.50		B&A	Primary	17.50
	90		OPEN	17.50		FLM	Primary	17.50

GROOM   Figurine   Sixth Issue "Bridal" Series   *See "Nobody's Perfect!" Section

E-2837	86	Groom	UPP	$15.00	4.50"	OLB*	Secondary	$45.00
(269)	87		UPP	15.00		CED	Secondary	20.00
	88		UPP	18.00		FLW	Secondary	20.00
	89		UPP	20.00		B&A	Primary	20.00
	90		OPEN	20.00		FLM	Primary	20.00

THIS IS THE DAY WHICH THE LORD HAS MADE   Figurine   Eighth & Final Issue "Bridal" Series

E-2838	87	Complete Wedding Party	Annual	$175.00	5.25"	CED	Secondary	$200.00
(312)								

BABY'S FIRST STEP   Figurine   First Issue "Baby's First" Series

E-2840	84	Angel Carrying Baby	UPP	$35.00	5.25"	CRS	Susp/Sec	$65.00
(173)	85		UPP	35.00		DVE	Susp/Sec	50.00
	86		UPP	35.00		OLB	Susp/Sec	50.00
	87		UPP	35.00		CED	Susp/Sec	50.00
	88		UPP	40.00		FLW	Susp/Sec	50.00

BABY'S FIRST PICTURE   Figurine   Second Issue "Baby's First" Series

E-2841	84	Angel Taking Baby's Picture	UPP	$45.00	5.00"	CRS	Retired/Sec	$95.00
(174)	85		UPP	45.00		DVE	Retired/Sec	90.00
	86		UPP	45.00		OLB	Retired/Sec	90.00

JUNIOR BRIDESMAID   Figurine   Fifth Issue "Bridal" Series

E-2845	86	Junior Bridesmaid	UPP	$12.50	3.75"	OLB	Secondary	$20.00
(210)	87		UPP	12.50		CED	Secondary	17.00
	88		UPP	15.00		FLW	Secondary	17.00
	89		UPP	17.00		B&A	Primary	17.00
	90		OPEN	17.00		FLM	Primary	17.00

BRIDE	Figurine	Seventh Issue "Bridal" Series						
E-2846	87	Bride		UPP	$18.00	4.75"	CED	Secondary	$30.00
(313)	88			UPP	22.50		FLW	Secondary	25.00
	89			UPP	25.00		B&A	Primary	25.00
	90			OPEN	25.00		FLM	Primary	25.00

LOVE IS KIND	Plate	Fourth Issue "Inspired Thoughts" Series		Individually Numbered				
E-2847	84	Boy Pushing Girl on Swing	15,000	$40.00	8.50"	UM	Secondary	$45.00
(175)						CRS	Secondary	40.00

LOVING THY NEIGHBOR	Plate	Fourth Issue "Mother's Love" Series		Individually Numbered			
E-2848	84	Mother Wrapping Bread	15,000	$40.00	8.50"	CRS	Secondary	$40.00
(176)								

MOTHER SEW DEAR	Doll						
E-2850	*	Mother Needlepointing	UPP	$350.00	16.00"	UM	Retired/Prim	$350.00
(30)	84		UPP	350.00		CRS	Retired/Prim	350.00
	85		UPP	350.00		DVE	Retired/Prim	350.00

* UNMARKED (UM) pieces could have been produced in any of the years of production.

KRISTY	Doll						
E-2851	84	Baby Collector Doll	UPP	$150.00	12.00"	CRS	Susp/Sec	$180.00
(177)	85		UPP	150.00		DVE	Susp/Sec	170.00
	86		UPP	150.00		OLB	Susp/Sec	170.00
	87		UPP	150.00		CED	Susp/Sec	170.00
	88		UPP	160.00		FLW	Susp/Sec	170.00
	89		UPP	170.00		B&A	Susp/Sec	170.00

BABY FIGURINES	Figurines	Set of 6					
E-2852	84	Baby Figurines	UPP	$72.00	3.50"	CRS	Secondary	$120.00
(178)	85		UPP	72.00		DVE	Secondary	90.00
	86		UPP	72.00		OLB	Secondary	90.00
	87		UPP	72.00		CED	Secondary	90.00

IN 1988 INDIVIDUAL NUMBERS WERE ASSIGNED FOR EACH OF THE 6:

E-2852A	88	Baby Boy Standing	UPP	$14.00	3.75"	FLW	Secondary	$15.00
(401)	89		UPP	15.00		B&A	Primary	15.00
	90		OPEN	15.00		FLM	Primary	15.00

E-2852B	88	Baby Girl with Bow in Hair	UPP	$14.00	3.75"	FLW	Secondary	$15.00
(402)	89		UPP	15.00		B&A	Primary	15.00
	90		OPEN	15.00		FLM	Primary	15.00

E-2852C	88	Baby Boy Sitting	UPP	$14.00	3.00"	FLW	Secondary	$15.00
(403)	89		UPP	15.00		B&A	Primary	15.00
	90		OPEN	15.00		FLM	Primary	15.00

E-2852D	88	Baby Girl Clapping Hands	UPP	$14.00	3.25"	FLW	Secondary	$15.00
(404)	89		UPP	15.00		B&A	Primary	15.00
	90		OPEN	15.00		FLM	Primary	15.00

E-2852E	88	Baby Boy Crawling	UPP	$14.00	2.75"	FLW	Secondary	$15.00
(405)	89		UPP	15.00		B&A	Primary	15.00
	90		OPEN	15.00		FLM	Primary	15.00

E-2852F	88	Baby Girl Lying Down	UPP	$14.00	2.50"	FLW	Secondary	$15.00
(406)	89		UPP	15.00		B&A	Primary	15.00
	90		OPEN	15.00		FLM	Primary	15.00

GOD BLESSED OUR YEARS TOGETHER WITH SO MUCH LOVE & HAPPINESS					Figurine		
E-2853	84	Happy Anniversary	UPP	$35.00	5.50"	CRS	Secondary	$50.00
(179)	85		UPP	35.00		DVE	Secondary	45.00
	86		UPP	35.00		OLB	Secondary	45.00
	87		UPP	35.00		CED	Secondary	45.00
	88		UPP	40.00		FLW	Secondary	45.00
	89		UPP	45.00		B&A	Primary	45.00
	90		OPEN	45.00		FLM	Primary	45.00

GOD BLESSED OUR YEAR TOGETHER WITH SO MUCH LOVE & HAPPINESS — Figurine

E-2854	84	First Anniversary	UPP	$35.00	5.50"	CRS	Secondary	$55.00
(180)	85		UPP	35.00		DVE	Secondary	45.00
	86		UPP	35.00		OLB	Secondary	45.00
	87		UPP	35.00		CED	Secondary	45.00
	88		UPP	40.00		FLW	Secondary	45.00
	89		UPP	45.00		B&A	Primary	45.00
	90		OPEN	45.00		FLM	Primary	45.00

GOD BLESSED OUR YEARS TOGETHER WITH SO MUCH LOVE & HAPPINESS — Figurine

E-2855	84	5th Anniversary	UPP	$35.00	5.50"	CRS	Secondary	$50.00
(181)	85		UPP	35.00		DVE	Secondary	45.00
	86		UPP	35.00		OLB	Secondary	45.00
	87		UPP	35.00		CED	Secondary	45.00
	88		UPP	40.00		FLW	Secondary	45.00
	89		UPP	45.00		B&A	Primary	45.00
	90		OPEN	45.00		FLM	Primary	45.00

GOD BLESSED OUR YEARS TOGETHER WITH SO MUCH LOVE & HAPPINESS — Figurine

E-2856	84	10th Anniversary	UPP	$35.00	5.50"	CRS	Secondary	$50.00
(182)	85		UPP	35.00		DVE	Secondary	45.00
	86		UPP	35.00		OLB	Secondary	45.00
	87		UPP	35.00		CED	Secondary	45.00
	88		UPP	40.00		FLW	Secondary	45.00
	89		UPP	45.00		B&A	Primary	45.00
	90		OPEN	45.00		FLM	Primary	45.00

GOD BLESSED OUR YEARS TOGETHER WITH SO MUCH LOVE & HAPPINESS — Figurine

E-2857	84	25th Anniversary	UPP	$35.00	5.50"	CRS	Secondary	$55.00
(183)	85		UPP	35.00		DVE	Secondary	45.00
	86		UPP	35.00		OLB	Secondary	45.00
	87		UPP	35.00		CED	Secondary	45.00
	88		UPP	40.00		FLW	Secondary	45.00
	89		UPP	45.00		B&A	Secondary	45.00
	90		OPEN	45.00		FLM	Primary	45.00

GOD BLESSED OUR YEARS TOGETHER WITH SO MUCH LOVE & HAPPINESS — Figurine

E-2859	84	40th Anniversary	UPP	$35.00	5.50"	CRS	Secondary	$50.00
(184)	85		UPP	35.00		DVE	Secondary	45.00
	86		UPP	35.00		OLB	Secondary	45.00
	87		UPP	35.00		CED	Secondary	45.00
	88		UPP	40.00		FLW	Secondary	45.00
	89		UPP	45.00		B&A	Secondary	45.00
	90		OPEN	45.00		FLM	Primary	45.00

GOD BLESSED OUR YEARS TOGETHER WITH SO MUCH LOVE & HAPPINESS — Figurine

E-2860	84	50th Anniversary	UPP	$35.00	5.50"	CRS	Secondary	$45.00
(185)	85		UPP	35.00		DVE	Secondary	45.00
	86		UPP	35.00		OLB	Secondary	45.00
	87		UPP	35.00		CED	Secondary	45.00
	88		UPP	40.00		FLW	Secondary	45.00
	89		UPP	45.00		B&A	Secondary	45.00
	90		OPEN	45.00		FLM	Primary	45.00

BLESSED ARE THE PURE IN HEART — Figurine

E-3104	80	Rocking Cradle	UPP	$ 9.00	2.75"	NM	Secondary	$45.00
(28)	81		UPP	10.50		TRI	Secondary	35.00
	82		UPP	12.00		HRG	Secondary	30.00
	83		UPP	12.00		FSH	Secondary	25.00
	84		UPP	13.50		CRS	Secondary	17.50
	85		UPP	13.50		DVE	Secondary	17.50
	86		UPP	13.50		OLB	Secondary	17.50
	87		UPP	13.50		CED	Secondary	17.50
	88		UPP	16.00		FLW	Secondary	17.50
	89		UPP	17.50		B&A	Primary	17.50
	90		OPEN	17.50		FLM	Primary	17.50

HE WATCHES OVER US ALL   Figurine

E-3105	80	Boy on Crutches with Bible	UPP	$11.00	5.25"	NM	Susp/Sec	$85.00
(29)	81		UPP	11.00		TRI	Susp/Sec	75.00
	82		UPP	15.00		HRG	Susp/Sec	65.00
	83		UPP	15.00		FSH	Susp/Sec	60.00
	84		UPP	17.00		CRS	Susp/Sec	60.00

MOTHER SEW DEAR   Figurine

E-3106	80	Mother Needlepointing	UPP	$11.00	5.00"	NM	Secondary	$70.00
(30)	81		UPP	13.00		TRI	Secondary	65.00
	82		UPP	16.00		HRG	Secondary	50.00
	83		UPP	16.00		FSH	Secondary	35.00
	84		UPP	17.00		CRS	Secondary	25.00
	85		UPP	17.00		DVE	Secondary	25.00
	86		UPP	17.00		OLB	Secondary	25.00
	87		UPP	17.00		CED	Secondary	25.00
	88		UPP	22.50		FLW	Secondary	25.00
	89		UPP	25.00		B&A	Primary	25.00
	90		OPEN	25.00		FLM	Primary	25.00

BLESSED ARE THE PEACEMAKERS   Figurine

E-3107	80	Boy Holding Cat & Dog	UPP	$13.00	5.25"	NM	Retired/Sec	$105.00
(31)	81		UPP	15.00		TRI	Retired/Sec	90.00
	82		UPP	17.00		HRG	Retired/Sec	80.00
	83		UPP	17.00		FSH	Retired/Sec	75.00
	84		UPP	19.00		CRS	Retired/Sec	65.00
	85		UPP	19.00		DVE	Retired/Sec	65.00

THE HAND THAT ROCKS THE FUTURE   Figurine

E-3108	80	Girl Rocking Cradle	UPP	$13.00	4.50"	NM	Susp/Sec	$80.00
(32)	81		UPP	15.00		TRI	Susp/Sec	75.00
	82		UPP	17.00		HRG	Susp/Sec	70.00
	83		UPP	17.00		FSH	Susp/Sec	65.00
	84		UPP	17.00		CRS	Susp/Sec	60.00

THE PURR-FECT GRANDMA   Figurine

E-3109	80	Grandma in Rocker	UPP	$13.00	4.75"	NM	Secondary	$70.00
(33)	81		UPP	15.00		TRI	Secondary	55.00
	82		UPP	17.00		HRG	Secondary	35.00
	83		UPP	17.00		FSH	Secondary	30.00
	84		UPP	19.00		CRS	Secondary	25.00
	85		UPP	19.00		DVE	Secondary	25.00
	86		UPP	19.00		OLB	Secondary	25.00
	87		UPP	19.00		CED	Secondary	25.00
	88		UPP	23.00		FLW	Secondary	25.00
	89		UPP	25.00		B&A	Primary	25.00
	90		OPEN	25.00		FLM	Primary	25.00

LOVING IS SHARING   Figurine

E-3110B	80	Boy Sharing with Puppy	UPP	$13.00	4.50"	NM	Secondary	$80.00
(34)	81		UPP	15.00		TRI	Secondary	70.00
	82		UPP	17.00		HRG	Secondary	50.00
	83		UPP	17.00		FSH	Secondary	40.00
	84		UPP	19.00		CRS	Secondary	27.50
	85		UPP	19.00		DVE	Secondary	27.50
	86		UPP	19.00		OLB	Secondary	27.50
	87		UPP	19.00		CED	Secondary	27.50
	88		UPP	24.00		FLW	Secondary	27.50
	89		UPP	27.50		B&A	Primary	27.50
	90		OPEN	27.50		FLM	Primary	27.50

LOVING IS SHARING — Figurine

E-3110G	80	Girl Sharing with Puppy	UPP	$13.00	4.50"	NM	Secondary	$90.00
(35)	81		UPP	15.00		TRI	Secondary	75.00
	82		UPP	17.00		HRG	Secondary	55.00
	83		UPP	17.00		FSH	Secondary	35.00
	84		UPP	19.00		CRS	Secondary	27.50
	85		UPP	19.00		DVE	Secondary	27.50
	86		UPP	19.00		OLB	Secondary	27.50
	87		UPP	19.00		CED	Secondary	27.50
	88		UPP	24.00		FLW	Secondary	27.50
	89		UPP	27.50		B&A	Primary	27.50
	90		OPEN	27.50		FLM	Primary	27.50

BE NOT WEARY IN WELL DOING — Figurine *See "Nobody's Perfect!" Section

E-3111	80	Girl Helper	UPP	$14.00	4.00"	NM*	Retired/Sec	$115.00
(36)	81		UPP	16.00		TRI	Retired/Sec	100.00
	82		UPP	18.00		HRG	Retired/Sec	75.00
	83		UPP	18.00		FSH	Retired/Sec	75.00
	84		UPP	19.00		CRS	Retired/Sec	60.00
	85		UPP	19.00		DVE	Retired/Sec	60.00

GOD'S SPEED — Figurine

E-3112	80	Boy Jogging with Dog	UPP	$14.00	4.75"	NM	Retired/Sec	$100.00
(44)	81		UPP	16.00		TRI	Retired/Sec	90.00
	82		UPP	18.00		HRG	Retired/Sec	80.00
	83		UPP	18.00		FSH	Retired/Sec	75.00

[NOTE: Exists in a double mark TRI & HRG.]

THOU ART MINE — Figurine

E-3113	80	Boy with Girl Writing	UPP	$16.00	5.00"	NM	Secondary	$85.00
(37)	81	in Sand	UPP	19.00		TRI	Secondary	75.00
	82		UPP	22.50		HRG	Secondary	60.00
	83		UPP	22.50		FSH	Secondary	40.00
	84		UPP	25.00		CRS	Secondary	35.00
	85		UPP	25.00		DVE	Secondary	33.00
	86		UPP	25.00		OLB	Secondary	33.00
	87		UPP	25.00		CED	Secondary	33.00
	88		UPP	30.00		FLW	Secondary	33.00
	89		UPP	33.00		B&A	Primary	33.00
	90		OPEN	33.00		FLM	Primary	33.00

THE LORD BLESS YOU AND KEEP YOU — Figurine

E-3114	80	Bride and Groom	UPP	$16.00	5.00"	NM	Secondary	$80.00
(38)	81		UPP	19.00		TRI	Secondary	60.00
	82		UPP	22.50		HRG	Secondary	55.00
	83		UPP	22.50		FSH	Secondary	40.00
	84		UPP	25.00		CRS	Secondary	37.50
	85		UPP	25.00		DVE	Secondary	37.50
	86		UPP	25.00		OLB	Secondary	37.50
	87		UPP	25.00		CED	Secondary	37.50
	88		UPP	32.50		FLW	Secondary	37.50
	89		UPP	37.50		B&A	Primary	37.50
	90		OPEN	37.50		FLM	Primary	37.50

BUT LOVE GOES ON FOREVER — Figurine

E-3115	80	Boy and Girl Angels on Cloud	UPP	$16.50	5.25"	NM	Secondary	$85.00
(39)	81		UPP	19.00		TRI	Secondary	70.00
	82		UPP	22.50		HRG	Secondary	55.00
	83		UPP	22.50		FSH	Secondary	40.00
	84		UPP	25.00		CRS	Secondary	33.00
	85		UPP	25.00		DVE	Secondary	33.00
	86		UPP	25.00		OLB	Secondary	33.00
	87		UPP	25.00		CED	Secondary	33.00
	88		UPP	30.00		FLW	Secondary	33.00
	89		UPP	33.00		B&A	Primary	33.00
	90		OPEN	33.00		FLM	Primary	33.00

THEE I LOVE — Figurine

E-3116		Boy Carving Tree for Girl						
(40)	80		UPP	$16.50	6.00"	NM	Secondary	$90.00
	81		UPP	19.00		TRI	Secondary	85.00
	82		UPP	22.50		HRG	Secondary	65.00
	83		UPP	22.50		FSH	Secondary	45.00
	84		UPP	25.00		CRS	Secondary	36.00
	85		UPP	25.00		DVE	Secondary	36.00
	86		UPP	25.00		OLB	Secondary	36.00
	87		UPP	25.00		CED	Secondary	36.00
	88		UPP	32.50		FLW	Secondary	36.00
	89		UPP	36.00		B&A	Primary	36.00
	90		OPEN	36.00		FLM	Primary	36.00

WALKING BY FAITH — Figurine — See "Nobody's Perfect!" Section

E-3117		Boy Pulling Wagon with Girl						
(41)	80		UPP	$35.00	7.25"	NM	Secondary	$105.00
	81		UPP	40.00		TRI	Secondary	90.00
	82		UPP	45.00		HRG	Secondary	80.00
	83		UPP	45.00		FSH	Secondary	75.00
	84		UPP	50.00		CRS	Secondary	67.50
	85		UPP	50.00		DVE	Secondary	67.50
	86		UPP	50.00		OLB	Secondary	67.50
	87		UPP	50.00		CED	Secondary	67.50
	88		UPP	60.00		FLW	Secondary	67.50
	89		UPP	67.50		B&A	Primary	67.50
	90		OPEN	67.50		FLM	Primary	67.50

EGGS OVER EASY — Figurine

E-3118		Girl with Frypan						
(45)	80		UPP	$12.00	5.00"	NM	Retired/Sec	$110.00
	81		UPP	14.00		TRI	Retired/Sec	95.00
	82		UPP	15.00		HRG	Retired/Sec	80.00
	83		UPP	15.00		FSH	Retired/Sec	75.00

IT'S WHAT'S INSIDE THAT COUNTS — Figurine

E-3119		Boy with Books						
(42)	80		UPP	$13.00	5.25"	NM	Susp/Sec	$105.00
	81		UPP	15.00		TRI	Susp/Sec	90.00
	82		UPP	17.00		HRG	Susp/Sec	85.00
	83		UPP	17.00		FSH	Susp/Sec	80.00
	84		UPP	17.00		CRS	Susp/Sec	75.00

TO THEE WITH LOVE — Figurine

E-3120		Girl with Box of Kittens						
(43)	80		UPP	$13.00	5.75"	NM	Susp/Sec	$80.00
	81		UPP	15.00		TRI	Susp/Sec	65.00
	82		UPP	17.00		HRG	Susp/Sec	65.00
	83		UPP	17.00		FSH	Susp/Sec	60.00
	84		UPP	19.00		CRS	Susp/Sec	60.00
	85		UPP	19.00		DVE	Susp/Sec	55.00
	86		UPP	19.00		OLB	Susp/Sec	55.00

THE LORD BLESS YOU AND KEEP YOU — Figurine

E-4720		Boy Graduate						
(46)	81		UPP	$14.00	5.25"	NM	Susp/Sec	$45.00
	81		UPP	14.00		TRI	Susp/Sec	40.00
	82		UPP	17.00		HRG	Susp/Sec	37.00
	83		UPP	17.00		FSH	Susp/Sec	35.00
	84		UPP	19.00		CRS	Susp/Sec	30.00
	85		UPP	19.00		DVE	Susp/Sec	30.00
	86		UPP	19.00		OLB	Susp/Sec	30.00
	87		UPP	19.00		CED	Susp/Sec	30.00

THE LORD BLESS YOU AND KEEP YOU — Figurine

E-4721	81	Girl Graduate	UPP	$14.00	5.25"	NM	Secondary	$75.00
(47)	81		UPP	14.00		TRI	Secondary	60.00
	82		UPP	17.00		HRG	Secondary	45.00
	83		UPP	17.00		FSH	Secondary	35.00
	84		UPP	19.00		CRS	Secondary	30.00
	85		UPP	19.00		DVE	Secondary	27.00
	86		UPP	19.00		OLB	Secondary	27.00
	87		UPP	19.00		CED	Secondary	27.00
	88		UPP	24.00		FLW	Secondary	27.00
	89		UPP	27.00		B&A	Primary	27.00
	90		OPEN	27.00		FLM	Primary	27.00

LOVE CANNOT BREAK A TRUE FRIENDSHIP — Figurine

E-4722	81	Girl with Piggy Bank	UPP	$22.50	5.00"	NM	Susp/Sec	$90.00
(48)	81		UPP	22.50		TRI	Susp/Sec	85.00
	82		UPP	25.00		HRG	Susp/Sec	75.00
	83		UPP	25.00		FSH	Susp/Sec	65.00
	84		UPP	27.50		CRS	Susp/Sec	60.00
	85		UPP	27.50		DVE	Susp/Sec	60.00

PEACE AMID THE STORM — Figurine

E-4723	81	Boy Reading Holy Bible	UPP	$22.50	4.75"	NM	Susp/Sec	$70.00
(49)	81		UPP	22.50		TRI	Susp/Sec	65.00
	82		UPP	25.00		HRG	Susp/Sec	60.00
	83		UPP	25.00		FSH	Susp/Sec	55.00
	84		UPP	27.50		CRS	Susp/Sec	55.00

REJOICING WITH YOU — Figurine   *See "Nobody's Perfect!" Section

E-4724	81	Christening	UPP	$25.00	5.25"	NM*	Secondary	$80.00
(50)	81		UPP	25.00		TRI*	Secondary	70.00
	82		UPP	27.50		HRG*	Secondary	65.00
	83		UPP	27.50		FSH	Secondary	45.00
	84		UPP	30.00		CRS	Secondary	45.00
	85		UPP	30.00		DVE	Secondary	40.00
	86		UPP	30.00		OLB	Secondary	40.00
	87		UPP	30.00		CED	Secondary	40.00
	88		UPP	37.50		FLW	Secondary	40.00
	89		UPP	40.00		B&A	Primary	40.00
	90		OPEN	40.00		FLM	Primary	40.00

PEACE ON EARTH — Figurine

E-4725	81	Choir Boys with Bandages	UPP	$25.00	5.25"	NM	Susp/Sec	$80.00
(51)	81		UPP	25.00		TRI	Susp/Sec	75.00
	82		UPP	27.50		HRG	Susp/Sec	65.00
	83		UPP	27.50		FSH	Susp/Sec	60.00
	84		UPP	27.50		CRS	Susp/Sec	60.00

PEACE ON EARTH — Musical   TUNE: Jesus Loves Me

E-4726	81	Choir Boys with Bandages	UPP	$45.00	6.25"	NM	Susp/Sec	$85.00
(51)	81		UPP	45.00		TRI	Susp/Sec	75.00
	82		UPP	45.00		HRG	Susp/Sec	70.00
	83		UPP	45.00		FSH	Susp/Sec	70.00
	84		UPP	45.00		CRS	Susp/Sec	60.00

BEAR YE ONE ANOTHER'S BURDENS — Figurine

E-5200	81	Sad Boy with Teddy	UPP	$20.00	4.74"	NM	Susp/Sec	$90.00
(52)	81		UPP	20.00		TRI	Susp/Sec	85.00
	82		UPP	22.50		HRG	Susp/Sec	75.00
	83		UPP	22.50		FSH	Susp/Sec	65.00
	84		UPP	25.00		CRS	Susp/Sec	65.00

LOVE LIFTED ME Figurine

E-5201	81	Boy Helping Friend	UPP	$25.00	5.50"	NM	Susp/Sec	$90.00
(53)	81		UPP	25.00		TRI	Susp/Sec	85.00
	82		UPP	30.00		HRG	Susp/Sec	70.00
	83		UPP	30.00		FSH	Susp/Sec	65.00
	84		UPP	33.00		CRS	Susp/Sec	65.00

THANK YOU FOR COMING TO MY ADE Figurine

E-5202	81	Lemonade Stand	UPP	$22.50	5.50"	NM	Susp/Sec	$90.00
(54)	81		UPP	22.50		TRI	Susp/Sec	85.00
	82		UPP	27.50		HRG	Susp/Sec	70.00
	83		UPP	27.50		FSH	Susp/Sec	65.00
	84		UPP	30.00		CRS	Susp/Sec	65.00

LET NOT THE SUN GO DOWN UPON YOUR WRATH Figurine

E-5203	81	Boy with Dog on Stairs	UPP	$22.50	6.75"	NM	Susp/Sec	$130.00
(55)	81		UPP	22.50		TRI	Susp/Sec	105.00
	82		UPP	27.50		HRG	Susp/Sec	90.00
	83		UPP	30.00		FSH	Susp/Sec	75.00
	84		UPP	30.00		CRS	Susp/Sec	75.00

THE HAND THAT ROCKS THE FUTURE Musical TUNE: Mozart's Lullaby

E-5204	81	Girl Rocking Cradle	UPP	$30.00	5.50"	NM	Secondary	$70.00
(32)	81		UPP	30.00		TRI	Secondary	65.00
	82		UPP	35.00		HRG	Secondary	60.00
	83		UPP	35.00		FSH	Secondary	55.00
	84		UPP	37.50		CRS	Secondary	50.00
	85		UPP	37.50		DVE	Secondary	50.00
	86		UPP	37.50		OLB	Secondary	50.00
	87		UPP	37.50		CED	Secondary	50.00
	88		UPP	45.00		FLW	Primary	50.00
	89		UPP	50.00		B&A	Primary	50.00
	90		OPEN	50.00		FLM	Primary	50.00

MY GUARDIAN ANGEL Musical TUNE: Brahm's Lullaby

E-5205	81	Boy Angel on Cloud	UPP	$22.50	5.50"	NM	Susp/Sec	$65.00
(56)	84		UPP	27.50		CRS	Susp/Sec	55.00
	85		UPP	27.50		DVE	Susp/Sec	55.00

MY GUARDIAN ANGEL Musical TUNE: Brahm's Lullaby

E-5206	81	Girl Angel on Cloud	UPP	$22.50	5.50"	NM	Susp/Sec	$75.00
(57)	84		UPP	27.50		CRS	Susp/Sec	55.00
	85		UPP	27.50		DVE	Susp/Sec	55.00
	86		UPP	27.50		OLB	Susp/Sec	50.00
	87		UPP	27.50		CED	Susp/Sec	50.00
	88		UPP	33.00		FLW	Susp/Sec	50.00

MY GUARDIAN ANGELS Night Light

E-5207	81	Boy & Girl Angels on Cloud	UPP	$30.00	3.50"	NM	Susp/Sec	$125.00
(39)	84		UPP	35.00		CRS	Susp/Sec	100.00

JESUS LOVES ME Bell

E-5208	81	Boy with Teddy	UPP	$15.00	5.75"	NM	Susp/Sec	$45.00
(1)	84		UPP	19.00		CRS	Susp/Sec	40.00
	85		UPP	19.00		DVE	Susp/Sec	35.00

JESUS LOVES ME Bell

E-5209	81	Girl with Bunny	UPP	$15.00	5.75"	NM	Susp/Sec	$50.00
(2)	84		UPP	19.00		CRS	Susp/Sec	45.00
	85		UPP	19.00		DVE	Susp/Sec	40.00

PRAYER CHANGES THINGS Bell

E-5210	81	Girl Praying	UPP	$15.00	5.75"	NM	Susp/Sec	$50.00
(58)	84		UPP	19.00		CRS	Susp/Sec	40.00

GOD UNDERSTANDS Bell

E-5211	81	Boy with Report Card	UPP	$15.00	5.75"	UM	Retired/Sec	$55.00
(12)	84		UPP	19.00		CRS	Retired/Sec	50.00

TO A SPECIAL DAD Figurine

E-5212	81	Boy in Dad's Duds	UPP	$20.00	5.50"	NM	Secondary	$70.00
(59)	81		UPP	20.00		TRI	Secondary	65.00
	82		UPP	22.50		HRG	Secondary	50.00
	83		UPP	22.50		FSH	Secondary	35.00
	84		UPP	25.00		CRS	Secondary	33.00
	85		UPP	25.00		DVE	Secondary	33.00
	86		UPP	25.00		OLB	Secondary	33.00
	87		UPP	25.00		CED	Secondary	33.00
	88		UPP	30.00		FLW	Secondary	33.00
	89		UPP	33.00		B&A	Primary	33.00
	90		OPEN	33.00		FLM	Primary	33.00

GOD IS LOVE Figurine

E-5213	81	Girl with Goose in Lap	UPP	$17.00	5.00"	NM	Susp/Sec	$80.00
(60)	81		UPP	17.00		TRI	Susp/Sec	75.00
	82		UPP	20.00		HRG	Susp/Sec	70.00
	83		UPP	20.00		FSH	Susp/Sec	65.00
	84		UPP	22.50		CRS	Susp/Sec	60.00
	85		UPP	22.50		DVE	Susp/Sec	55.00
	86		UPP	22.50		OLB	Susp/Sec	50.00
	87		UPP	22.50		CED	Susp/Sec	50.00
	88		UPP	27.00		FLW	Susp/Sec	45.00
	89		UPP	30.00		B&A	Susp/Sec	45.00

[NOTE: This piece was re-sculpted in 1985. On the original mold the girl had no chin.]

PRAYER CHANGES THINGS Figurine *See "Nobody's Perfect!" Section

E-5214	81	Boy & Girl Praying at Table	UPP	$35.00	5.15"	NM	Susp/Sec	*
(61)	81	with Bible	UPP	35.00		TRI	Susp/Sec	*
	82		UPP	35.00		HRG	Susp/Sec	*
	83		UPP	35.00		FSH	Susp/Sec	$80.00
	84		UPP	37.50		CRS	Susp/Sec	80.00

LOVE ONE ANOTHER Plate First Issue "Inspired Thoughts" Series Individually Numbered

E-5215	81	Boy and Girl on Stump	15,000	$40.00	8.50"	UM	Secondary	$70.00
(8)								

THE LORD BLESS YOU AND KEEP YOU Plate

E-5216	81	Bride and Groom	UPP	$30.00	7.00"	UM	Susp/Sec	$40.00
(38)	84		UPP	30.00		CRS	Susp/Sec	40.00
	85		UPP	30.00		DVE	Susp/Sec	40.00
	86		UPP	30.00		OLB	Susp/Sec	40.00
	87		UPP	35.00		CED	Susp/Sec	40.00

MOTHER SEW DEAR Plate First Issue "Mother's Love" Series Individually Numbered

E-5217	81	Mother Needlepointing	15,000	$40.00	8.50"	UM	Secondary	$70.00
(30)								

MAY YOUR CHRISTMAS BE BLESSED Figurine

E-5376	84	Girl with Long Hair & Bible	UPP	$37.50	5.75"	CRS	Susp/Sec	$60.00
(186)	85		UPP	37.50		DVE	Susp/Sec	55.00
	86		UPP	37.50		OLB	Susp/Sec	55.00

LOVE IS KIND Figurine

E-5377	84	Girl with Mouse	UPP	$27.50	4.00"	CRS	Retired/Sec	$85.00
(187)	85		UPP	27.50		DVE	Retired/Sec	75.00
	86		UPP	27.50		OLB	Retired/Sec	70.00
	87		UPP	27.50		CED	Retired/Sec	70.00

JOY TO THE WORLD — Figurine — Nativity Addition

E-5378	84	Boy Playing Harp	UPP	$18.00	4.00"	CRS	Susp/Sec	$35.00
(188)	85		UPP	18.00		DVE	Susp/Sec	30.00
	86		UPP	18.00		OLB	Susp/Sec	30.00
	87		UPP	18.00		CED	Susp/Sec	30.00
	88		UPP	20.00		FLW	Susp/Sec	30.00
	89		UPP	25.00		B&A	Susp/Sec	30.00

ISN'T HE PRECIOUS — Figurine — Nativity Addition — See "Nobody's Perfect!" Section

E-5379	84	Girl with Broom	UPP	$20.00	5.00"	CRS	Secondary	$35.00
(189)	85		UPP	20.00		DVE	Secondary	27.50
	86		UPP	20.00		OLB	Secondary	27.50
	87		UPP	20.00		CED	Secondary	27.50
	88		UPP	22.50		FLW	Secondary	27.50
	89		UPP	27.50		B&A	Primary	27.50
	90		OPEN	27.50		FLM	Primary	27.50

A MONARCH IS BORN — Figurine

E-5380	84	Boy with Butterfly at Manger	UPP	$33.00	5.00"	CRS	Susp/Sec	$50.00
(190)	85		UPP	33.00		DVE	Susp/Sec	45.00
	86		UPP	33.00		OLB	Susp/Sec	45.00

HIS NAME IS JESUS — Figurine

E-5381	84	Boys at Manger	UPP	$45.00	5.00"	CRS	Susp/Sec	$70.00
(191)	85		UPP	45.00		DVE	Susp/Sec	65.00
	86		UPP	45.00		OLB	Susp/Sec	60.00
	87		UPP	45.00		CED	Susp/Sec	60.00

FOR GOD SO LOVED THE WORLD — Figurines — Set of 4

E-5382	84	Deluxe 4 Piece Nativity	UPP	$70.00	5.00"	CRS	Susp/Sec	$90.00
(192)	85		UPP	70.00		DVE	Susp/Sec	80.00
	86		UPP	70.00		OLB	Susp/Sec	75.00

WISHING YOU A MERRY CHRISTMAS — Figurine, Dated

E-5383	84	Girl with Songbook	Annual	$17.00	4.75"	CRS	Secondary	$45.00
(193)								

I'LL PLAY MY DRUM FOR HIM — Figurine — Nativity Addition

E-5384	84	Drummer Boy	UPP	$10.00	3.50"	CRS	Secondary	$20.00
(87)	85		UPP	10.00		DVE	Secondary	15.00
	86		UPP	10.00		OLB	Secondary	13.50
	87		UPP	10.00		CED	Secondary	13.50
	88		UPP	11.00		FLW	Secondary	13.50
	89		UPP	13.50		B&A	Primary	13.50
	90		OPEN	13.50		FLM	Primary	13.50

OH WORSHIP THE LORD — Figurine — Nativity Addition

E-5385	84	Boy Angel with Candle	UPP	$10.00	3.25"	CRS	Susp/Sec	$30.00
(194)	85		UPP	10.00		DVE	Susp/Sec	28.00
	86		UPP	10.00		OLB	Susp/Sec	28.00

OH WORSHIP THE LORD — Figurine — Nativity Addition

E-5386	84	Girl Angel Praying	UPP	$10.00	3.25"	CRS	Susp/Sec	$35.00
(195)	85		UPP	10.00		DVE	Susp/Sec	30.00
	86		UPP	10.00		OLB	Susp/Sec	30.00

WISHING YOU A MERRY CHRISTMAS — Ornament, Dated

E-5387	84	Girl with Songbook	Annual	$10.00	3.00"	CRS	Secondary	$35.00
(193)								

JOY TO THE WORLD — Ornament

E-5388	84	Boy Playing Harp	UPP	$10.00	2.50"	CRS	Retired/Sec	$45.00
(188)	85		UPP	10.00		DVE	Retired/Sec	40.00
	86		UPP	10.00		OLB	Retired/Sec	35.00
	87		UPP	10.00		CED	Retired/Sec	35.00

PEACE ON EARTH   Ornament

E-5389	84	Boy in Choir	UPP	$10.00	3.00"	CRS	Susp/Sec	$35.00
(196)	85		UPP	10.00		DVE	Susp/Sec	30.00
	86		UPP	10.00		OLB	Susp/Sec	30.00

MAY GOD BLESS YOU WITH A PERFECT SEASON   Ornament

E-5390	84	Girl in Scarf and Hat	UPP	$10.00	3.00"	CRS	Susp/Sec	$30.00
(197)	85		UPP	10.00		DVE	Susp/Sec	28.00
	86		UPP	10.00		OLB	Susp/Sec	28.00
	87		UPP	10.00		CED	Susp/Sec	25.00
	88		UPP	11.00		FLW	Susp/Sec	25.00
	89		UPP	13.50		B&A	Susp/Sec	25.00

LOVE IS KIND   Ornament

E-5391	84	Girl with Gift	UPP	$10.00	2.50"	CRS	Susp/Sec	$35.00
(198)	85		UPP	10.00		DVE	Susp/Sec	32.00
	86		UPP	10.00		OLB	Susp/Sec	30.00
	87		UPP	10.00		CED	Susp/Sec	30.00
	88		UPP	11.00		FLW	Susp/Sec	28.00
	89		UPP	13.50		B&A	Susp/Sec	28.00

BLESSED ARE THE PURE IN HEART   Ornament, Dated

E-5392	84	Baby in Cradle	Annual	$10.00	2.00"	CRS	Secondary	$35.00
(28)								

WISHING YOU A MERRY CHRISTMAS   Bell, Dated

E-5393	84	Girl with Songbook	Annual	$19.00	5.75"	CRS	Secondary	$40.00
(193)								

WISHING YOU A MERRY CHRISTMAS   Musical   TUNE: We Wish You A Merry Christmas

E-5394	84	Carollers with Puppy	UPP	$55.00	6.50"	CRS	Susp/Sec	$80.00
(200)	85		UPP	55.00		DVE	Susp/Sec	75.00
	86		UPP	55.00		OLB	Susp/Sec	70.00

UNTO US A CHILD IS BORN   Plate   Fourth Issue "Christmas Collection" Series
Individually Numbered

E-5395	84	Shepherds and Lambs	15,000	$40.00	8.50"	UM	Secondary	$40.00
(201)		on Hillside				CRS	Secondary	40.00

THE WONDER OF CHRISTMAS   Plate, Dated   Third Issue "Joy of Christmas" Series

E-5396	84	Boy Pulling Girl and Tree	Annual	$40.00	8.50"	CRS	Secondary	$60.00
(202)		on Sled						

TIMMY   Doll

E-5397	84	Boy Jogger	UPP	$125.00	10.00"	CRS	Secondary	$155.00
(203)	85		UPP	125.00		DVE	Secondary	145.00
	86		UPP	125.00		OLB	Primary	145.00
	87		UPP	125.00		CED	Primary	145.00
	88		UPP	135.00		FLW	Primary	145.00
	89		UPP	145.00		B&A	Primary	145.00
	90		OPEN	145.00		FLM	Primary	145.00

COME LET US ADORE HIM   Figurine

E-5619	*	Manger Child	UPP	$10.00	2.00"	UM	Susp/Sec	$45.00
(62)	81		UPP	10.00		TRI	Susp/Sec	35.00
	82		UPP	10.50		HRG	Susp/Sec	30.00
	83		UPP	10.50		FSH	Susp/Sec	30.00
	84		UPP	11.00		CRS	Susp/Sec	30.00
	85		UPP	11.00		DVE	Susp/Sec	30.00

* UNMARKED pieces could have been produced in any of the years of production.

WE HAVE SEEN HIS STAR   Bell

E-5620	81	Boy Holding Lamb	UPP	$15.00	5.50"	UM	Susp/Sec	$40.00
(16)	84		UPP	15.00		CRS	Susp/Sec	35.00

[NOTE: Piece was suspended in 1985, however it appears there are no DOVE pieces.]

DONKEY   Figurine   Nativity Addition

E-5621	81	Donkey	UPP	$ 6.00	2.75"	UM	Secondary	$25.00
(63)	84		UPP	9.00		CRS	Secondary	15.00
	85		UPP	9.00		DVE	Secondary	12.00
	86		UPP	9.00		OLB	Secondary	12.00
	87		UPP	10.00		CED	Secondary	12.00
	88		UPP	11.00		FLW	Primary	12.00
	89		UPP	12.00		B&A	Primary	12.00
	90		OPEN	12.00		FLM	Primary	12.00

LET THE HEAVENS REJOICE   Bell, Dated

E-5622	81	Praying Angel Boy	Annual	$15.00	5.75"	UM	Secondary	$165.00
(77)								

JESUS IS BORN   Bell

E-5623	81	Shepherd	UPP	$15.00	5.75"	UM	Susp/Sec	$40.00
(64)	84		UPP	15.00		CRS	Susp/Sec	35.00

THEY FOLLOWED THE STAR   Figurines   Set of 3

E-5624	*	3 Kings on Camels	UPP	$130.00	8.75"	UM	Secondary	$250.00
(65)	81		UPP	130.00		TRI	Secondary	225.00
	82		UPP	150.00		HRG	Secondary	210.00
	83		UPP	150.00		FSH	Secondary	200.00
	84		UPP	165.00		CRS	Secondary	190.00
	85		UPP	165.00		DVE	Secondary	190.00
	86		UPP	165.00		OLB	Secondary	190.00
	87		UPP	165.00		CED	Secondary	190.00
	88		UPP	175.00		FLW	Secondary	190.00
	89		UPP	190.00		B&A	Primary	190.00
	90		OPEN	190.00		FLM	Primary	190.00

* UNMARKED (UM) pieces could have been produced in any of the years of production.

BUT LOVE GOES ON FOREVER   Ornament

E-5627	*	Boy Angel on Cloud	UPP	$ 6.00	3.00"	UM	Susp/Sec	$65.00
(56)	81		UPP	6.00		TRI	Susp/Sec	90.00
	82		UPP	6.00		HRG	Susp/Sec	80.00
	83		UPP	9.00		FSH	Susp/Sec	65.00
	84		UPP	10.00		CRS	Susp/Sec	60.00
	85		UPP	10.00		DVE	Susp/Sec	55.00

* UNMARKED (UM) pieces could have been produced in any of the years of production.

BUT LOVE GOES ON FOREVER   Ornament

E-5628	*	Girl Angel on Cloud	UPP	$ 6.00	3.00"	UM	Susp/Sec	$ 70.00
(57)	81		UPP	6.00		TRI	Susp/Sec	125.00
	82		UPP	6.00		HRG	Susp/Sec	95.00
	83		UPP	9.00		FSH	Susp/Sec	80.00
	84		UPP	10.00		CRS	Susp/Sec	75.00
	85		UPP	10.00		DVE	Susp/Sec	70.00

* UNMARKED (UM) pieces could have been produced in any of the years of production.

LET THE HEAVENS REJOICE   Ornament, Dated   See "Nobody's Perfect!" Section

E-5629	81	Praying Angel Boy	Annual	$6.00	3.10"	TRI	Secondary	$195.00
(77)								

UNTO US A CHILD IS BORN   Ornament

E-5630	*	Shepherd	UPP	$ 6.00	3.25"	UM	Susp/Sec	$50.00
(64)	81		UPP	6.00		TRI	Susp/Sec	60.00
	82		UPP	6.00		HRG	Susp/Sec	55.00
	83		UPP	9.00		FSH	Susp/Sec	50.00
	84		UPP	10.00		CRS	Susp/Sec	45.00
	85		UPP	10.00		DVE	Susp/Sec	45.00

* UNMARKED (UM) pieces could have been produced in any of the years of production.

BABY'S FIRST CHRISTMAS   Ornament

E-5631	*	Boy with Teddy	UPP	$ 6.00	3.00"	UM	Susp/Sec	$50.00
(1)	81		UPP	6.00		TRI	Susp/Sec	60.00
	82		UPP	6.50		HRG	Susp/Sec	55.00
	83		UPP	9.00		FSH	Susp/Sec	50.00
	84		UPP	10.00		CRS	Susp/Sec	45.00
	85		UPP	10.00		DVE	Susp/Sec	45.00

* UNMARKED (UM) pieces could have been produced in any of the years of production.

BABY'S FIRST CHRISTMAS   Ornament

E-5632	*	Girl with Bunny	UPP	$ 6.00	3.00"	UM	Susp/Sec	$50.00
(2)	81		UPP	6.00		TRI	Susp/Sec	60.00
	82		UPP	6.50		HRG	Susp/Sec	55.00
	83		UPP	9.00		FSH	Susp/Sec	50.00
	84		UPP	10.00		CRS	Susp/Sec	45.00
	85		UPP	10.00		DVE	Susp/Sec	45.00

* UNMARKED (UM) pieces could have been produced in any of the years of production.

COME LET US ADORE HIM   Ornaments   Set of 4

E-5633	*	Jesus, Mary, Joseph & Lamb	UPP	$22.00	2.50"	UM	Susp/Sec	$80.00
(22)	81		UPP	22.00		TRI	Susp/Sec	90.00
	82		UPP	25.00		HRG	Susp/Sec	80.00
	83		UPP	31.50		FSH	Susp/Sec	75.00
	84		UPP	31.50		CRS	Susp/Sec	70.00

* UNMARKED (UM) pieces could have been produced in any of the years of production.

WEE THREE KINGS   Ornaments   Set of 3

E-5634	*	Three Kings	UPP	$19.00	3.50"	UM	Susp/Sec	$85.00
(66)	81		UPP	19.00		TRI	Susp/Sec	95.00
	82		UPP	19.00		HRG	Susp/Sec	85.00
	83		UPP	25.00		FSH	Susp/Sec	80.00
	84		UPP	27.50		CRS	Susp/Sec	75.00

* UNMARKED (UM) pieces could have been produced in any of the years of production.

WEE THREE KINGS   Figurines   Set of 3   Nativity Addition

E-5635	*	Three Kings	UPP	$40.00	5.50"	UM	Secondary	$90.00
(66)	81		UPP	40.00		TRI	Secondary	95.00
	82		UPP	50.00		HRG	Secondary	85.00
	83		UPP	50.00		FSH	Secondary	80.00
	84		UPP	55.00		CRS	Secondary	70.00
	85		UPP	55.00		DVE	Secondary	70.00
	86		UPP	55.00		OLB	Secondary	70.00
	87		UPP	55.00		CED	Secondary	70.00
	88		UPP	60.00		FLW	Secondary	70.00
	89		UPP	70.00		B&A	Primary	70.00
	90		OPEN	70.00		FLM	Primary	70.00

* UNMARKED (UM) pieces could have been produced in any of the years of production.

REJOICE O EARTH   Figurine   Nativity Addition

E-5636	*	Angel with Trumpet	UPP	$15.00	5.00"	UM	Secondary	$60.00
(67)	81		UPP	15.00		TRI	Secondary	65.00
	82		UPP	19.00		HRG	Secondary	40.00
	83		UPP	19.00		FSH	Secondary	35.00
	84		UPP	20.00		CRS	Secondary	27.50
	85		UPP	20.00		DVE	Secondary	27.50
	86		UPP	20.00		OLB	Secondary	27.50
	87		UPP	20.00		CED	Secondary	27.50
	88		UPP	22.50		FLW	Secondary	27.50
	89		UPP	27.50		B&A	Primary	27.50
	90		OPEN	27.50		FLM	Primary	27.50

* UNMARKED (UM) pieces could have been produced in any of the years of production.

THE HEAVENLY LIGHT   Figurine   Nativity Addition

E-5637	*	Angel with Flashlight	UPP	$15.00	4.85"	UM	Secondary	$60.00
(68)	81		UPP	15.00		TRI	Secondary	65.00
	82		UPP	17.00		HRG	Secondary	45.00
	83		UPP	17.00		FSH	Secondary	30.00
	84		UPP	19.00		CRS	Secondary	25.00
	85		UPP	19.00		DVE	Secondary	25.00
	86		UPP	19.00		OLB	Secondary	25.00
	87		UPP	19.00		CED	Secondary	25.00
	88		UPP	21.00		FLW	Secondary	25.00
	89		UPP	25.00		B&A	Primary	25.00
	90		OPEN	25.00		FLM	Primary	25.00

* UNMARKED (UM) pieces could have been produced in any of the years of production.

COW   Figurine   Nativity Addition

E-5638	*	Cow with Bell	UPP	$16.00	3.50"	UM	Secondary	$40.00
(69)	84		UPP	21.00		CRS	Secondary	30.00
	85		UPP	21.00		DVE	Secondary	30.00
	86		UPP	22.50		OLB	Secondary	30.00
	87		UPP	22.50		CED	Secondary	30.00
	88		UPP	27.50		FLW	Secondary	30.00
	89		UPP	30.00		B&A	Primary	30.00
	90		OPEN	30.00		FLM	Primary	30.0

* UNMARKED (UM) pieces could have been produced in any of the years of production.

ISN'T HE WONDERFUL   Figurine   Nativity Addition

E-5639	*	Boy Angel Praying with Harp	UPP	$12.00	4.75"	UM	Susp/Sec	$60.00
(70)	81		UPP	12.00		TRI	Susp/Sec	65.00
	82		UPP	15.00		HRG	Susp/Sec	55.00
	83		UPP	15.00		FSH	Susp/Sec	50.00
	84		UPP	17.00		CRS	Susp/Sec	45.00
	85		UPP	17.00		DVE	Susp/Sec	40.00

* UNMARKED (UM) pieces could have been produced in any of the years of production.

ISN'T HE WONDERFUL   Figurine   Nativity Addition

E-5640	*	Girl Angel Praying with Harp	UPP	$12.00	4.75"	UM	Susp/Sec	$60.00
(71)	81		UPP	12.00		TRI	Susp/Sec	65.00
	82		UPP	15.00		HRG	Susp/Sec	55.00
	83		UPP	15.00		FSH	Susp/Sec	50.00
	84		UPP	17.00		CRS	Susp/Sec	45.00
	85		UPP	17.00		DVE	Susp/Sec	45.00

* UNMARKED (UM) pieces could have been produced in any of the years of production.

THEY FOLLOWED THE STAR   Figurine

E-5641	*	"Follow Me" Angel with	UPP	$75.00	6.00"	UM	Susp/Sec	$165.00
(72)	81	Three Kings	UPP	75.00		TRI	Susp/Sec	170.00
	82		UPP	90.00		HRG	Susp/Sec	160.00
	83		UPP	90.00		FSH	Susp/Sec	155.00
	84		UPP	100.00		CRS	Susp/Sec	150.00
	85		UPP	100.00		DVE	Susp/Sec	150.00

* UNMARKED (UM) pieces could have been produced in any of the years of production.

SILENT KNIGHT   Musical   TUNE: Silent Night

E-5642	*	Boy Angel & Knight	UPP	$45.00	6.25"	UM	Susp/Sec	$110.00
(73)	81		UPP	45.00		TRI	Susp/Sec	110.00
	82		UPP	55.00		HRG	Susp/Sec	95.00
	83		UPP	55.00		FSH	Susp/Sec	90.00
	84		UPP	60.00		CRS	Susp/Sec	90.00
	85		UPP	60.00		DVE	Susp/Sec	90.00

[NOTE: Exists in a double mark TRI & HRG.]
* UNMARKED (UM) pieces could have been produced in any of the years of production.

TWO SECTION WALL   Figurines   Set of 2   Nativity Addition

E-5644	*	Two Section Wall	UPP	$60.00	6.00"	UM	Secondary	$130.00
(74)	81		UPP	60.00		TRI	Secondary	140.00
	82		UPP	80.00		HRG	Secondary	135.00
	83		UPP	80.00		FSH	Secondary	130.00
	84		UPP	90.00		CRS	Secondary	110.00
	85		UPP	90.00		DVE	Secondary	110.00
	86		UPP	90.00		OLB	Secondary	110.00
	87		UPP	90.00		CED	Secondary	110.00
	88		UPP	100.00		FLW	Secondary	110.00
	89		UPP	110.00		B&A	Primary	110.00
	90		OPEN	110.00		FLM	Primary	110.00

* UNMARKED (UM) pieces could have been produced in any of the years of production.

REJOICE O EARTH   Musical   TUNE: Joy To The World

E-5645	*	Angel with Trumpet	UPP	$35.00	6.25"	UM	Retired/Sec	$100.00
(67)	81		UPP	35.00		TRI	Retired/Sec	105.00
	82		UPP	40.00		HRG	Retired/Sec	95.00
	83		UPP	40.00		FSH	Retired/Sec	90.00
	84		UPP	45.00		CRS	Retired/Sec	90.00
	85		UPP	45.00		DVE	Retired/Sec	85.00
	86		UPP	45.00		OLB	Retired/Sec	85.00
	87		UPP	45.00		CED	Retired/Sec	80.00
	88		UPP	50.00		FLW	Retired/Sec	80.00

* UNMARKED (UM) pieces could have been produced in any of the years of production.

COME LET US ADORE HIM   Plate   First Issue "Christmas Collection" Series
Individually Numbered

E-5646	81	Nativity Scene	15,000	$40.00	8.50"	UM	Secondary	$60.00
(22)								

BUT LOVE GOES ON FOREVER   Candle Climbers   Set of 2

E-6118	81	Angels on Clouds	UPP	$14.00	2.50"	UM	Susp/Sec	$55.00
(56 & 57)	84		UPP	20.00		CRS	Susp/Sec	45.00
	85		UPP	20.00		DVE	Susp/Sec	40.00
	86		UPP	20.00		OLB	Susp/Sec	40.00
	87		UPP	22.50		CED	Susp/Sec	35.00
	88		UPP	25.00		FLW	Susp/Sec	35.00

WE HAVE SEEN HIS STAR   Ornament

E-6120	*	Boy Holding Lamb	UPP	$ 6.00	3.00"	UM	Retired/Sec	$60.00
(16)	81		UPP	6.00		TRI	Retired/Sec	65.00
	82		UPP	6.00		HRG	Retired/Sec	60.00
	83		UPP	9.00		FSH	Retired/Sec	60.00
	84		UPP	10.00		CRS	Retired/Sec	55.00

* UNMARKED (UM) pieces could have been produced in any of the years of production.

MIKEY   Doll

E-6214B	81	Mikey	UPP	$150.00	16.50"	UM	Susp/Sec	$200.00
(75)	83		UPP	175.00		FSH	Susp/Sec	200.00
	84		UPP	200.00		CRS	Susp/Sec	200.00
	85		UPP	200.00		DVE	Susp/Sec	200.00

DEBBIE   Doll

E-6214G	81	Debbie	UPP	$150.00	16.50"	UM	Susp/Sec	$200.00
(76)	83		UPP	175.00		FSH	Susp/Sec	200.00
	84		UPP	200.00		CRS	Susp/Sec	200.00
	85		UPP	200.00		DVE	Susp/Sec	200.00

GOD SENDS THE GIFT OF HIS LOVE   Figurine

E-6613	84	Girl with Present and Kitten	UPP	$22.50	5.75"	FSH	Susp/Sec	$60.00
(204)	84		UPP	22.50		CRS	Susp/Sec	50.00
	85		UPP	22.50		DVE	Susp/Sec	45.00
	86		UPP	22.50		OLB	Susp/Sec	40.00
	87		UPP	22.50		CED	Susp/Sec	40.00

COLLECTION PLAQUE   Plaque
E-6901	82	Boy Angel on Cloud	UPP	$19.00	3.50"	HRG	Susp/Sec	$125.00
(56)	83		UPP	19.00		FSH	Susp/Sec	45.00
	84		UPP	20.00		CRS	Susp/Sec	40.00
	85		UPP	20.00		DVE	Susp/Sec	35.00
	86		UPP	20.00		OLB	Susp/Sec	35.00

[NOTE: Exists in a double mark HRG & FSH.]

GOD IS LOVE, DEAR VALENTINE   Figurine
E-7153	82	Boy Holding Heart	UPP	$16.00	5.50"	TRI	Susp/Sec	$60.00
(102)	82		UPP	16.00		HRG	Susp/Sec	45.00
	83		UPP	16.00		FSH	Susp/Sec	40.00
	84		UPP	17.00		CRS	Susp/Sec	35.00
	85		UPP	17.00		DVE	Susp/Sec	35.00
	86		UPP	17.00		OLB	Susp/Sec	30.00

GOD IS LOVE, DEAR VALENTINE   Figurine
E-7154	82	Girl Holding Heart	UPP	$16.00	5.50"	TRI	Susp/Sec	$65.00
(103)	82		UPP	16.00		HRG	Susp/Sec	50.00
	83		UPP	16.00		FSH	Susp/Sec	40.00
	84		UPP	17.00		CRS	Susp/Sec	35.00
	85		UPP	17.00		DVE	Susp/Sec	35.00
	86		UPP	17.00		OLB	Susp/Sec	35.00

THANKING HIM FOR YOU   Figurine
E-7155	82	Girl Praying in Field	UPP	$16.00	5.50"	HRG	Susp/Sec	$65.00
(58)	83		UPP	16.00		FSH	Susp/Sec	55.00
	84		UPP	17.00		CRS	Susp/Sec	50.00

I BELIEVE IN MIRACLES   Figurine
E-7156	82	Boy Holding Chick	UPP	$17.00	4.25"	HRG	Susp/Sec	$110.00
(105)	83		UPP	17.00		FSH	Susp/Sec	90.00
	84		UPP	19.00		CRS	Susp/Sec	85.00
	85		UPP	19.00		DVE	Susp/Sec	80.00

PIECE WAS RE-INTRODUCED IN JULY 1987:

I BELIEVE IN MIRACLES   Figurine   *See "Nobody's Perfect!" Section
E-7156R	87	Boy Holding Bluebird	UPP	$22.50	4.50"	CED*	Secondary	$30.00
(374)	88		UPP	22.50		FLW	Secondary	25.00
	89		UPP	25.00		B&A	Primary	25.00
	90		OPEN	25.00		FLM	Primary	25.00

THERE IS JOY IN SERVING JESUS   Figurine
E-7157	82	Waitress Carrying Food	UPP	$17.00	5.50"	HRG	Retired/Sec	$65.00
(106)	83		UPP	17.00		FSH	Retired/Sec	50.00
	84		UPP	19.00		CRS	Retired/Sec	45.00
	85		UPP	19.00		DVE	Retired/Sec	45.00
	86		UPP	19.00		OLB	Retired/Sec	45.00

LOVE BEARETH ALL THINGS   Figurine
E-7158	82	Nurse Giving Shot to Bear	UPP	$25.00	5.15"	HRG	Secondary	$55.00
(107)	83		UPP	25.00		FSH	Secondary	40.00
	84		UPP	27.50		CRS	Secondary	36.00
	85		UPP	27.50		DVE	Secondary	36.00
	86		UPP	27.50		OLB	Secondary	36.00
	87		UPP	27.50		CED	Secondary	36.00
	88		UPP	32.50		FLW	Secondary	36.00
	89		UPP	36.00		B&A	Primary	36.00
	90		OPEN	36.00		FLM	Primary	36.00

LORD GIVE ME PATIENCE   Figurine
E-7159	82	Bandaged Boy by Sign	UPP	$25.00	5.50"	HRG	Susp/Sec	$60.00
(108)	83		UPP	25.00		FSH	Susp/Sec	50.00
	84		UPP	27.50		CRS	Susp/Sec	45.00
	85		UPP	27.50		DVE	Susp/Sec	45.00

THE PERFECT GRANDPA   Figurine
E-7160	82	Grandpa in Rocking Chair	UPP	$25.00	5.00"	HRG	Susp/Sec	$55.00
(109)	83		UPP	25.00		FSH	Susp/Sec	45.00
	84		UPP	27.50		CRS	Susp/Sec	45.00
	85		UPP	27.50		DVE	Susp/Sec	45.00
	86		UPP	27.50		OLB	Susp/Sec	45.00

HIS SHEEP AM I   Figurine
E-7161	82	Shepherd Painting Lamb	UPP	$25.00	5.25"	HRG	Susp/Sec	$55.00
(110)	83		UPP	25.00		FSH	Susp/Sec	50.00
	84		UPP	27.50		CRS	Susp/Sec	45.00

LOVE IS SHARING   Figurine
E-7162	82	Girl at School Desk	UPP	$25.00	4.75"	HRG	Susp/Sec	$135.00
(111)	83		UPP	25.00		FSH	Susp/Sec	105.00
	84		UPP	27.50		CRS	Susp/Sec	100.00

GOD IS WATCHING OVER YOU   Figurine
E-7163	82	Boy with Ice Bag on Head	UPP	$27.50	5.25"	HRG	Susp/Sec	$65.00
(112)	83		UPP	27.50		FSH	Susp/Sec	55.00
	84		UPP	30.00		CRS	Susp/Sec	50.00

BLESS THIS HOUSE   Figurine
E-7164	82	Boy & Girl Painting Dog House	UPP	$45.00	5.50"	HRG	Susp/Sec	$125.00
(113)	83		UPP	45.00		FSH	Susp/Sec	95.00
	84		UPP	50.00		CRS	Susp/Sec	90.00

LET THE WHOLE WORLD KNOW   Figurine
E-7165	82	Boy & Girl in Baptism Bucket	UPP	$45.00	6.00"	HRG	Susp/Sec	$80.00
(114)	83		UPP	45.00		FSH	Susp/Sec	70.00
	84		UPP	50.00		CRS	Susp/Sec	65.00
	85		UPP	50.00		DVE	Susp/Sec	60.00
	86		UPP	50.00		OLB	Susp/Sec	60.00
	87		UPP	50.00		CED	Susp/Sec	60.00

THE LORD BLESS YOU AND KEEP YOU   Frame
E-7166	82	Bride and Groom	UPP	$22.50	5.50"	HRG	Secondary	$40.00
(38)	83		UPP	22.50		FSH	Secondary	30.00
	84		UPP	25.00		CRS	Secondary	30.00
	85		UPP	25.00		DVE	Secondary	30.00
	86		UPP	25.00		OLB	Secondary	30.00
	87		UPP	25.00		CED	Secondary	30.00
	88		UPP	27.50		FLW	Secondary	30.00
	89		UPP	30.00		B&A	Primary	30.00
	90		OPEN	30.00		FLM	Primary	30.00

THE LORD BLESS YOU AND KEEP YOU   Covered Box
E-7167	82	Bride and Groom	UPP	$22.50	5.00"	HRG	Susp/Sec	$40.00
(38)	83		UPP	22.50		FSH	Susp/Sec	35.00
	84		UPP	25.00		CRS	Susp/Sec	30.00
	85		UPP	25.00		DVE	Susp/Sec	30.00

MY GUARDIAN ANGEL   Frame
E-7168	82	Boy Angel	UPP	$18.00	5.50"	HRG	Susp/Sec	$40.00
(265)	83		UPP	18.00		FSH	Susp/Sec	35.00
	84		UPP	19.00		CRS	Susp/Sec	30.00

MY GUARDIAN ANGEL   Frame
E-7169	82	Girl Angel	UPP	$18.00	5.50"	HRG	Susp/Sec	$40.00
(266)	83		UPP	18.00		FSH	Susp/Sec	35.00
	84		UPP	19.00		CRS	Susp/Sec	35.00

JESUS LOVES ME   Frame

E-7170	82	Boy with Teddy	UPP	$17.00	4.25"	HRG	Susp/Sec	$45.00
(1)	83		UPP	17.00		FSH	Susp/Sec	40.00
	84		UPP	19.00		CRS	Susp/Sec	30.00
	85		UPP	19.00		DVE	Susp/Sec	30.00

JESUS LOVES ME   Frame

E-7171	82	Girl with Bunny	UPP	$17.00	4.25"	HRG	Susp/Sec	$45.00
(2)	83		UPP	17.00		FSH	Susp/Sec	40.00
	84		UPP	19.00		CRS	Susp/Sec	40.00
	85		UPP	19.00		DVE	Susp/Sec	35.00

REJOICING WITH YOU   Plate

E-7172	82	Christening	UPP	$30.00	7.25"	UM	Susp/Sec	$40.00
(50)	84		UPP			CRS	Susp/Sec	40.00
	85		UPP			DVE	Susp/Sec	40.00

THE PURR-FECT GRANDMA   Plate

Second Issue "Mother's Love" Series
Individually Numbered

E-7173	82	Grandma in Rocker	15,000	$40.00	8.50"	UM	Secondary	$40.00
(33)								

MAKE A JOYFUL NOISE   Plate

Second Issue "Inspired Thoughts" Series
Individually Numbered

E-7174	82	Girl with Goose	15,000	$40.00	8.50"	UM	Secondary	$50.00
(5)								

THE LORD BLESS YOU AND KEEP YOU   Bell

E-7175	82	Boy Graduate	UPP	$17.00	5.75"	UM	Susp/Sec	$30.00
(46)	84		UPP			CRS	Susp/Sec	30.00
	85		UPP			DVE	Susp/Sec	30.00

THE LORD BLESS YOU AND KEEP YOU   Bell

E-7176	82	Girl Graduate	UPP	$17.00	5.75"	UM	Susp/Sec	$35.00
(47)	84		UPP			CRS	Susp/Sec	35.00
	85		UPP			DVE	Susp/Sec	35.00

THE LORD BLESS YOU AND KEEP YOU   Frame

E-7177	82	Boy Graduate	UPP	$18.00	5.50"	HRG	Susp/Sec	$30.00
(46)	83		UPP	18.00		FSH	Susp/Sec	25.00
	84		UPP	19.00		CRS	Susp/Sec	25.00
	85		UPP	19.00		DVE	Susp/Sec	25.00
	86		UPP	19.00		OLB	Susp/Sec	25.00
	87		UPP	19.00		CED	Susp/Sec	20.00

THE LORD BLESS YOU AND KEEP YOU   Frame

E-7178	82	Girl Graduate	UPP	$18.00	5.25"	UM	Susp/Sec	$35.00
(47)	84		UPP	19.00		CRS	Susp/Sec	30.00
	85		UPP	19.00		DVE	Susp/Sec	30.00
	86		UPP	19.00		OLB	Susp/Sec	30.00
	87		UPP	19.00		CED	Susp/Sec	30.00

THE LORD BLESS YOU AND KEEP YOU   Bell

E-7179	82	Bride and Groom	UPP	$22.50	5.50"	UM	Secondary	$40.00
(38)	84		UPP	25.00		CRS	Secondary	35.00
	85		UPP	25.00		DVE	Secondary	33.00
	86		UPP	25.00		OLB	Secondary	33.00
	87		UPP	25.00		CED	Secondary	33.00
	88		UPP	30.00		FLW	Primary	33.00
	89		UPP	33.00		B&A	Primary	33.00
	90		OPEN	33.00		FLM	Primary	33.00

THE LORD BLESS YOU AND KEEP YOU — Musical — TUNE: Wedding March

E-7180	82	Bride and Groom	UPP	$55.00	6.00"	UM	Secondary	$80.00
(38)	84	on Cake	UPP	55.00		CRS	Secondary	75.00
	85		UPP	60.00		DVE	Secondary	75.00
	86		UPP	60.00		OLB	Secondary	75.00
	87		UPP	60.00		CED	Secondary	75.00
	88		UPP	70.00		FLW	Secondary	75.00
	89		UPP	75.00		B&A	Primary	75.00
	90		OPEN	75.00		FLM	Primary	75.00

MOTHER SEW DEAR — Bell

E-7181	82	Mother Needlepointing	UPP	$17.00	5.50"	UM	Susp/Sec	$40.00
(30)	84		UPP	19.00		CRS	Susp/Sec	35.00
	85		UPP	19.00		DVE	Susp/Sec	30.00
	86		UPP	19.00		OLB	Susp/Sec	30.00
	87		UPP	19.00		CED	Susp/Sec	30.00
	88		UPP	22.50		FLW	Susp/Sec	25.00

MOTHER SEW DEAR — Musical — TUNE: You Light Up My Life

E-7182	82	Mother Needlepointing	UPP	$35.00	6.25"	UM	Secondary	$70.00
(30)	84		UPP	37.50		CRS	Secondary	50.00
	85		UPP	37.50		DVE	Secondary	50.00
	86		UPP	37.50		OLB	Secondary	50.00
	87		UPP	37.50		CED	Secondary	50.00
	88		UPP	45.00		FLW	Secondary	50.00
	89		UPP	50.00		B&A	Primary	50.00
	90		OPEN	50.00		FLM	Primary	50.00

THE PURR-FECT GRANDMA — Bell

E-7183	82	Grandma in Rocker	UPP	$17.00	5.50"	UM	Susp/Sec	$40.00
(33)	84		UPP	19.00		CRS	Susp/Sec	30.00
	85		UPP	19.00		DVE	Susp/Sec	30.00
	86		UPP	19.00		OLB	Susp/Sec	30.00
	87		UPP	19.00		CED	Susp/Sec	30.00
	88		UPP	22.50		FLW	Susp/Sec	30.00

THE PURR-FECT GRANDMA — Musical — TUNE: Always In My Heart

E-7184	82	Grandma in Rocker	UPP	$35.00	6.00"	UM	Secondary	$70.00
(33)	84		UPP	37.50		CRS	Secondary	55.00
	85		UPP	37.50		DVE	Secondary	50.00
	86		UPP	37.50		OLB	Secondary	50.00
	87		UPP	37.50		CED	Secondary	50.00
	88		UPP	45.00		FLW	Secondary	50.00
	89		UPP	50.00		B&A	Primary	50.00
	90		OPEN	50.00		FLM	Primary	50.00

LOVE IS SHARING — Musical — TUNE: School Days

E-7185	82	Girl at School Desk	UPP	$40.00	5.75"	HRG	Retired/Sec	$145.00
(111)	83		UPP	40.00		FSH	Retired/Sec	120.00
	84		UPP	45.00		CRS	Retired/Sec	100.00
	85		UPP	45.00		DVE	Retired/Sec	100.00

LET THE WHOLE WORLD KNOW — Musical — TUNE: What A Friend We Have In Jesus

E-7186	*	Boy & Girl in Baptism Bucket	UPP	$60.00	6.25"	UM	Susp/Sec	$80.00
(114)	82		UPP	60.00		HRG	Susp/Sec	85.00
	83		UPP	60.00		FSH	Susp/Sec	75.00
	84		UPP	65.00		CRS	Susp/Sec	70.00
	85		UPP	65.00		DVE	Susp/Sec	70.00
	86		UPP	65.00		OLB	Susp/Sec	70.00

* UNMARKED (UM) pieces could have been produced in any of the years of production.

MOTHER SEW DEAR		Frame						
E-7241	82	Mother Needlepointing	UPP	$18.00	5.50"	HRG	Susp/Sec	$35.00
(30)	83		UPP	18.00		FSH	Susp/Sec	25.00
	84		UPP	19.00		CRS	Susp/Sec	25.00
	85		UPP	19.00		DVE	Susp/Sec	25.00
	86		UPP	19.00		OLB	Susp/Sec	25.00

THE PURR-FECT GRANDMA		Frame						
E-7242	82	Grandma in Rocker	UPP	$18.00	5.50"	HRG	Susp/Sec	$35.00
(33)	83		UPP	18.00		FSH	Susp/Sec	30.00
	84		UPP	19.00		CRS	Susp/Sec	25.00
	85		UPP	19.00		DVE	Susp/Sec	25.00
	86		UPP	19.00		OLB	Susp/Sec	25.00
	87		UPP	19.00		CED	Susp/Sec	25.00
	88		UPP	22.50		FLW	Susp/Sec	25.00

CUBBY		Doll	Individually Numbered on Bottom of Foot					
E-7267B	82	Groom Doll	5,000	$200.00	18.00"	UM	Secondary	$400.00
(115)								

TAMMY		Doll	Individually Numbered on Bottom of Foot					
E-7267G	82	Bride Doll	5,000	$300.00	18.00"	UM	Secondary	$700.00
(116)								

RETAILER'S DOME		Figurine under Dome	Gift to Centers					
E-7350	84	Kids on Cloud under Dome	UPP	GIFT	9.00"	CRS	Secondary	$950.00
(411)								

LOVE IS PATIENT		Figurine						
E-9251	83	Boy Holding Blackboard	UPP	$35.00	5.00"	FSH	Susp/Sec	$60.00
(135)	84	with Teacher	UPP	35.00		CRS	Susp/Sec	55.00
	85		UPP	35.00		DVE	Susp/Sec	50.00

FORGIVING IS FORGETTING		Figurine						
E-9252	83	Boy & Girl with Bandage	UPP	$37.50	5.75"	FSH	Susp/Sec	$70.00
(136)	84		UPP	37.50		CRS	Susp/Sec	65.00
	85		UPP	37.50		DVE	Susp/Sec	60.00
	86		UPP	37.50		OLB	Susp/Sec	60.00
	87		UPP	37.50		CED	Susp/Sec	60.00
	88		UPP	42.50		FLW	Susp/Sec	60.00
	89		UPP	47.50		B&A	Susp/Sec	60.00

THE END IS IN SIGHT		Figurine						
E-9253	*	Boy with Dog Ripping Pants	UPP	$25.00	5.25"	UM	Susp/Sec	$135.00
(137)	83		UPP	25.00		HRG	Susp/Sec	60.00
	83		UPP	25.00		FSH	Susp/Sec	55.00
	84		UPP	25.00		CRS	Susp/Sec	50.00
	85		UPP	25.00		DVE	Susp/Sec	50.00

* UNMARKED (UM) pieces could have been produced in any of the years of production.

PRAISE THE LORD ANYHOW		Figurine	*See "Nobody's Perfect!" Section					
E-9254	83	Girl at Typewriter	UPP	$35.00	4.75"	HRG	Secondary	$70.00
(138)	83		UPP	35.00		FSH*	Secondary	55.00
	84		UPP	35.00		CRS	Secondary	47.50
	85		UPP	35.00		DVE	Secondary	47.50
	86		UPP	35.00		OLB	Secondary	47.50
	87		UPP	35.00		CED	Secondary	47.50
	88		UPP	40.00		FLW	Secondary	47.50
	89		UPP	47.50		B&A	Primary	47.50
	90		OPEN	47.50		FLM	Primary	47.50

BLESS YOU TWO   Figurine

E-9255	83	Groom Carrying Bride	UPP	$21.00	5.25"	FSH	Secondary	$40.00
(139)	84		UPP	21.00		CRS	Secondary	30.00
	85		UPP	21.00		DVE	Secondary	30.00
	86		UPP	21.00		OLB	Secondary	30.00
	87		UPP	21.00		CED	Secondary	30.00
	88		UPP	25.00		FLW	Secondary	30.00
	89		UPP	30.00		B&A	Primary	30.00
	90		OPEN	30.00		FLM	Primary	30.00

THE HAND THAT ROCKS THE FUTURE   Plate   Third Issue "Mother's Love" Series
Individually Numbered

E-9256	83	Girl Rocking Cradle	15,000	$40.00	8.50"	UM	Secondary	$40.00
(32)								

I BELIEVE IN MIRACLES   Plate   Third Issue "Inspired Thoughts" Series   Individually Numbered

E-9257	83	Boy Holding Chick	15,000	$40.00	8.50"	UM	Secondary	$45.00
(105)	84			40.00		CRS	Secondary	40.00

WE ARE GOD'S WORKMANSHIP   Figurine

E-9258	83	Bonnet Girl with Butterfly	UPP	$19.00	5.25"	HRG	Secondary	$40.00
(140)	83		UPP	19.00		FSH	Secondary	30.00
	84		UPP	19.00		CRS	Secondary	25.00
	85		UPP	19.00		DVE	Secondary	25.00
	86		UPP	19.00		OLB	Secondary	25.00
	87		UPP	19.00		CED	Secondary	25.00
	88		UPP	22.50		FLW	Secondary	25.00
	89		UPP	25.00		B&A	Primary	25.00
	90		OPEN	25.00		FLM	Primary	25.00

WE'RE IN IT TOGETHER   Figurine

E-9259	83	Boy with Piggy	UPP	$24.00	3.75"	HRG	Secondary	$45.00
(141)	83		UPP	24.00		FSH	Secondary	35.00
	84		UPP	24.00		CRS	Secondary	33.00
	85		UPP	24.00		DVE	Secondary	33.00
	86		UPP	24.00		OLB	Secondary	33.00
	87		UPP	24.00		CED	Secondary	33.00
	88		UPP	30.00		FLW	Secondary	33.00
	89		UPP	33.00		B&A	Primary	33.00
	90		OPEN	33.00		FLM	Primary	33.00

GOD'S PROMISES ARE SURE   Figurine

E-9260	83	Boy Angel Winding Rainbow	UPP	$30.00	5.50"	FSH	Susp/Sec	$55.00
(142)	84		UPP	30.00		CRS	Susp/Sec	50.00
	85		UPP	30.00		DVE	Susp/Sec	50.00
	86		UPP	30.00		OLB	Susp/Sec	50.00
	87		UPP	30.00		CED	Susp/Sec	50.00

SEEK YE THE LORD   Figurine   *See "Nobody's Perfect!" Section

E-9261	83	Boy Graduate with Scroll	UPP	$21.00	4.75"	FSH*	Susp/Sec	$45.00
(143)	84		UPP	21.00		CRS	Susp/Sec	35.00
	85		UPP	21.00		DVE	Susp/Sec	35.00
	86		UPP	21.00		OLB	Susp/Sec	35.00

SEEK YE THE LORD   Figurine   *See "Nobody's Perfect!" Section

E-9262	83	Girl Graduate with Scroll	UPP	$21.00	4.75"	FSH*	Susp/Sec	$45.00
(144)	84		UPP	21.00		CRS	Susp/Sec	40.00
	85		UPP	21.00		DVE	Susp/Sec	40.00
	86		UPP	21.00		OLB	Susp/Sec	40.00

HOW CAN TWO WALK TOGETHER EXCEPT THEY AGREE   Figurine

E-9263	83	Boy and Girl in Horse	UPP	$35.00	5.25"	HRG	Susp/Sec	$120.00
(145)	83	Costume	UPP	35.00		FSH	Susp/Sec	80.00
	84		UPP	35.00		CRS	Susp/Sec	75.00
	85		UPP	35.00		DVE	Susp/Sec	75.00

PRESS ON — Figurine

E-9265	83	Girl Ironing Clothes	UPP	$40.00	5.75"	HRG	Secondary	$70.00
(146)	83		UPP	40.00		FSH	Secondary	55.00
	84		UPP	40.00		CRS	Secondary	50.00
	85		UPP	40.00		DVE	Secondary	50.00
	86		UPP	40.00		OLB	Secondary	50.00
	87		UPP	40.00		CED	Secondary	50.00
	88		UPP	45.00		FLW	Secondary	50.00
	89		UPP	50.00		B&A	Primary	50.00
	90		OPEN	50.00		FLM	Primary	50.00

I'M FALLING FOR SOMEBUNNY — Box

E-9266	*	Lamb and Bunny	UPP	$13.50	3.00"	UM	Susp/Sec	$35.00
(308)	83		UPP	13.50		HRG	Susp/Sec	30.00
	83		UPP	13.50		FSH	Susp/Sec	30.00
	84		UPP	16.00		CRS	Susp/Sec	30.00
	85		UPP	16.00		DVE	Susp/Sec	25.00
	86		UPP	16.00		OLB	Susp/Sec	25.00
	87		UPP	16.00		CED	Susp/Sec	25.00
	88		UPP	18.50		FLW	Susp/Sec	25.00

* UMMARKED (UM) pieces could have been produced in any of the years of production.

OUR LOVE IS HEAVEN SCENT — Box

E-9266	*	Lamb and Skunk	UPP	$13.50	3.00"	UM	Susp/Sec	$35.00
(308)	83		UPP	13.50		HRG	Susp/Sec	30.00
	83		UPP	13.50		FSH	Susp/Sec	30.00
	84		UPP	16.00		CRS	Susp/Sec	30.00
	85		UPP	16.00		DVE	Susp/Sec	25.00
	86		UPP	16.00		OLB	Susp/Sec	25.00
	87		UPP	16.00		CED	Susp/Sec	25.00
	88		UPP	18.50		FLW	Susp/Sec	25.00

* UNMARKED (UM) pieces could have been produced in any of the years of production.

ANIMAL COLLECTION — Figurines — Set of 6

E-9267	83	Animals	UPP	$39.00	2.50"	UM	Secondary	$80.00
(147)	84		UPP	45.00		CRS	Secondary	72.00
	85		UPP	45.00		DVE	Secondary	60.00
	86		UPP	45.00		OLB	Secondary	60.00
	87		UPP	45.00		CED	Secondary	60.00

IN 1988 INDIVIDUAL NUMBERS WERE ASSIGNED FOR EACH OF THE 6:

E-9267A	88	Teddy Bear	UPP	$ 8.50	2.50"	FLW	Secondary	$10.00
(414)	89		UPP	10.00		B&A	Primary	10.00
	90		OPEN	10.00		FLM	Primary	10.00

E-9267B	88	Dog with Slippers	UPP	$ 8.50	3.00"	FLW	Secondary	$10.00
(407)	89		UPP	10.00		B&A	Primary	10.00
	90		OPEN	10.00		FLM	Primary	10.00

E-9267C	88	Bunny with Carrot	UPP	$ 8.50	2.60"	FLW	Secondary	$10.00
(408)	89		UPP	10.00		B&A	Primary	10.00
	90		OPEN	10.00		FLM	Primary	10.00

E-9267D	88	Cat with Bow Tie	UPP	$ 8.50	2.40"	FLW	Secondary	$10.00
(413)	89		UPP	10.00		B&A	Primary	10.00
	90		OPEN	10.00		FLM	Primary	10.00

E-9267E	88	Lamb with Bird on Back	UPP	$ 8.50	2.60"	FLW	Secondary	$10.00
(409)	89		UPP	10.00		B&A	Primary	10.00
	90		OPEN	10.00		FLM	Primary	10.00

E-9267F	88	Pig with Patches	UPP	$ 8.50	2.10"	FLW	Secondary	$10.00
(412)	89		UPP	10.00		B&A	Primary	10.00
	90		OPEN	10.00		FLM	Primary	10.00

NOBODY'S PERFECT!   Figurine   *See "Nobody's Perfect!" Section

E-9268	83	Boy with Dunce Cap	UPP	$21.00	7.00"	HRG*	Secondary	$45.00
(148)	83		UPP	21.00		FSH	Secondary	35.00
	84		UPP	21.00		CRS	Secondary	27.00
	85		UPP	21.00		DVE	Secondary	27.00
	86		UPP	21.00		OLB	Secondary	27.00
	87		UPP	21.00		CED	Secondary	27.00
	88		UPP	24.00		FLW	Secondary	27.00
	89		UPP	27.00		B&A	Primary	27.00
	90		OPEN	27.00		FLM	Primary	27.00

LET LOVE REIGN   Figurine

E-9273	83	Girl with Chicks in Umbrella	UPP	$27.50	5.25"	HRG	Retired/Sec	*
(149)	83		UPP	27.50		FSH	Retired/Sec	$75.00
	84		UPP	27.50		CRS	Retired/Sec	65.00
	85		UPP	27.50		DVE	Retired/Sec	60.00
	86		UPP	27.50		OLB	Retired/Sec	60.00
	87		UPP	27.50		CED	Retired/Sec	60.00
	* Extremely rare							

TASTE AND SEE THAT THE LORD IS GOOD   Figurine

E-9274	83	Girl Angel Making Food	UPP	$22.50	6.25"	FSH	Retired/Sec	$60.00
(150)	84		UPP	22.50		CRS	Retired/Sec	55.00
	85		UPP	22.50		DVE	Retired/Sec	55.00
	86		UPP	22.50		OLB	Retired/Sec	50.00

JESUS LOVES ME   Plate

E-9275	83	Boy with Teddy	UPP	$30.00	7.25"	UM	Susp/Sec	$40.00
(1)	84		UPP	30.00		CRS	Susp/Sec	45.00

JESUS LOVES ME   Plate

E-9276	83	Girl with Bunny	UPP	$30.00	7.25"	UM	Susp/Sec	$45.00
(2)	84		UPP	30.00		CRS	Susp/Sec	45.00

JESUS LOVES ME   Figurine

E-9278	83	Boy with Teddy	UPP	$ 9.00	3.00"	HRG	Secondary	$20.00
(1)	83		UPP	9.00		FSH	Secondary	15.00
	84		UPP	10.00		CRS	Secondary	13.50
	85		UPP	10.00		DVE	Secondary	13.50
	86		UPP	10.00		OLB	Secondary	13.50
	87		UPP	10.00		CED	Secondary	13.50
	88		UPP	12.50		FLW	Secondary	13.50
	89		UPP	13.50		B&A	Primary	13.50
	90		OPEN	13.50		FLM	Primary	13.50

JESUS LOVES ME   Figurine

E-9279	83	Girl with Bunny	UPP	$ 9.00	3.00"	HRG	Secondary	$20.00
(2)	83		UPP	9.00		FSH	Secondary	15.00
	84		UPP	10.00		CRS	Secondary	15.00
	85		UPP	10.00		DVE	Secondary	13.50
	86		UPP	10.00		OLB	Secondary	13.50
	87		UPP	10.00		CED	Secondary	13.50
	88		UPP	12.50		FLW	Secondary	13.50
	89		UPP	13.50		B&A	Primary	13.50
	90		OPEN	13.50		FLM	Primary	13.50

JESUS LOVES ME   Box

E-9280	83	Boy with Teddy	UPP	$17.50	5.00"	HRG	Susp/Sec	$30.00
(1)	83		UPP	17.50		FSH	Susp/Sec	25.00
	84		UPP	19.00		CRS	Susp/Sec	25.00
	85		UPP	19.00		DVE	Susp/Sec	25.00

JESUS LOVES ME   Box

E-9281	83	Girl with Bunny	UPP	$17.50	5.00"	HRG	Susp/Sec	$30.00
(2)	83		UPP	17.50		FSH	Susp/Sec	25.00
	84		UPP	19.00		CRS	Susp/Sec	25.00
	85		UPP	19.00		DVE	Susp/Sec	25.00

YOU'RE WORTH YOUR WEIGHT IN GOLD   Figurine

E-9282	*	Pig with Patches on Base	UPP	$ 8.00	2.50"	UM	Secondary	$25.00
(151)	83		UPP	8.00		HRG	Secondary	20.00
	83		UPP	8.00		FSH	Secondary	18.00
	84		UPP	9.00		CRS	Secondary	12.00
	85		UPP	9.00		DVE	Secondary	12.00
	86		UPP	9.00		OLB	Secondary	12.00
	87		UPP	9.00		CED	Secondary	12.00

* UNMARKED (UM) pieces could have been produced in any of the years of production.

E-9282B	88	Pig with Patches on Base	UPP	$10.50	2.50"	FLW	Primary	$12.00
(151)	89		UPP	12.00		B&A	Primary	12.00
	90		OPEN	12.00		FLM	Primary	12.00

TO SOMEBUNNY SPECIAL   Figurine

E-9282	*	Bunny on Heart Base	UPP	$ 8.00	3.00"	UM	Secondary	$25.00
(152)	83		UPP	8.00		HRG	Secondary	20.00
	83		UPP	8.00		FSH	Secondary	18.00
	84		UPP	9.00		CRS	Secondary	12.00
	85		UPP	9.00		DVE	Secondary	12.00
	86		UPP	9.00		OLB	Secondary	12.00
	87		UPP	9.00		CED	Secondary	12.00

* UNMARKED (UM) pieces could have been produced in any of the years of production.

E-9282A	88	Bunny on Heart Base	UPP	$10.50	3.00"	FLW	Secondary	$12.00
(152)	89		UPP	12.00		B&A	Primary	12.00
	90		OPEN	12.00		FLM	Primary	12.00

ESPECIALLY FOR EWE   Figurine   See "Nobody's Perfect!" Section

E-9282	*	Lamb with Bird	UPP	$ 8.00	3.00"	UM	Secondary	$25.00
(153)	83		UPP	8.00		HRG	Secondary	20.00
	83		UPP	8.00		FSH	Secondary	18.00
	84		UPP	9.00		CRS	Secondary	12.00
	85		UPP	9.00		DVE	Secondary	12.00
	86		UPP	9.00		OLB	Secondary	12.00
	87		UPP	9.00		CED	Secondary	12.00

* UNMARKED (UM) pieces could have been produced in any of the years of production.

E-9282C	88	Lamb with Bird	UPP	$10.50	3.00"	FLW	Secondary	$12.00
(153)	89		UPP	12.00		B&A	Primary	12.00
	90		OPEN	12.00		FLM	Primary	12.00

FOREVER FRIENDS   Box

E-9283	83	Dog	UPP	$15.00	4.25"	HRG	Susp/Sec	$40.00
(309)	83		UPP	15.00		FSH	Susp/Sec	35.00
	84		UPP	17.00		CRS	Susp/Sec	30.00

FOREVER FRIENDS   Box

E-9283	83	Cat	UPP	$15.00	4.10"	HRG	Susp/Sec	$45.00
(309)	83		UPP	15.00		FSH	Susp/Sec	40.00
	84		UPP	17.00		CRS	Susp/Sec	35.00

IF GOD BE FOR US, WHO CAN BE AGAINST US   Figurine

E-9285	83	Boy at Pulpit	UPP	$27.50	5.85"	FSH	Susp/Sec	$50.00
(154)	84		UPP	27.50		CRS	Susp/Sec	45.00
	85		UPP	27.50		DVE	Susp/Sec	40.00

PEACE ON EARTH   Figurine

E-9287	83	Girl with Lion & Lamb	UPP	$37.50	5.25"	FSH	Susp/Sec	$65.00
(155)	84		UPP	37.50		CRS	Susp/Sec	55.00
	85		UPP	37.50		DVE	Susp/Sec	50.00
	86		UPP	37.50		OLB	Susp/Sec	50.00

SENDING YOU A RAINBOW — Figurine

E-9288	83	Girl Angel with Sprinkler	UPP	$22.50	5.50"	FSH	Susp/Sec	$50.00
(156)	84		UPP	22.50		CRS	Susp/Sec	45.00
	85		UPP	22.50		DVE	Susp/Sec	45.00
	86		UPP	22.50		OLB	Susp/Sec	40.00

TRUST IN THE LORD — Figurine

E-9289	83	Boy Angel Taking	UPP	$20.00	5.90"	FSH	Susp/Sec	$50.00
(157)	84	Flying Lessons	UPP	21.00		CRS	Susp/Sec	40.00
	85		UPP	21.00		DVE	Susp/Sec	35.00
	86		UPP	21.00		OLB	Susp/Sec	35.00
	87		UPP	21.00		CED	Susp/Sec	35.00

LOVE COVERS ALL — Figurine

12009	85	Girl Making Heart Quilt	UPP	$27.50	4.50"	CRS	Secondary	$40.00
(225)	85		UPP	27.50		DVE	Secondary	35.00
	86		UPP	27.50		OLB	Secondary	35.00
	87		UPP	27.50		CED	Secondary	35.00
	88		UPP	32.50		FLW	Secondary	35.00
	89		UPP	35.00		B&A	Primary	35.00
	90		OPEN	35.00		FLM	Primary	35.00

LOVING YOU — Frame

12017	85	Boy Holding Heart	UPP	$19.00	4.50"	CRS	Susp/Sec	$35.00
(102)	85		UPP	19.00		DVE	Susp/Sec	30.00
	86		UPP	19.00		OLB	Susp/Sec	30.00
	87		UPP	19.00		CED	Susp/Sec	30.00

LOVING YOU — Frame

12025	85	Girl Holding Heart	UPP	$19.00	4.50"	CRS	Susp/Sec	$40.00
(103)	85		UPP	19.00		DVE	Susp/Sec	35.00
	86		UPP	19.00		OLB	Susp/Sec	35.00
	87		UPP	19.00		CED	Susp/Sec	35.00

GOD'S PRECIOUS GIFT — Frame

12033	85	Baby Boy	UPP	$19.00	4.50"	DVE	Susp/Sec	$35.00
(310)	86		UPP	19.00		OLB	Susp/Sec	30.00
	87		UPP	19.00		CED	Susp/Sec	30.00

GOD'S PRECIOUS GIFT — Frame

12041	85	Baby Girl	UPP	$19.00	4.50"	DVE	Secondary	$30.00
(311)	86		UPP	19.00		OLB	Secondary	25.00
	87		UPP	19.00		CED	Secondary	25.00
	88		UPP	22.50		FLW	Primary	25.00
	89		UPP	25.00		B&A	Primary	25.00
	90		OPEN	25.00		FLM	Primary	25.00

THE VOICE OF SPRING — Figurine — First Issue "The Four Seasons" Series

12068	85	Girl with Bible	Annual	$30.00	6.40"	CRS	Secondary	$275.00
(226)	85			30.00		DVE	Secondary	260.00

SUMMER'S JOY — Figurine — Second Issue "The Four Seasons" Series

12076	85	Girl with Ducklings	Annual	$30.00	6.40"	CRS	Secondary	$100.00
(227)	85			30.00		DVE	Secondary	95.00

AUTUMN'S PRAISE — Figurine — Third Issue "The Four Seasons" Series

12084	86	Girl in Field of Flowers	Annual	$30.00	6.40"	DVE	Secondary	$70.00
(228)	86			30.00		OLB	Secondary	60.00

WINTER'S SONG — Figurine — Fourth Issue "The Four Seasons" Series

12092	86	Girl in Snow with Birds	Annual	$40.00	6.40"	DVE	Secondary	$95.00
(229)	86			40.00		OLB	Secondary	90.00

THE VOICE OF SPRING — Plate — First Issue "The Four Seasons" Series

12106	85	Girl with Bible	Annual	$40.00	8.50"	CRS	Secondary	$80.00
(226)	85			40.00		DVE	Secondary	75.00

SUMMER'S JOY   Plate   Second Issue "The Four Seasons" Series

12114	85	Girl with Ducklings		Annual	$40.00	8.50"	CRS	Secondary	$80.00
(227)	85				40.00		DVE	Secondary	75.00

AUTUMN'S PRAISE   Plate   Third Issue "The Four Seasons" Series

12122	86	Girl in Field of Flowers		Annual	$40.00	8.50"	OLB	Secondary	$55.00
(228)									

WINTER'S SONG   Plate   Fourth Issue "The Four Seasons" Series

12130	86	Girl in Snow with Birds		Annual	$40.00	8.50"	DVE	Secondary	$65.00
(229)	86				40.00		OLB	Secondary	60.00

PART OF ME WANTS TO BE GOOD   Figurine

12149	85	Angel Boy in Devil Suit	UPP	$19.00	5.10"	CRS	Susp/Sec	$35.00
(230)	85		UPP	19.00		DVE	Susp/Sec	25.00
	86		UPP	19.00		OLB	Susp/Sec	25.00
	87		UPP	19.00		CED	Susp/Sec	25.00
	88		UPP	22.50		FLW	Susp/Sec	25.00
	89		UPP	25.00		B&A	Susp/Prim	25.00

THIS IS THE DAY THE LORD HAS MADE   Figurine

12157	87	Birthday Boy	UPP	$20.00	5.00"	OLB	Secondary	$30.00
(314)	87		UPP	20.00		CED	Secondary	27.00
	88		UPP	24.00		FLW	Secondary	27.00
	89		UPP	27.00		B&A	Primary	27.00
	90		OPEN	27.00		FLM	Primary	27.00

LORD, KEEP MY LIFE IN TUNE   Musical   "Rejoice In The Lord" Band Series   TUNE: Amazing Grace   Set of 2

12165	85	Boy Playing Piano	UPP	$37.50	4.50"	DVE	Susp/Sec	$55.00
(231)	86		UPP	37.50		OLB	Susp/Sec	50.00
	87		UPP	37.50		CED	Susp/Sec	50.00
	88		UPP	45.00		FLW	Susp/Sec	50.00
	89		UPP	50.00		B&A	Susp/Sec	50.00

THERE'S A SONG IN MY HEART   Figurine   "Rejoice In The Lord" Band Series

12173	85	Girl Playing Triangle	UPP	$11.00	3.50"	DVE	Secondary	$20.00
(232)	86		UPP	11.00		OLB	Secondary	15.00
	87		UPP	11.00		CED	Secondary	15.00
	88		UPP	13.00		FLW	Secondary	15.00
	89		UPP	15.00		B&A	Primary	15.00
	90		OPEN	15.00		FLM	Primary	15.00

GET INTO THE HABIT OF PRAYER   Figurine

12203	85	Nun	UPP	$19.00	5.10"	CRS	Susp/Sec	$35.00
(233)	85		UPP	19.00		DVE	Susp/Sec	30.00
	86		UPP	19.00		OLB	Susp/Sec	30.00

BABY'S FIRST HAIRCUT   Figurine   Third Issue "Baby's First " Series

12211	85	Angel Cutting Baby's Hair	UPP	$32.50	4.50"	DVE	Susp/Sec	$60.00
(234)	86		UPP	32.50		OLB	Susp/Sec	55.00
	87		UPP	32.50		CED	Susp/Sec	55.00

CLOWN FIGURINES   Figurines   Set of 4   See "Nobody's Perfect!" Section

12238	85	Mini Clowns	UPP	$54.00	4.25"	DVE	Secondary	$80.00
(235)	86		UPP	54.00		OLB	Secondary	72.00
	87		UPP	54.00		CED	Secondary	72.00

IN 1988 INDIVIDUAL NUMBERS WERE ASSIGNED FOR EACH OF THE 4 PIECES:

12238A	88	Boy Balancing Ball	UPP	$16.00	3.00"	FLW	Secondary	$17.50
(416)	89		UPP	17.50		B&A	Primary	17.50
	90		OPEN	17.50		FLM	Primary	17.50

12238B (417)	88 89 90	Girl Holding Balloon	UPP UPP OPEN	$16.00 17.50 17.50	4.40"	FLW B&A FLM	Secondary Primary Primary	$17.50 17.50 17.50
12238C (418)	88 89 90	Boy Bending Over Ball	UPP UPP OPEN	$16.00 17.50 17.50	3.75"	FLW B&A FLM	Secondary Primary Primary	$17.50 17.50 17.50
12238D (419)	88 89 90	Girl with Flower Pot	UPP UPP OPEN	$16.00 17.50 17.50	3.75"	FLW B&A FLM	Secondary Primary Primary	$17.50 17.50 17.50

PRECIOUS MOMENTS LAST FOREVER   Medallion

12246 (365)	84	Medallion	UPP	$10.00		CRS	Secondary	$125.00

LOVE COVERS ALL   Thimble

12254 (225)	85 86 87 88 89 90	Girl Making Heart Quilt	UPP UPP UPP UPP UPP OPEN	$ 5.50 5.50 5.50 7.00 8.00 8.00	2.25"	DVE OLB CED FLW B&A FLM	Secondary Secondary Secondary Secondary Primary Primary	$12.00 8.00 8.00 8.00 8.00 8.00

I GET A BANG OUT OF YOU   Figurine   First Issue "Clown" Series

12262 (236)	85 86 87 88 89 90	Clown Holding Balloons	UPP UPP UPP UPP UPP OPEN	$30.00 30.00 30.00 35.00 40.00 40.00	6.60"	DVE OLB CED FLW B&A FLM	Secondary Secondary Secondary Secondary Primary Primary	$45.00 40.00 40.00 40.00 40.00 40.00

LORD KEEP ME ON THE BALL   Figurine   Fourth Issue "Clown" Series

12270 (270)	86 87 88 89 90	Clown Sitting on Ball	UPP UPP UPP UPP OPEN	$30.00 30.00 35.00 40.00 40.00	7.00"	OLB CED FLW B&A FLM	Secondary Secondary Secondary Primary Primary	$45.00 40.00 40.00 40.00 40.00

IT IS BETTER TO GIVE THAN TO RECEIVE   Figurine

12297 (237)	85 86 87	Policeman Writing Ticket	UPP UPP UPP	$19.00 19.00 19.00	5.25"	DVE OLB CED	Susp/Sec Susp/Sec Susp/Sec	$40.00 35.00 30.00

LOVE NEVER FAILS   Figurine

12300 (238)	85 86 87 88 89 90	Teacher at Desk with Report Card	UPP UPP UPP UPP UPP OPEN	$25.00 25.00 25.00 30.00 33.00 33.00	5.50"	DVE OLB CED FLW B&A FLM	Secondary Secondary Secondary Secondary Primary Primary	$35.00 33.00 33.00 33.00 33.00 33.00

GOD BLESS OUR HOME   Figurine

12319 (239)	85 86 87 88 89 90	Boy & Girl Building Sandcastle	UPP UPP UPP UPP UPP OPEN	$40.00 40.00 40.00 45.00 50.00 50.00	4.40"	DVE OLB CED FLW B&A FLM	Secondary Secondary Secondary Secondary Primary Primary	$55.00 50.00 50.00 50.00 50.00 50.00

YOU CAN FLY   Figurine

12335 (271)	86 87 88	Boy Angel on Cloud	UPP UPP UPP	$25.00 25.00 30.00	5.50"	OLB CED FLW	Susp/Sec Susp/Sec Susp/Sec	$45.00 40.00 40.00

JESUS IS COMING SOON   Figurine

12343	85	Mary Knitting Booties	UPP	$22.50	4.75"	DVE	Susp/Sec	$30.00
(240)	86		UPP	22.50		OLB	Susp/Sec	28.00

HALO, AND MERRY CHRISTMAS   Figurine

12351	85	Angels Making Snowman	UPP	$40.00	6.10"	DVE	Susp/Sec	$85.00
(241)	86		UPP	40.00		OLB	Susp/Sec	75.00
	87		UPP	40.00		CED	Susp/Sec	75.00
	88		UPP	45.00		FLW	Susp/Sec	75.00

HAPPINESS IS THE LORD   Figurine   "Rejoice In The Lord" Band Series

12378	85	Boy Playing Banjo	UPP	$15.00	4.75"	DVE	Secondary	$25.00
(242)	86		UPP	15.00		OLB	Secondary	20.00
	87		UPP	15.00		CED	Secondary	20.00
	88		UPP	18.00		FLW	Secondary	20.00
	89		UPP	20.00		B&A	Primary	20.00
	90		OPEN	20.00		FLM	Primary	20.00

LORD GIVE ME A SONG   Figurine   "Rejoice In The Lord" Band Series

12386	85	Girl Playing Harmonica	UPP	$15.00	4.90"	DVE	Secondary	$25.00
(243)	86		UPP	15.00		OLB	Secondary	20.00
	87		UPP	15.00		CED	Secondary	20.00
	88		UPP	18.00		FLW	Secondary	20.00
	89		UPP	20.00		B&A	Primary	20.00
	90		OPEN	20.00		FLM	Primary	20.00

HE IS MY SONG   Figurine   "Rejoice In The Lord" Band Series   Set of 2

12394	85	Boy Playing Trumpet	UPP	$17.50	4.50"	DVE	Secondary	$30.00
(244)	86	with Dog	UPP	17.50		OLB	Secondary	25.00
	87		UPP	17.50		CED	Secondary	25.00
	88		UPP	22.50		FLW	Secondary	25.00
	89		UPP	25.00		B&A	Primary	25.00
	90		OPEN	25.00		FLM	Primary	25.00

WE SAW A STAR   Musical   Set of 3   TUNE: Joy To The World

12408	85	Two Angels Sawing Star	UPP	$50.00	4.75"	DVE	Susp/Sec	$60.00
(245)	86		UPP	50.00		OLB	Susp/Sec	60.00
	87		UPP	50.00		CED	Susp/Sec	55.00

HAVE A HEAVENLY CHRISTMAS   Ornament   See "Nobody's Perfect!" Section

12416	85	Boy in Airplane	UPP	$12.00	2.60"	DVE	Secondary	$20.00
(246)	86		UPP	12.00		OLB	Secondary	15.00
	87		UPP	12.00		CED	Secondary	15.00
	88		UPP	13.50		FLW	Secondary	15.00
	89		UPP	15.00		B&A	Primary	15.00
	90		OPEN	15.00		FLM	Primary	15.00

AARON   Doll

12424	85	Boy Angel	UPP	$135.00	12.00"	DVE	Susp/Sec	$135.00
(247)	86		UPP	135.00		OLB	Susp/Prim	135.00

BETHANY   Doll

12432	85	Girl Angel	UPP	$135.00	12.00"	DVE	Susp/Sec	$135.00
(248)	86		UPP	135.00		OLB	Susp/Prim	135.00

WADDLE I DO WITHOUT YOU   Figurine   Second Issue "Clown" Series

12459	85	Girl Clown with Basket	UPP	$30.00	5.50"	DVE	Retired/Sec	$70.00
(250)	86	with Goose	UPP	30.00		OLB	Retired/Sec	60.00
	87		UPP	30.00		CED	Retired/Sec	60.00
	88		UPP	35.00		FLW	Retired/Sec	60.00
	89		UPP	35.00		B&A	Retired/Sec	60.00

THE LORD WILL CARRY YOU THROUGH   Figurine   Third Issue "Clown" Series

12467	86	Clown with Dog in Mud	UPP	$30.00	5.75"	OLB	Retired/Sec	$70.00
(251)	87		UPP	30.00		CED	Retired/Sec	65.00
	88		UPP	35.00		FLW	Retired/Sec	65.00

P.D.   Doll

12475	85	Baby Boy		UPP	$50.00	7.00"	DVE	Susp/Sec	$60.00
(252)	86			UPP	50.00		OLB	Susp/Prim	50.00

TRISH   Doll

12483	85	Baby Girl		UPP	$50.00	7.00"	DVE	Susp/Sec	$65.00
(253)	86			UPP	50.00		OLB	Susp/Prim	50.00

ANGIE, THE ANGEL OF MERCY   Doll   Individually Numbered

12491	87	Nurse	12,500	$160.00	12.00"	CED	Secondary	$160.00
(339)								

LORD KEEP MY LIFE IN TUNE   Musical   "Rejoice In The Lord" Band Series   Set of 2
TUNE: I'd Like To Teach The World To Sing

12580	87	Girl with Piano	UPP	$37.50	4.00"	OLB	Secondary	$55.00
(315)	87		UPP	37.50		CED	Secondary	50.00
	88		UPP	45.00		FLW	Secondary	50.00
	89		UPP	50.00		B&A	Primary	50.00
	90		OPEN	50.00		FLM	Primary	50.00

MOTHER SEW DEAR   Thimble

13293	85	Mother Needlepointing	UPP	$ 5.50	2.25"	DVE	Secondary	$12.00
(30)	86		UPP	5.50		OLB	Secondary	8.00
	87		UPP	5.50		CED	Secondary	8.00
	88		UPP	7.00		FLW	Secondary	8.00
	89		UPP	8.00		B&A	Primary	8.00
	90		OPEN	8.00		FLM	Primary	8.00

THE PURR-FECT GRANDMA   Thimble

13307	85	Grandma in Rocker	UPP	$ 5.50	2.25"	DVE	Secondary	$12.00
(33)	86		UPP	5.50		OLB	Secondary	8.00
	87		UPP	5.50		CED	Secondary	8.00
	88		UPP	7.00		FLW	Secondary	8.00
	89		UPP	8.00		B&A	Primary	8.00
	90		OPEN	8.00		FLM	Primary	8.00

TELL ME THE STORY OF JESUS   Plate, Dated   Fourth Issue "Joy Of Christmas" Series

15237	85	Girl with Doll Reading Book	Annual	$40.00	8.50"	DVE	Secondary	$90.00
(83)								

MAY YOUR CHRISTMAS BE DELIGHTFUL   Figurine

15482	85	Boy Tangled in	UPP	$25.00	5.00"	DVE	Secondary	$40.00
(254)	86	Christmas Lights	UPP	25.00		OLB	Secondary	33.00
	87		UPP	25.00		CED	Secondary	33.00
	88		UPP	27.50		FLW	Secondary	33.00
	89		UPP	33.00		B&A	Primary	33.00
	90		OPEN	33.00		FLM	Primary	33.00

HONK IF YOU LOVE JESUS   Figurine   Set of 2   Nativity Addition

15490	85	Mother Goose in Bonnet	UPP	$13.00	3.25"	DVE	Secondary	$25.00
(255)	86	with Babies	UPP	13.00		OLB	Secondary	17.50
	87		UPP	13.00		CED	Secondary	17.50
	88		UPP	15.00		FLW	Secondary	17.50
	89		UPP	17.50		B&A	Primary	17.50
	90		OPEN	17.50		FLM	Primary	17.50

GOD SENT YOU JUST IN TIME   Musical   TUNE: We Wish You A Merry Christmas

15504	85	Clown Holding a	UPP	$45.00	6.25"	DVE	Retired/Sec	$85.00
(256)	86	Jack- in- the- Box	UPP	45.00		OLB	Retired/Sec	80.00
	87		UPP	45.00		CED	Retired/Sec	75.00
	88		UPP	50.00		FLW	Retired/Sec	75.00
	89		UPP	60.00		B&A	Retired/Sec	70.00

BABY'S FIRST CHRISTMAS   Figurine, Dated

15539	85	Baby Boy with Bottle	Annual	$13.00	3.00"	DVE	Secondary	$45.00
(257)								

BABY'S FIRST CHRISTMAS   Figurine, Dated

15547	85	Baby Girl with Bottle	Annual	$13.00	3.00"	DVE	Secondary	$45.00
(258)								

GOD SENT HIS LOVE   Ornament, Dated

15768	85	Boy Holding Heart	Annual	$10.00	3.00"	DVE	Secondary	$40.00
(259)								

MAY YOU HAVE THE SWEETEST CHRISTMAS   Figurine   "Family Christmas Scene" Series

15776	85	Mother with Cookie Sheet	UPP	$17.00	4.90"	DVE	Secondary	$25.00
(260)	86		UPP	17.00		OLB	Secondary	23.00
	87		UPP	17.00		CED	Secondary	23.00
	88		UPP	19.00		FLW	Secondary	23.00
	89		UPP	23.00		B&A	Primary	23.00
	90		OPEN	23.00		FLM	Primary	23.00

THE STORY OF GOD'S LOVE   Figurine   "Family Christmas Scene" Series

15784	85	Father Reading Bible	UPP	22.50	4.00"	DVE	Secondary	$35.00
(261)	86		UPP	22.50		OLB	Secondary	32.50
	87		UPP	22.50		CED	Secondary	32.50
	88		UPP	25.00		FLW	Secondary	32.50
	89		UPP	32.50		B&A	Primary	32.50
	90		OPEN	32.50		FLM	Primary	32.50

TELL ME A STORY   Figurine   "Family Christmas Scene" Series

15792	85	Boy Sitting Listening to	UPP	$10.00	2.00"	DVE	Secondary	$15.00
(262)	86	Story	UPP	10.00		OLB	Secondary	13.50
	87		UPP	10.00		CED	Secondary	13.50
	88		UPP	11.00		FLW	Secondary	13.50
	89		UPP	13.50		B&A	Primary	13.50
	90		OPEN	13.50		FLM	Primary	13.50

GOD GAVE HIS BEST   Figurine   "Family Christmas Scene" Series

15806	85	Girl with Ornament	UPP	$13.00	3.50"	DVE	Secondary	$20.00
(263)	86		UPP	13.00		OLB	Secondary	17.50
	87		UPP	13.00		CED	Secondary	17.50
	88		UPP	15.00		FLW	Secondary	17.50
	89		UPP	17.50		B&A	Primary	17.50
	90		OPEN	17.50		FLM	Primary	17.50

SILENT NIGHT   Musical   "Family Christmas Scene" Series   TUNE: Silent Night

15814	85	Christmas Tree	UPP	$37.50	5.60"	DVE	Secondary	$55.00
(264)	86		UPP	37.50		OLB	Secondary	50.00
	87		UPP	37.50		CED	Secondary	50.00
	88		UPP	40.00		FLW	Secondary	50.00
	89		UPP	50.00		B&A	Primary	50.00
	90		OPEN	50.00		FLM	Primary	50.00

MAY YOUR CHRISTMAS BE HAPPY   Ornament

15822	85	Girl Clown with Balloon	UPP	$10.00	3.25"	DVE	Susp/Sec	$30.00
(235)	86		UPP	10.00		OLB	Susp/Sec	25.00
	87		UPP	10.00		CED	Susp/Sec	25.00
	88		UPP	11.00		FLW	Susp/Sec	25.00
	89		UPP	13.50		B&A	Susp/Sec	25.00

HAPPINESS IS THE LORD   Ornament

15830	85	Boy Clown with Ball	UPP	$10.00	2.10"	DVE	Susp/Sec	$25.00
(235)	86		UPP	10.00		OLB	Susp/Sec	20.00
	87		UPP	10.00		CED	Susp/Sec	20.00
	88		UPP	11.00		FLW	Susp/Sec	20.00
	89		UPP	13.50		B&A	Susp/Sec	20.00

MAY YOUR CHRISTMAS BE DELIGHTFUL — Ornament

15849	85	Boy Tangled in	UPP	$10.00	3.00"	DVE	Secondary	$18.00
(254)	86	Christmas Lights	UPP	10.00		OLB	Secondary	13.50
	87		UPP	10.00		CED	Secondary	13.50
	88		UPP	11.00		FLW	Secondary	13.50
	89		UPP	13.50		B&A	Primary	13.50
	90		OPEN	13.50		FLM	Primary	13.50

HONK IF YOU LOVE JESUS — Ornament

15857	85	Mother Goose in Bonnet	UPP	$10.00	3.60"	DVE	Secondary	$15.00
(255)	86		UPP	10.00		OLB	Secondary	13.50
	87		UPP	10.00		CED	Secondary	13.50
	88		UPP	11.00		FLW	Secondary	13.50
	89		UPP	13.50		B&A	Primary	13.50
	90		OPEN	13.50		FLM	Primary	13.50

GOD SENT HIS LOVE — Thimble, Dated

15865	85	Boy Holding Heart	Annual	$5.50	2.20"	DVE	Secondary	$25.00
(259)								

GOD SENT HIS LOVE — Bell, Dated

15873	85	Boy Holding Heart	Annual	$19.00	5.40"	DVE	Secondary	$35.00
(259)								

GOD SENT HIS LOVE — Figurine, Dated

15881	85	Boy Holding Heart	Annual	$17.00	4.50"	DVE	Secondary	$35.00
(259)								

BABY'S FIRST CHRISTMAS — Ornament, Dated

15903	85	Baby Boy with Bottle	Annual	$10.00	2.40"	DVE	Secondary	$35.00
(257)								

BABY'S FIRST CHRISTMAS — Ornament, Dated

15911	85	Baby Girl with Bottle	Annual	$10.00	2.40"	DVE	Secondary	$30.00
(258)								

MAY YOUR BIRTHDAY BE WARM — Figurine — "Birthday Train" Series

15938	86	Teddy on Caboose -	UPP	$10.00	2.75"	DVE	Secondary	$30.00
(296)	86	"For Baby"	UPP	10.00		OLB	Secondary	13.50
	87		UPP	10.00		CED	Secondary	13.50
	88		UPP	12.00		FLW	Secondary	13.50
	89		UPP	13.50		B&A	Secondary	13.50
	90		OPEN	13.50		FLM	Primary	13.50

HAPPY BIRTHDAY LITTLE LAMB — Figurine — "Birthday Train" Series

15946	86	Lamb - Age 1	UPP	$10.00	3.00"	DVE	Secondary	$30.00
(297)	86		UPP	10.00		OLB	Secondary	13.50
	87		UPP	10.00		CED	Secondary	13.50
	88		UPP	12.00		FLW	Secondary	13.50
	89		UPP	13.50		B&A	Secondary	13.50
	90		OPEN	13.50		FLM	Primary	13.50

HEAVEN BLESS YOUR SPECIAL DAY — Figurine — "Birthday Train" Series

15954	86	Pig - Age 3	UPP	$11.00	3.50"	DVE	Secondary	$30.00
(299)	86		UPP	11.00		OLB	Secondary	15.00
	87		UPP	11.00		CED	Secondary	15.00
	88		UPP	13.50		FLW	Secondary	15.00
	89		UPP	15.00		B&A	Secondary	15.00
	90		OPEN	15.00		FLM	Primary	15.00

GOD BLESS YOU ON YOUR BIRTHDAY — Figurine — "Birthday Train" Series

15962	86	Seal - Age 2	UPP	$11.00	3.75"	DVE	Secondary	$30.00
(298)	86		UPP	11.00		OLB	Secondary	15.00
	87		UPP	11.00		CED	Secondary	15.00
	88		UPP	13.50		FLW	Secondary	15.00
	89		UPP	15.00		B&A	Secondary	15.00
	90		OPEN	15.00		FLM	Primary	15.00

MAY YOUR BIRTHDAY BE GIGANTIC　Figurine　"Birthday Train" Series

15970	86	Elephant - Age 4	UPP	$12.50	3.50"	DVE	Secondary	$35.00
(300)	86		UPP	12.50		OLB	Secondary	17.00
	87		UPP	12.50		CED	Secondary	17.00
	88		UPP	15.00		FLW	Secondary	17.00
	89		UPP	17.00		B&A	Secondary	17.00
	90		OPEN	17.00		FLM	Primary	17.00

THIS DAY IS SOMETHING TO ROAR ABOUT　Figurine　"Birthday Train" Series

15989	86	Lion - Age 5	UPP	$13.50	4.00"	DVE	Secondary	$35.00
(301)	86		UPP	13.50		OLB	Secondary	20.00
	87		UPP	13.50		CED	Secondary	20.00
	88		UPP	17.50		FLW	Secondary	20.00
	89		UPP	20.00		B&A	Primary	20.00
	90		OPEN	20.00		FLM	Primary	20.00

KEEP LOOKING UP　Figurine　"Birthday Train" Series

15997	86	Giraffe - Age 6	UPP	$13.50	5.50"	DVE	Secondary	$35.00
(302)	86		UPP	13.50		OLB	Secondary	20.00
	87	•	UPP	13.50		CED	Secondary	20.00
	88		UPP	17.50		FLW	Secondary	20.00
	89		UPP	20.00		B&A	Primary	20.00
	90		OPEN	20.00		FLM	Primary	20.00

BLESS THE DAYS OF OUR YOUTH　Figurine　"Birthday Train" Series

16004	86	Clown with Pull Rope	UPP	$15.00	5.25"	DVE	Secondary	$40.00
(303)	86		UPP	15.00		OLB	Secondary	22.50
	87		UPP	15.00		CED	Secondary	22.50
	88		UPP	19.50		FLW	Secondary	22.50
	89		UPP	22.50		B&A	Primary	22.50
	90		OPEN	22.50		FLM	Primary	22.50

BABY'S FIRST TRIP　Figurine　Fourth Issue "Baby's First" Series

16012	86	Angel Pushing Buggy	UPP	$32.50	5.00"	OLB	Susp/Sec	$65.00
(267)	87		UPP	32.50		CED	Susp/Sec	60.00
	88		UPP	40.00		FLW	Susp/Sec	55.00
	89		UPP	45.00		B&A	Susp/Sec	55.00

GOD BLESS YOU WITH RAINBOWS　Night Light

16020	86	Angel Behind Rainbow	UPP	$45.00	5.00"	DVE	Susp/Sec	$70.00
(199)	86		UPP	45.00		OLB	Susp/Sec	65.00
	87		UPP	45.00		CED	Susp/Sec	65.00
	88		UPP	52.50		FLW	Susp/Sec	65.00
	89		UPP	57.50		B&A	Susp/Sec	65.00

TO MY FAVORITE PAW　Figurine

100021	86	Boy Sitting with Teddy	UPP	$22.50	3.50"	OLB	Susp/Sec	$45.00
(211)	87		UPP	22.50		CED	Susp/Sec	40.00
	88		UPP	27.00		FLW	Susp/Sec	40.00

TO MY DEER FRIEND　Figurine

100048	87	Girl with Flowers and Deer	UPP	$33.00	5.75"	OLB	Secondary	$60.00
(316)	87		UPP	33.00		CED	Secondary	45.00
	88		UPP	40.00		FLW	Secondary	45.00
	89		UPP	45.00		B&A	Primary	45.00
	90		OPEN	45.00		FLM	Primary	45.00

SENDING MY LOVE　Figurine

100056	86	Boy with Bow & Arrow	UPP	$22.50	5.75"	DVE	Secondary	$35.00
(212)	86	on Cloud	UPP	22.50		OLB	Secondary	30.00
	87		UPP	22.50		CED	Secondary	30.00
	88		UPP	27.00		FLW	Secondary	30.00
	89		UPP	30.00		B&A	Primary	30.00
	90		OPEN	30.00		FLM	Primary	30.00

WORSHIP THE LORD — Figurine

100064	86	Girl Kneeling at	UPP	$24.00	5.25"	DVE	Secondary	$35.00
(213)	86	Church Window	UPP	24.00		OLB	Secondary	33.00
	87		UPP	24.00		CED	Secondary	33.00
	88		UPP	30.00		FLW	Secondary	33.00
	89		UPP	33.00		B&A	Primary	33.00
	90		OPEN	33.00		FLM	Primary	33.00

TO MY FOREVER FRIEND — Figurine

100072	86	Two Girls with Flowers	UPP	$33.00	5.50"	DVE	Secondary	$55.00
(214)	86		UPP	33.00		OLB	Secondary	45.00
	87		UPP	33.00		CED	Secondary	45.00
	88		UPP	40.00		FLW	Secondary	45.00
	89		UPP	45.00		B&A	Primary	45.00
	90		OPEN	45.00		FLM	Primary	45.00

HE'S THE HEALER OF BROKEN HEARTS — Figurine

100080	87	Girl & Boy with	UPP	$33.00	5.50"	OLB	Secondary	$50.00
(317)	87	Bandaged Heart	UPP	33.00		CED	Secondary	45.00
	88		UPP	40.00		FLW	Secondary	45.00
	89		UPP	45.00		B&A	Primary	45.00
	90		OPEN	45.00		FLM	Primary	45.00

MAKE ME A BLESSING — Figurine

100102	87	Girl with Sick Bear	UPP	$35.00	5.50"	CED	Secondary	$50.00
(323)	88		UPP	40.00		FLW	Secondary	45.00
	89		UPP	45.00		B&A	Primary	45.00
	90		OPEN	45.00		FLM	Primary	45.00

LORD I'M COMING HOME — Figurine

100110	86	Baseball Player with Bat	UPP	$22.50	5.00"	DVE	Secondary	$50.00
(215)	86		UPP	22.50		OLB	Secondary	30.00
	87		UPP	22.50		CED	Secondary	30.00
	88		UPP	27.00		FLW	Secondary	30.00
	89		UPP	30.00		B&A	Primary	30.00
	90		OPEN	30.00		FLM	Primary	30.00

LORD KEEP ME ON MY TOES — Figurine

100129	86	Ballerina	UPP	$22.50	5.75"	DVE	Retired/Sec	$70.00
(216)	86		UPP	22.50		OLB	Retired/Sec	60.00
	87		UPP	22.50		CED	Retired/Sec	55.00
	88		UPP	27.00		FLW	Retired/Sec	50.00

THE JOY OF THE LORD IS MY STRENGTH — Figurine

100137	86	Mother with Babies	UPP	$35.00	5.40"	OLB	Secondary	$50.00
(217)	87		UPP	35.00		CED	Secondary	47.50
	88		UPP	40.00		FLW	Secondary	47.50
	89		UPP	47.50		B&A	Primary	47.50
	90		OPEN	47.50		FLM	Primary	47.50

GOD BLESS THE DAY WE FOUND YOU — Figurine

100145	86	Mom & Dad with	UPP	$40.00	5.50"	OLB	Secondary	$50.00
(272)	87	Adopted Daughter	UPP	40.00		CED	Secondary	50.00
	88		UPP	47.50		FLW	Primary	50.00
	89		UPP	50.00		B&A	Primary	50.00
	90		OPEN	50.00		FLM	Primary	50.00

GOD BLESS THE DAY WE FOUND YOU — Figurine

100153	86	Mom & Dad with	UPP	$40.00	5.50"	OLB	Secondary	$50.00
(273)	87	Adopted Son	UPP	40.00		CED	Secondary	50.00
	88		UPP	47.50		FLW	Primary	50.00
	89		UPP	50.00		B&A	Primary	50.00
	90		OPEN	50.00		FLM	Primary	50.00

SERVING THE LORD Figurine
100161	86	Tennis Girl	UPP	$19.00	5.00"	DVE	Secondary	$30.00
(218)	86		UPP	19.00		OLB	Secondary	25.00
	87		UPP	19.00		CED	Secondary	25.00
	88		UPP	22.50		FLW	Secondary	25.00
	89		UPP	25.00		B&A	Primary	25.00
	90		OPEN	25.00		FLM	Primary	25.00

I'M A POSSIBILITY Figurine
100188	86	Boy with Football	UPP	$22.00	5.25"	OLB	Secondary	$30.00
(274)	87		UPP	22.00		CED	Secondary	30.00
	88		UPP	27.00		FLW	Primary	30.00
	89		UPP	30.00		B&A	Primary	30.00
	90		OPEN	30.00		FLM	Primary	30.00

THE SPIRIT IS WILLING BUT THE FLESH IS WEAK Figurine
100196	87	Girl on Scale	UPP	$19.00	5.50"	CED	Secondary	$35.00
(324)	88		UPP	24.00		FLW	Secondary	27.00
	89		UPP	27.00		B&A	Primary	27.00
	90		OPEN	27.00		FLM	Primary	27.00

THE LORD GIVETH AND THE LORD TAKETH AWAY Figurine
100226	87	Girl with Cat & Bird Cage	UPP	$33.50	5.25"	CED	Secondary	38.50
(340)	88		UPP	36.00		FLW	Secondary	38.50
	89		UPP	38.50		B&A	Primary	38.50
	90		OPEN	38.50		FLM	Primary	38.50

FRIENDS NEVER DRIFT APART Figurine
100250	86	Kids in Boat	UPP	$35.00	4.25"	DVE	Secondary	$50.00
(219)	86		UPP	35.00		OLB	Secondary	47.50
	87		UPP	35.00		CED	Secondary	47.50
	88		UPP	42.50		FLW	Secondary	47.50
	89		UPP	47.50		B&A	Primary	47.50
	90		OPEN	47.50		FLM	Primary	47.50

HELP LORD, I'M IN A SPOT Figurine
100269	86	Boy Standing in Ink Spot	UPP	$18.50	5.25"	OLB	Retired/Sec	$55.00
(275)	87		UPP	18.50		CED	Retired/Sec	50.00
	88		UPP	22.50		FLW	Retired/Sec	50.00
	89		UPP	25.00		B&A	Retired/Sec	45.00

HE CLEANSED MY SOUL Figurine
100277	86	Girl in Old Bath Tub	UPP	$24.00	4.90"	DVE	Secondary	$35.00
(220)	86		UPP	24.00		OLB	Secondary	33.00
	87		UPP	24.00		CED	Secondary	33.00
	88		UPP	30.00		FLW	Secondary	33.00
	89		UPP	33.00		B&A	Primary	33.00
	90		OPEN	33.00		FLM	Primary	33.00

HEAVEN BLESS YOU Musical TUNE: Brahm's Lullaby
100285	86	Baby with Bunny & Turtle	UPP	$45.00	5.00"	OLB	Secondary	$60.00
(221)	87		UPP	45.00		CED	Secondary	57.50
	88		UPP	52.50		FLW	Secondary	57.50
	89		UPP	57.50		B&A	Primary	57.50
	90		OPEN	57.50		FLM	Primary	57.50

SERVING THE LORD Figurine
100293	86	Tennis Boy	UPP	$19.00	5.25"	DVE	Secondary	$30.00
(222)	86		UPP	19.00		OLB	Secondary	25.00
	87		UPP	19.00		CED	Secondary	25.00
	88		UPP	22.50		FLW	Primary	25.00
	89		UPP	25.00		B&A	Primary	25.00
	90		OPEN	25.00		FLM	Primary	25.00

BONG BONG   Doll   Individually Numbered
100455 86 Boy Clown   12,000 $150.00 13.00" OLB Secondary $165.00
(289)

CANDY   Doll   Individually Numbered
100463 86 Girl Clown   12,000 $150.00 13.00" OLB Secondary $160.00
(290)

GOD BLESS OUR FAMILY   Figurine
100498 87 Parents of the Groom   UPP $35.00 5.50" CED Secondary $45.00
(325)   88   UPP   40.00   FLW Primary   45.00
          89   UPP   45.00   B&A Primary   45.00
          90   OPEN 45.00   FLM Primary   45.00

GOD BLESS OUR FAMILY   Figurine
100501 87 Parents of the Bride   UPP $35.00 5.50" CED Secondary $45.00
(326)   88   UPP   40.00   FLW Primary   45.00
          89   UPP   45.00   B&A Primary   45.00
          90   OPEN 45.00   FLM Primary   45.00

SCENT FROM ABOVE   Figurine
100528 87 Girl with Skunk   UPP $19.00 5.25" OLB Secondary $30.00
(327)   87   UPP   19.00   CED Secondary 25.00
          88   UPP   23.00   FLW Secondary 25.00
          89   UPP   25.00   B&A Primary   25.00
          90   OPEN 25.00   FLM Primary   25.00

I PICKED A VERY SPECIAL MOM   Figurine   See "Nobody's Perfect!" Section
100536 87 Boy with His   Annual $37.50 5.50" CED Secondary $45.00
(328)   Gardening Mother

BROTHERLY LOVE   Figurine
100544 86 Pilgrim & Indian with Turkey UPP $37.00 4.50" OLB Susp/Sec $60.00
(276)   87   UPP   37.00   CED Susp/Sec 55.00
          88   UPP   42.50   FLW Susp/Sec 47.50
          89   UPP   47.50   B&A Susp/Prim 47.50

GOD IS LOVE, DEAR VALENTINE   Thimble
100625 86 Girl Holding Heart   UPP $5.50 2.25" DVE Susp/Sec $15.00
(103)   86   UPP   5.50   OLB Susp/Sec 10.00
          87   UPP   5.50   CED Susp/Sec 10.00
          88   UPP   7.00   FLW Susp/Sec 8.00
          89   UPP   8.00   B&A Susp/Prim 8.00

THE LORD BLESS YOU AND KEEP YOU   Thimble
100633 86 Bride   UPP $5.50 2.25" DVE Secondary $10.00
(313)   86   UPP   5.50   OLB Secondary 8.00
          87   UPP   5.50   CED Secondary 8.00
          88   UPP   7.00   FLW Secondary 8.00
          89   UPP   8.00   B&A Primary   8.00
          90   OPEN 8.00   FLM Primary   8.00

FOUR SEASONS THIMBLES   Thimbles   Set of 4
100641 86 Four Seasons Thimbles Annual $20.00 2.00" OLB Secondary $45.00
(226-229)

CLOWN THIMBLES   Thimbles   Set of 2
100668 86 Clowns   UPP $11.00 2.00" OLB Susp/Sec $25.00
(235)   87   UPP   11.00   CED Susp/Sec 20.00
          88   UPP   14.00   FLW Susp/Sec 20.00

OUR FIRST CHRISTMAS TOGETHER   Musical   TUNE: We Wish You A Merry Christmas

101702	86	Boy & Girl in Box	UPP	$50.00	5.50"	OLB	Secondary	$67.50
(277)	87		UPP	50.00		CED	Secondary	67.50
	88		UPP	55.00		FLW	Secondary	67.50
	89		UPP	67.50		B&A	Primary	67.50
	90		OPEN	67.50		FLM	Primary	67.50

NO TEARS PAST THE GATE   Figurine

101826	87	Girl at Gate to Heaven	UPP	$40.00	6.25"	CED	Secondary	$55.00
(329)	88		UPP	47.50		FLW	Primary	55.00
	89		UPP	55.00		B&A	Primary	55.00
	90		OPEN	55.00		FLM	Primary	55.00

I'M SENDING YOU A WHITE CHRISTMAS   Plate, Dated   First Issue "Christmas Love" Series

101834	86	Girl Mailing Snowball	Annual	$45.00	8.50"	OLB	Secondary	$70.00
(169)								

SMILE ALONG THE WAY   Figurine

101842	87	Clown Balancing	UPP	$30.00	6.75"	CED	Secondary	$45.00
(330)	88	Upside Down	UPP	35.00		FLW	Secondary	40.00
	89		UPP	40.00		B&A	Primary	40.00
	90		OPEN	40.00		FLM	Primary	40.00

LORD HELP US KEEP OUR ACT TOGETHER   Figurine

101850	87	Clowns on Unicycle	UPP	$35.00	7.00"	OLB	Secondary	$50.00
(331)	87		UPP	35.00		CED	Secondary	45.00
	88		UPP	40.00		FLW	Secondary	45.00
	89		UPP	45.00		B&A	Primary	45.00
	90		OPEN	45.00		FLM	Primary	45.00

WORSHIP THE LORD   Figurine

102229	86	Boy Kneeling at	UPP	$24.00	5.50"	DVE	Secondary	$35.00
(223)	86	Church Window	UPP	24.00		OLB	Secondary	33.00
	87		UPP	24.00		CED	Secondary	33.00
	88		UPP	30.00		FLW	Secondary	33.00
	89		UPP	33.00		B&A	Primary	33.00
	90		OPEN	33.00		FLM	Primary	33.00

CONNIE   Doll   Individually Numbered

102253	86	Doll with Stand	7,500	$160.00	12.00"	OLB	Secondary	175.00
(291)								

SHEPHERD OF LOVE   Figurine   Mini Nativity Addition

102261	86	Angel with Black Lamb	UPP	$10.00	3.25"	OLB	Secondary	$18.00
(278)	87		UPP	10.00		CED	Secondary	13.50
	88		UPP	11.00		FLW	Secondary	13.50
	89		UPP	13.50		B&A	Primary	13.50
	90		OPEN	13.50		FLM	Primary	13.50

SHEPHERD OF LOVE   Ornament

102288	86	Angel with Black Lamb	UPP	$10.00	3.25"	OLB	Secondary	$18.00
(278)	87		UPP	10.00		CED	Secondary	13.50
	88		UPP	11.00		FLW	Secondary	13.50
	89		UPP	13.50		B&A	Primary	13.50
	90		OPEN	13.50		FLM	Primary	13.50

MINI ANIMAL FIGURINES   Figurines   Set of 3   Mini Nativity Addition

102296	86	Black Sheep, Bunny & Turtle	UPP	$13.50	1.75"	OLB	Secondary	$22.00
(279)	87		UPP	13.50		CED	Secondary	17.50
	88		UPP	15.00		FLW	Secondary	17.50
	89		UPP	17.50		B&A	Primary	17.50
	90		OPEN	17.50		FLM	Primary	17.50

WISHING YOU A COZY CHRISTMAS   Bell, Dated

102318	86	Girl with Muff	Annual	$20.00	5.50"	OLB	Secondary	$30.00
(280)								

WISHING YOU A COZY CHRISTMAS — Ornament, Dated

102326	86	Girl with Muff	Annual	$10.00	3.00"	OLB	Secondary	$35.00
(280)							

WISHING YOU A COZY CHRISTMAS — Thimble, Dated

102334	86	Girl with Muff	Annual	$5.50	2.25"	OLB	Secondary	$15.00
(280)							

WISHING YOU A COZY CHRISTMAS — Figurine, Dated

102342	86	Girl with Muff	Annual	$17.00	4.75"	OLB	Secondary	$35.00
(280)							

OUR FIRST CHRISTMAS TOGETHER — Ornament, Dated

102350	86	Boy and Girl in Package	Annual	$10.00	2.74"	OLB	Secondary	$25.00
(277)							

WEDDING ARCH — Figurine

102369	86	Bridal Arch	UPP	$22.50	7.75"	OLB	Secondary	$30.00
(332)	87		UPP	22.50		CED	Secondary	27.50
	88		UPP	25.00		FLW	Secondary	27.50
	89		UPP	27.50		B&A	Primary	27.50
	90		OPEN	27.50		FLM	Primary	27.50

TRUST AND OBEY — Ornament

102377	86	Policeman Writing Ticket	UPP	$10.00	3.00"	OLB	Secondary	$18.00
(237)	87		UPP	10.00		CED	Secondary	13.50
	88		UPP	11.00		FLW	Secondary	13.50
	89		UPP	13.50		B&A	Primary	13.50
	90		OPEN	13.50		FLM	Primary	13.50

LOVE RESCUED ME — Ornament

102385	86	Fireman Holding Puppy	UPP	$10.00	3.00"	OLB	Secondary	$18.00
(281)	87		UPP	10.00		CED	Secondary	13.50
	88		UPP	11.00		FLW	Secondary	13.50
	89		UPP	13.50		B&A	Primary	13.50
	90		OPEN	13.50		FLM	Primary	13.50

LOVE RESCUED ME — Figurine

102393	86	Fireman Holding Puppy	UPP	$22.50	5.50"	OLB	Secondary	$35.00
(281)	87		UPP	22.50		CED	Secondary	30.00
	88		UPP	27.00		FLW	Secondary	30.00
	89		UPP	30.00		B&A	Primary	30.00
	90		OPEN	30.00		FLM	Primary	30.00

ANGEL OF MERCY — Ornament

102407	86	Nurse with Potted Plant	UPP	$10.00	3.00"	OLB	Secondary	$20.00
(282)	87		UPP	10.00		CED	Secondary	13.50
	88		UPP	11.00		FLW	Secondary	13.50
	89		UPP	13.50		B&A	Primary	13.50
	90		OPEN	13.50		FLM	Primary	13.50

IT'S A PERFECT BOY — Ornament

102415	86	Boy Angel with	UPP	$10.00	3.00"	OLB	Susp/Sec	$20.00
(127)	87	Red Cross Bag	UPP	10.00		CED	Susp/Sec	18.00
	88		UPP	11.00		FLW	Susp/Sec	18.00
	89		UPP	13.50		B&A	Susp/Sec	18.00

LORD KEEP ME ON MY TOES — Ornament

102423	86	Ballerina	UPP	$10.00	3.50"	OLB	Secondary	$15.00
(216)	87		UPP	10.00		CED	Secondary	13.50
	88		UPP	11.00		FLW	Secondary	13.50
	89		UPP	13.50		B&A	Primary	13.50
	90		OPEN	13.50		FLM	Primary	13.50

SERVE WITH A SMILE   Ornament

102431	86	Tennis Boy		UPP	$10.00	3.25"	OLB	Susp/Sec	$20.00
(222)	87			UPP	10.00		CED	Susp/Sec	18.00
	88			UPP	11.00		FLW	Susp/Sec	18.00

SERVE WITH A SMILE   Ornament

102458	86	Tennis Girl	UPP	$10.00	3.25"	OLB	Susp/Sec	$22.00
(218)	87		UPP	10.00		CED	Susp/Sec	20.00
	88		UPP	11.00		FLW	Susp/Sec	20.00

REINDEER   Ornament, Dated   Birthday Collection

102466	86	Reindeer and Teddy Bear	Annual	$11.00	3.25"	OLB	Secondary	$165.00
(306)								

ROCKING HORSE   Ornament

102474	86	Rocking Horse	UPP	$10.00	2.50"	OLB	Secondary	$15.00
(283)	87		UPP	10.00		CED	Secondary	13.50
	88		UPP	11.00		FLW	Secondary	13.50
	89		UPP	13.50		B&A	Primary	13.50
	90		OPEN	13.50		FLM	Primary	13.50

ANGEL OF MERCY   Figurine

102482	86	Nurse with Potted Plant	UPP	$20.00	5.50"	OLB	Secondary	$30.00
(282)	87		UPP	20.00		CED	Secondary	27.00
	88		UPP	24.00		FLW	Secondary	27.00
	89		UPP	27.00		B&A	Primary	27.00
	90		OPEN	27.00		FLM	Primary	27.00

SHARING OUR CHRISTMAS TOGETHER   Figurine

102490	86	Husband & Wife with	UPP	$37.00	5.25"	OLB	Susp/Sec	$50.00
(284)	87	Cookies & Pup	UPP	37.00		CED	Susp/Sec	45.00
	88		UPP	40.00		FLW	Susp/Sec	45.00

BABY'S FIRST CHRISTMAS   Ornament, Dated

102504	86	Girl with Candy Cane	Annual	$10.00	2.75"	OLB	Secondary	$25.00
(285)								

BABY'S FIRST CHRISTMAS   Ornament, Dated

102512	86	Boy with Candy Cane	Annual	$10.00	2.75"	OLB	Secondary	$25.00
(286)								

LET'S KEEP IN TOUCH   Musical   TUNE: Be A Clown

102520	86	Clown on Elephant	UPP	$65.00	7.00"	OLB	Secondary	$85.00
(287)	87		UPP	65.00		CED	Secondary	80.00
	88		UPP	75.00		FLW	Secondary	80.00
	89		UPP	80.00		B&A	Primary	80.00
	90		OPEN	80.00		FLM	Primary	80.00

WE ARE ALL PRECIOUS IN HIS SIGHT   Figurine   See "Nobody's Perfect!" Section

102903	87	Girl with Pearl	Annual	$30.00	7.10"	CED	Secondary	$75.00
(373)								

GOD BLESS AMERICA   Figurine

102938	86	Uncle Sam Holding Bible	Annual	$30.00	5.50"	OLB	Secondary	$60.00
(292)		with Dog						

MY PEACE I GIVE UNTO THEE   Plate, Dated   Second Issue "Christmas Love" Series

102954	87	Children around Lamppost	Annual	$45.00	8.50"	CED	Secondary	$90.00
(341)								

IT'S THE BIRTHDAY OF A KING   Figurine   Nativity Addition

102962	86	Boy Angel with	UPP	$18.50	5.50"	OLB	Susp/Sec	$35.00
(288)	87	Birthday Cake	UPP	18.50		CED	Susp/Sec	30.00
	88		UPP	21.00		FLW	Susp/Sec	30.00
	89		UPP	25.00		B&A	Susp/Sec	30.00

I WOULD BE SUNK WITHOUT YOU — Figurine

102970	87	Baby Boy in Tub	UPP	$15.00	3.25"	CED	Secondary	$20.00
(342)	88		UPP	16.00		FLW	Secondary	17.50
	89		UPP	17.50		B&A	Primary	17.50
	90		OPEN	17.50		FLM	Primary	17.50

WE BELONG TO THE LORD — Figurine — Special Damien-Dutton Piece

103004	86	Shepherd & Lambs	UPP	$29.50	4.90"	DIA	Secondary	$150.00
(338)								

MY LOVE WILL NEVER LET YOU GO — Figurine

103497	87	Boy with Hat & Fish	UPP	$25.00	5.50"	CED	Secondary	$35.00
(333)	88		UPP	30.00		FLW	Secondary	33.00
	89		UPP	33.00		B&A	Primary	33.00
	90		OPEN	33.00		FLM	Primary	33.00

I BELIEVE IN THE OLD RUGGED CROSS — Figurine

103632	86	Girl Holding Cross	UPP	$25.00	5.25"	DVE	Secondary	$40.00
(224)	86		UPP	25.00		OLB	Secondary	33.00
	87		UPP	25.00		CED	Secondary	33.00
	88		UPP	30.00		FLW	Primary	33.00
	89		UPP	33.00		B&A	Primary	33.00
	90		OPEN	33.00		FLM	Primary	33.00

COME LET US ADORE HIM — Figurines — Set of 9

104000	86	Nativity Set with Cassette	UPP	$ 95.00	4.75"	OLB	Secondary	$120.00
(307)	87		UPP	95.00		CED	Secondary	110.00
	88		UPP	100.00		FLW	Secondary	110.00
	89		UPP	110.00		B&A	Primary	110.00
	90		OPEN	110.00		FLM	Primary	110.00

WITH THIS RING I... — Figurine

104019	87	Boy Giving Girl Ring	UPP	$40.00	5.00"	CED	Secondary	$55.00
(343)	88		UPP	45.00		FLW	Primary	50.00
	89		UPP	50.00		B&A	Primary	50.00
	90		OPEN	50.00		FLM	Primary	50.00

LOVE IS THE GLUE THAT MENDS — Figurine

104027	87	Boy Mending Hobby Horse	UPP	$33.50	4.00"	CED	Secondary	$40.00
(344)	88		UPP	36.00		FLW	Secondary	38.50
	89		UPP	38.50		B&A	Primary	38.50
	90		OPEN	38.50		FLM	Primary	38.50

CHEERS TO THE LEADER — Figurine

104035	87	Girl Cheerleader	UPP	$22.50	5.25"	CED	Secondary	$30.00
(345)	88		UPP	24.00		FLW	Secondary	27.00
	89		UPP	27.00		B&A	Primary	27.00
	90		OPEN	27.00		FLM	Primary	27.00

HAPPY DAYS ARE HERE AGAIN — Figurine

104396	87	Girl Clown with Books	UPP	$25.00	5.25"	CED	Secondary	$35.00
(346)	88		UPP	27.00		FLW	Secondary	30.00
	89		UPP	30.00		B&A	Primary	30.00
	90		OPEN	30.00		FLM	Primary	30.00

FRIENDS TO THE END — Figurine — Birthday Collection

104418	88	Rhino with Bird	UPP	$15.00	2.50"	UM	Secondary	$20.00
(420)	88		UPP	17.00		FLW	Secondary	20.00
	89		UPP	17.00		B&A	Primary	17.00
	90		OPEN	17.00		FLM	Primary	17.00

BEAR THE GOOD NEWS OF CHRISTMAS — Ornament, Dated — Birthday Collection

104515	87	Teddy Bear in Cup on Skis	Annual	$11.00	2.10"	CED	Secondary	$30.00
(347)								

"DEALERS ONLY" NATIVITY   Figurines   Set of 9
104523   86   Nativity with Backdrop   UPP $400.00   9.00"   OLB   Secondary $500.00
(337)   and Video

JESUS LOVES ME   Figurine   Easter Seal Raffle Piece   Individually Numbered
104531   88   Girl with Bunny   1,000 $500.00   9.00"   CED   Secondary $1500.00
(2)

A TUB FULL OF LOVE   Figurine
104817   87   Baby Boy in Wood Tub   UPP $22.50   3.75"   CED   Secondary $30.00
(348)   88   UPP   24.00   FLW   Secondary   27.50
         89   UPP   27.50   B&A   Primary   27.50
         90   OPEN   27.50   FLM   Primary   27.50

SITTING PRETTY   Figurine
104825   87   Girl Angel on Stool   UPP $22.50   5.50"   CED   Secondary $30.00
(349)   88   UPP   24.00   FLW   Secondary   27.00
         89   UPP   27.00   B&A   Primary   27.00
         90   OPEN   27.00   FLM   Primary   27.00

HAVE I GOT NEWS FOR YOU   Figurine   Nativity Addition
105635   87   Boy Reading Scroll   UPP $22.50   4.75"   CED   Secondary $30.00
(350)   88   UPP   22.50   FLW   Secondary   27.50
         89   UPP   27.50   B&A   Primary   27.50
         90   OPEN   27.50   FLM   Primary   27.50

SOMETHING'S MISSING WHEN YOU'RE NOT AROUND   Figurine
105643   88   Girl Holding Doll with Dog   UPP $32.50   5.50"   FLW   Secondary $40.00
(421)   89   UPP   36.00   B&A   Primary   36.00
         90   OPEN   36.00   FLM   Primary   36.00

TO TELL THE TOOTH YOU'RE SPECIAL   Figurine
105813   87   Dentist and Patient with   UPP $38.50   5.00"   CED   Secondary $50.00
(351)   88   Pulled Tooth   UPP   42.50   FLW   Secondary   47.50
         89   UPP   47.50   B&A   Primary   47.50
         90   OPEN   47.50   FLM   Primary   47.50

HALLELUJAH COUNTRY   Figurine
105821   88   Cowboy on Fence with Guitar   UPP $35.00   5.50"   CED   Secondary   *
(377)   88   UPP   35.00   FLW   Secondary $40.00
         89   UPP   40.00   B&A   Primary   40.00
         90   OPEN   40.00   FLM   Primary   40.00
         * Extremely rare

SHOWERS OF BLESSINGS   Figurine   Birthday Collection
105945   87   Elephant Showering   UPP $16.00   3.25"   CED   Secondary $25.00
(352)   88   Mouse   UPP   18.50   FLW   Secondary   20.00
         89   UPP   20.00   B&A   Primary   20.00
         90   OPEN   20.00   FLM   Primary   20.00

BRIGHTEN SOMEONE'S DAY   Figurine   Birthday Collection
105953   88   Skunk & Mouse   UPP $12.50   2.50"   CED   Secondary $18.00
(395)   88   UPP   12.50   FLW   Secondary   13.50
         89   UPP   13.50   B&A   Primary   13.50
         90   OPEN   13.50   FLM   Primary   13.50

WE'RE PULLING FOR YOU   Figurine
106151   87   Boy with Donkey   UPP $40.00   5.00"   CED   Secondary $55.00
(353)   88   UPP   45.00   FLW   Primary   50.00
         89   UPP   50.00   B&A   Primary   50.00
         90   OPEN   50.00   FLM   Primary   50.00

GOD BLESS YOU GRADUATE — Figurine

106194	86	Boy Graduate	UPP	$20.00	5.00"	OLB	Secondary	$30.00
(334)	87		UPP	20.00		CED	Secondary	27.00
	88		UPP	24.00		FLW	Primary	27.00
	89		UPP	27.00		B&A	Primary	27.00
	90		OPEN	27.00		FLM	Primary	27.00

CONGRATULATIONS, PRINCESS — Figurine

106208	86	Girl Graduate	UPP	$20.00	5.50"	OLB	Secondary	$32.00
(318)	87		UPP	20.00		CED	Secondary	27.00
	88		UPP	24.00		FLW	Secondary	27.00
	89		UPP	27.00		B&A	Primary	27.00
	90		OPEN	27.00		FLM	Primary	27.00

LORD HELP ME MAKE THE GRADE — Figurine

106216	87	Schoolboy Clown	UPP	$25.00	5.00"	CED	Secondary	$35.00
(354)	88		UPP	27.00		FLW	Secondary	30.00
	89		UPP	30.00		B&A	Primary	30.00
	90		OPEN	30.00		FLM	Primary	30.00

HEAVEN BLESS YOUR TOGETHERNESS — Figurine

106755	88	Groom Popping Out of	UPP	$65.00	5.50"	CED	Secondary	$80.00
(378)	88	Trunk at Bride	UPP	65.00		FLW	Secondary	75.00
	89		UPP	75.00		B&A	Primary	75.00
	90		OPEN	75.00		FLM	Primary	75.00

PRECIOUS MEMORIES — Figurine

106763	88	Couple on Couch Looking	UPP	$37.50	4.50"	CED	Secondary	$50.00
(379)	88	at Wedding Album	UPP	37.50		FLW	Secondary	45.00
	89		UPP	45.00		B&A	Primary	45.00
	90		OPEN	45.00		FLM	Primary	45.00

PUPPY LOVE IS FROM ABOVE — Figurine

106798	88	Anniversary Couple with Dog	UPP	$45.00	5.50"	CED	Secondary	$55.00
(380)	88		UPP	45.00		FLW	Secondary	50.00
	89		UPP	50.00		B&A	Primary	50.00
	90		OPEN	50.00		FLM	Primary	50.00

HAPPY BIRTHDAY POPPY — Figurine

106836	88	Girl Holding Poppy Plant	UPP	$27.50	5.50"	CED	Secondary	$35.00
(381)	88		UPP	27.50		FLW	Primary	31.50
	89		UPP	31.50		B&A	Primary	31.50
	90		OPEN	31.50		FLM	Primary	31.50

SEW IN LOVE — Figurine

106844	88	Girl Sewing Boy's Pants	UPP	$45.00	5.50"	CED	Secondary	$55.00
(382)	88		UPP	45.00		FLW	Secondary	50.00
	89		UPP	50.00		B&A	Primary	50.00
	90		OPEN	50.00		FLM	Primary	50.00

HE WALKS WITH ME — Figurine   Special Easter Seal Piece   Easter Seal Lily on Decal

107999	87	Girl on Crutches	Annual	$25.00	5.50"	CED	Secondary	$30.00
(319)								

THEY FOLLOWED THE STAR — Figurines   Set of 3   Mini Nativity Addition

108243	87·	Kings on Camels	UPP	$75.00	6.50"	CED	Secondary	$100.00
(65)	88		UPP	75.00		FLW	Secondary	95.00
	89		UPP	95.00		B&A	Primary	95.00
	90		OPEN	95.00		FLM	Primary	95.00

THE GREATEST GIFT IS A FRIEND   Figurine

109231	87	Baby Boy Sitting by Dog	UPP	$30.00	4.25"	CED	Secondary	$40.00
(355)	88		UPP	30.00		FLW	Secondary	36.00
	89		UPP	36.00		B&A	Primary	36.00
	90		OPEN	36.00		FLM	Primary	36.00

BABY'S FIRST CHRISTMAS   Ornament, Dated

109401	87	Girl on Rocking Horse	Annual	$12.00	3.25"	CED	Secondary	$35.00
(356)								

BABY'S FIRST CHRISTMAS   Ornament, Dated

109428	87	Boy on Rocking Horse	Annual	$12.00	3.25"	CED	Secondary	$35.00
(357)								

ISN'T EIGHT JUST GREAT   Figurine   "Birthday Train" Series

109460	88	Ostrich - Age 8	UPP	$18.50	4.50"	CED	Secondary	$25.00
(394)	88		UPP	18.50		FLW	Secondary	20.00
	89		UPP	20.00		B&A	Primary	20.00
	90		OPEN	20.00		FLM	Primary	20.00

WISHING YOU GRRR-EATNESS   Figurine   "Birthday Train" Series

109479	88	Leopard - Age 7	UPP	$18.50	4.25"	CED	Secondary	$25.00
(393)	88		UPP	18.50		FLW	Secondary	20.00
	89		UPP	20.00		B&A	Primary	20.00
	90		OPEN	20.00		FLM	Primary	20.00

BELIEVE THE IMPOSSIBLE   Figurine

109487	88	Boy with Barbells	UPP	$35.00	5.50"	CED	Secondary	$95.00
(383)	88		UPP	35.00		FLW	Secondary	45.00
	89		UPP	40.00		B&A	Primary	40.00
	90		OPEN	40.00		FLM	Primary	40.00

HAPPINESS DIVINE   Figurine

109584	88	Clown Angel with Flowers	UPP	$25.00	5.50"	FLW	Secondary	$30.00
(384)	89		UPP	27.50		B&A	Primary	27.50
	90		OPEN	27.50		FLM	Primary	27.50

PEACE ON EARTH   Musical   TUNE: Hark! The Herald Angels Sing

109746	88	Kids around Lamp Post	UPP	$100.00	6.50"	FLW	Secondary	$115.00
(341)	89		UPP	110.00		B&A	Primary	110.00
	90		OPEN	110.00		FLM	Primary	110.00

WISHING YOU A YUMMY CHRISTMAS   Figurine

109754	87	Girl with Ice Cream	UPP	$35.00	5.00"	CED	Secondary	$50.00
(358)	88		UPP	35.00		FLW	Secondary	42.50
	89		UPP	42.50		B&A	Primary	42.50
	90		OPEN	42.50		FLM	Primary	42.50

WE GATHER TOGETHER TO ASK THE LORD'S BLESSING   Figurines   Set of 6

109762	87	Family Thanksgiving Set	UPP	$130.00	5.00"	CED	Secondary	$150.00
(359)	88		UPP	130.00		FLW	Secondary	145.00
	89		UPP	145.00		B&A	Secondary	145.00
	90		OPEN	145.00		FLM	Primary	145.00

LOVE IS THE BEST GIFT OF ALL   Ornament, Dated

109770	87	Girl with Package and	Annual	$11.00	2.75"	CED	Secondary	$40.00
(360)		Doll						

MEOWIE CHRISTMAS   Figurine

109800	88	Girl with Kitten	UPP	$30.00	4.50"	FLW	Secondary	$35.00
(423)	89		UPP	33.00		B&A	Primary	33.00
	90		OPEN	33.00		FLM	Primary	33.00

OH WHAT FUN IT IS TO RIDE   Figurine

109819	87	Grandma on Sled	UPP	$85.00	6.25"	CED	Secondary	$100.00
(361)	88		UPP	85.00		FLW	Secondary	100.00
	89		UPP	100.00		B&A	Primary	100.00
	90		OPEN	100.00		FLM	Primary	100.00

LOVE IS THE BEST GIFT OF ALL   Bell, Dated

109835	87	Girl with Package and	Annual	$22.50	5.75"	CED	Secondary	$30.00
(360)		Doll						

LOVE IS THE BEST GIFT OF ALL   Thimble, Dated

109843	87	Girl with Package and	Annual	$6.00	2.25"	CED	Secondary	$15.00
(360)		Doll						

WISHING YOU A HAPPY EASTER   Figurine

109886	88	Girl Holding Bunny	UPP	$23.00	5.50"	CED	Secondary	$30.00
(388)	88		UPP	23.00		FLW	Secondary	25.00
	89		UPP	25.00		B&A	Primary	25.00
	90		OPEN	25.00		FLM	Primary	25.00

WISHING YOU A BASKETFUL OF BLESSINGS   Figurine

109924	88	Boy Holding Basket	UPP	$23.00	5.50"	CED	Secondary	$30.00
(385)	88		UPP	23.00		FLW	Secondary	25.00
	89		UPP	25.00		B&A	Primary	25.00
	90		OPEN	25.00		FLM	Primary	25.00

SENDING YOU MY LOVE   Figurine

109967	88	Girl with Hearts in Cloud	UPP	$35.00	5.00"	CED	Secondary	$45.00
(386)	88		UPP	35.00		FLW	Secondary	40.00
	89		UPP	40.00		B&A	Primary	40.00
	90		OPEN	40.00		FLM	Primary	40.00

MOMMY, I LOVE YOU   Figurine

109975	88	Boy with Flower	UPP	$22.50	5.50"	CED	Secondary	$30.00
(387)	88		UPP	22.50		FLW	Secondary	25.00
	89		UPP	25.00		B&A	Primary	25.00
	90		OPEN	25.00		FLM	Primary	25.00

JANUARY GIRL   Figurine   "Calendar Girl" Series

109983	88	Girl Pushing Doll in Sleigh	UPP	$37.50	5.50"	CED	Secondary	$65.00
(367)	88		UPP	37.50		FLW	Secondary	42.50
	89		UPP	42.50		B&A	Secondary	42.50
	90		OPEN	42.50		FLM	Primary	42.50

FEBRUARY GIRL   Figurine   "Calendar Girl" Series

109991	88	Girl Looking at Plant	UPP	$27.50	5.25"	CED	Secondary	$55.00
(368)	88	Peeking through Snow	UPP	27.50		FLW	Secondary	31.50
	89		UPP	31.50		B&A	Secondary	31.50
	90		OPEN	31.50		FLM	Primary	31.50

MARCH GIRL   Figurine   "Calendar Girl" Series

110019	88	Girl with Kite	UPP	$27.50	5.00"	CED	Secondary	$65.00
(369)	88		UPP	27.50		FLW	Secondary	31.50
	89		UPP	31.50		B&A	Secondary	31.50
	90		OPEN	31.50		FLM	Primary	31.50

APRIL GIRL   Figurine   "Calendar Girl" Series

110027	88	Girl with Umbrella	UPP	$30.00	6.00"	CED	Secondary	$110.00
(370)	88		UPP	30.00		FLW	Secondary	33.00
	89		UPP	33.00		B&A	Secondary	33.00
	90		OPEN	33.00		FLM	Primary	33.00

MAY GIRL   Figurine   "Calendar Girl" Series

110035	88	Girl with Potted Plant	UPP	$25.00	5.75"	CED	Secondary	$135.00
(371)	88		UPP	25.00		FLW	Secondary	27.50
	89		UPP	27.50		B&A	Secondary	27.50
	90		OPEN	27.50		FLM	Primary	27.50

JUNE GIRL   Figurine   "Calendar Girl" Series

110043	88	Girl Dressing Up as Bride	UPP	$40.00	5.50"	CED	Secondary	$85.00
(372)	88		UPP	40.00		FLW	Secondary	45.00
	89		UPP	45.00		B&A	Secondary	45.00
	90		OPEN	45.00		FLM	Primary	45.00

JULY GIRL   Figurine   "Calendar Girl" Series

110051	88	Girl with Puppy in Basket	UPP	$35.00	5.50"	FLW	Secondary	$50.00
(424)	89		UPP	40.00		B&A	Secondary	40.00
	90		OPEN	40.00		FLM	Primary	40.00

AUGUST GIRL   Figurine   "Calendar Girl" Series

110078	88	Girl in Pool	UPP	$40.00	4.00"	FLW	Secondary	$55.00
(425)	89		UPP	45.00		B&A	Primary	45.00
	90		OPEN	45.00		FLM	Primary	45.00

SEPTEMBER GIRL   Figurine   "Calendar Girl" Series

110086	88	Girl Balancing Books	UPP	$27.50	5.75"	FLW	Secondary	$40.00
(426)	89		UPP	31.50		B&A	Primary	31.50
	90		OPEN	31.50		FLM	Primary	31.50

OCTOBER GIRL   Figurine   "Calendar Girl" Series

110094	88	Girl with Pumpkins	UPP	$35.00	5.50"	FLW	Secondary	$50.00
(427)	89		UPP	40.00		B&A	Primary	40.00
	90		OPEN	40.00		FLM	Primary	40.00

NOVEMBER GIRL   Figurine   "Calendar Girl" Series

110108	88	Girl in Pilgrim Suit	UPP	$32.50	5.50"	FLW	Secondary	$45.00
(428)	89		UPP	35.00		B&A	Primary	35.00
	90		OPEN	35.00		FLM	Primary	35.00

DECEMBER GIRL   Figurine   "Calendar Girl" Series

110116	88	Girl with Christmas Candle	UPP	$27.50	5.50"	FLW	Secondary	$40.00
(429)	89		UPP	31.50		B&A	Primary	31.50
	90		OPEN	31.50		FLM	Primary	31.50

LOVE IS THE BEST GIFT OF ALL   Figurine, Dated

110930	87	Girl Holding Package with	Annual	$22.50	5.25"	CED	Secondary	$35.00
(360)		Doll						

I'M A POSSIBILITY   Ornament

111120	87	Football Player	UPP	$11.00	3.25"	CED	Secondary	$15.00
(274)	88		UPP	11.00		FLW	Secondary	13.50
	89		UPP	13.50		B&A	Primary	13.50
	90		OPEN	13.50		FLM	Primary	13.50

FAITH TAKES THE PLUNGE   Figurine   *See "Nobody's Perfect!" Section

111155	88	Girl with Plunger	UPP	$27.50	5.50"	CED*	Secondary	$50.00
(389)	88		UPP	27.50		FLW*	Secondary	31.50
	89		UPP	31.50		B&A	Primary	31.50
	90		OPEN	31.50		FLM	Primary	31.50

'TIS THE SEASON   Figurine

111163	88	Girl Adding Seasoning	UPP	$27.50	5.50"	FLW	Secondary	$35.00
(430)	89		UPP	31.50		B&A	Primary	31.50
	90		OPEN	31.50		FLM	Primary	31.50

O COME LET US ADORE HIM   Figurines   Set of 4

111333	87	Large Nativity	UPP	$200.00	9.00"	CED	Secondary	$225.00
(362)	88		UPP	200.00		FLW	Secondary	220.00
	89		UPP	220.00		B&A	Primary	220.00
	90		OPEN	220.00		FLM	Primary	220.00

RETAILER'S WREATH   Wreath   See "Nobody's Perfect!" Section

111465	87	Christmas Wreath	UPP	$150.00	16.0"	CED	Secondary	$190.00
(410)								

MOMMY, I LOVE YOU   Figurine

112143	88	Girl with Flower	UPP	$22.50	5.75"	CED	Secondary	$30.00
(390)	88		UPP	22.50		FLW	Secondary	25.00
	89		UPP	25.00		B&A	Primary	25.00
	90		OPEN	25.00		FLM	Primary	25.00

A TUB FULL OF LOVE   Figurine

112313	87	Baby Girl in Wood Tub	UPP	$22.50	3.50"	CED	Secondary	$30.00
(363)	88		UPP	22.50		FLW	Secondary	27.50
	89		UPP	27.50		B&A	Primary	27.50
	90		OPEN	27.50		FLM	Primary	27.50

RETAILER'S WREATH BELL   Bell

112348	87	Retailer's Wreath Bell	UPP		3.25"	CED	Secondary	$75.00
(415)		[NOTE: Bell from #111465 has its own Enesco Item Number.]						

YOU HAVE TOUCHED SO MANY HEARTS   Ornament

112356	87	Girl Holding Hearts	UPP	$11.00	3.25"	CED	Secondary	$15.00
(161)	88		UPP	11.00		FLW	Secondary	13.50
	89		UPP	13.50		B&A	Primary	13.50
	90		OPEN	13.50		FLM	Primary	13.50

WADDLE I DO WITHOUT YOU   Ornament

112364	87	Girl Clown with Goose	UPP	$11.00	3.50"	CED	Secondary	$15.00
(250)	88		UPP	11.00		FLW	Secondary	13.50
	89		UPP	13.50		B&A	Primary	13.50
	90		OPEN	13.50		FLM	Primary	13.50

I'M SENDING YOU A WHITE CHRISTMAS   Ornament

112372	87	Girl Mailing Snowball	UPP	$11.00	3.00"	CED	Secondary	$15.00
(169)	88		UPP	11.00		FLW	Secondary	13.50
	89		UPP	13.50		B&A	Primary	13.50
	90		OPEN	13.50		FLM	Primary	13.50

HE CLEANSED MY SOUL   Ornament

112380	87	Girl in Old Bathtub	UPP	$12.00	2.75"	CED	Secondary	$18.00
(220)	88		UPP	12.00		FLW	Secondary	15.00
	89		UPP	15.00		B&A	Primary	15.00
	90		OPEN	15.00		FLM	Primary	15.00

OUR FIRST CHRISTMAS TOGETHER   Ornament, Dated

112399	87	Boy and Girl in Package	Annual	$11.00	2.75"	CED	Secondary	$25.00
(277)								

I'M SENDING YOU A WHITE CHRISTMAS   Musical   TUNE: White Christmas

112402	87	Girl Mailing Snowball	UPP	$55.00	6.00"	CED	Secondary	$70.00
(169)	88		UPP	55.00		FLW	Secondary	67.50
	89		UPP	67.50		B&A	Primary	67.50
	90		OPEN	67.50		FLM	Primary	67.50

YOU HAVE TOUCHED SO MANY HEARTS   Musical   TUNE: Everybody Loves Somebody

112577	88	Girl with Hearts	UPP	$50.00	6.50"	CED	Secondary	$60.00
(161)	88		UPP	50.00		FLW	Primary	55.00
	89		UPP	55.00		B&A	Primary	55.00
	90		OPEN	55.00		FLM	Primary	55.00

TO MY FOREVER FRIEND   Ornament

113956	88	Girls with Flower Baskets	UPP	$16.00	3.00"	FLW	Secondary	$25.00
(214)	89		UPP	17.50		B&A	Secondary	17.50
	90		OPEN	17.50		FLM	Primary	17.50

SMILE ALONG THE WAY   Ornament

113964	88	Clown Doing Handstand	UPP	$15.00	3.50"	FLW	Secondary	$20.00
(330)	89		UPP	17.00		B&A	Secondary	17.00
	90		OPEN	17.00		FLM	Primary	17.00

GOD SENT YOU JUST IN TIME   Ornament

113972	88	Clown with Jack-in-the-Box	UPP	$13.50	3.00"	FLW	Secondary	$18.00
(256)	89		UPP	15.00		B&A	Primary	15.00
	90		OPEN	15.00		FLM	Primary	15.00

REJOICE O EARTH   Ornament

113980	88	Angel with Trumpet	UPP	$13.50	3.00"	FLW	Secondary	$18.00
(67)	89		UPP	15.00		B&A	Primary	15.00
	90		OPEN	15.00		FLM	Primary	15.00

CHEERS TO THE LEADER   Ornament

113999	88	Cheerleader	UPP	$13.50	3.00"	FLW	Secondary	$18.00
(345)	89		UPP	15.00		B&A	Primary	15.00
	90		OPEN	15.00		FLM	Primary	15.00

MY LOVE WILL NEVER LET YOU GO   Ornament

114006	88	Fisherman	UPP	$13.50	3.25"	FLW	Secondary	$18.00
(333)	89		UPP	15.00		B&A	Primary	15.00
	90		OPEN	15.00		FLM	Primary	15.00

THIS TOO SHALL PASS   Figurine

114014	88	Boy with Broken Heart	UPP	$23.00	5.50"	CED	Secondary	$30.00
(391)	88		UPP	23.00		FLW	Secondary	25.00
	89		UPP	25.00		B&A	Primary	25.00
	90		OPEN	25.00		FLM	Primary	25.00

THE GOOD LORD BLESSED US TENFOLD   Figurine

114022	88	Couple with Dogs	Annual	$90.00	5.75"	CED	Secondary	$100.00
(392)	88	and Puppies		90.00		FLW	Secondary	90.00

[NOTE: Special Tenth Anniversary Commemorative Edition.]

YOU ARE MY MAIN EVENT   Figurine   Special Events Piece   *See "Nobody's Perfect!" Section

115231	88	Girl Holding Balloons	Annual	$30.00	6.50"	CED*	Secondary	$70.00
(397)	88	and Bag		30.00		FLW	Secondary	45.00

SOME BUNNY'S SLEEPING   Figurines   Nativity Addition

115274	88	Bunnies	UPP	$15.00	2.75"	FLW	Secondary	$20.00
(431)	89		UPP	17.00		B&A	Primary	17.00
	90		OPEN	17.00		FLM	Primary	17.00

BABY'S FIRST CHRISTMAS   Ornament, Dated

115282	88	Boy in Sleigh	Annual	$15.00	2.25"	FLW	Secondary	$20.00
(432)								

OUR FIRST CHRISTMAS TOGETHER   Figurine
115290	88	Couple with Gifts	UPP	$50.00	5.50"	FLW	Secondary	$55.00
(433)	89		UPP	55.00		B&A	Primary	55.00
	90		OPEN	55.00		FLM	Primary	55.00

TIME TO WISH YOU A MERRY CHRISTMAS   Bell, Dated
115304	88	Girl Holding Clock with	Annual	$25.00	6.00"	FLW	Secondary	$40.00
(434)		Mouse						

TIME TO WISH YOU A MERRY CHRISTMAS   Thimble, Dated
115312	88	Girl with Clock and Mouse	Annual	$7.00	2.00"	FLW	Secondary	$20.00
(434)								

TIME TO WISH YOU A MERRY CHRISTMAS   Ornament, Dated
115320	88	Girl with Clock and Mouse	Annual	$13.00	3.00"	FLW	Secondary	$50.00
(434)								

TIME TO WISH YOU A MERRY CHRISTMAS   Figurine, Dated
115339	88	Girl Holding Clock with	Annual	$24.00	5.00"	FLW	Secondary	$35.00
(434)		Mouse						

BLESSED ARE THEY THAT OVERCOME   Figurine   Special Easter Seal Piece
115479	88	Boy On Crutches at Finish	Annual	$27.50	5.50"	CED	Secondary	$35.00
(396)	88	Line		27.50		FLW	Primary	35.00

[NOTE: Easter Seal Lily missing on all decals.]

THE VOICE OF SPRING   Musical Jack-in-the-Box   "The Four Seasons" Series   TUNE: April Love
408735	90	The Voice of Spring	2yr	$200.00	13.00"	FLM	Primary	$200.00
(226)								

SUMMER'S JOY   Musical Jack-in-the-Box   "The Four Seasons" Series   TUNE: You Are My Sunshine
408743	90	Summer's Joy	2yr	$200.00	13.00"	FLM	Primary	$200.00
(227)								

AUTUMN'S PRAISE   Musical Jack-in-the-Box   "The Four Seasons" Series   TUNE: Autumn Leaves
408751	90	Autumn's Praise	2yr	$200.00	13.00"	FLM	Primary	$200.00
(228)								

WINTER'S SONG   Musical Jack-in-the-Box   "The Four Seasons" Series   TUNE: Through The Eyes Of Love
408778	90	Winter's Son	2yr	$200.00	13.00"	FLM	Primary	$200.00
(229)								

THE VOICE OF SPRING   Doll   "The Four Seasons" Series
408786	90	The Voice of Spring	2yr	$150.00	15.00"	FLM	Primary	$150.00
(226)								

SUMMER'S JOY   Doll   "The Four Seasons" Series
408794	90	Summer's Joy	2yr	$150.00	15.00"	FLM	Primary	$150.00
(227)								

AUTUMN'S PRAISE   Doll   "The Four Seasons" Series
408808	90	Autumn's Praise	2yr	$150.00	15.00"	FLM	Primary	$150.00
(228)								

WINTER'S SONG   Doll   "The Four Seasons" Series
408816	90	Winter's Song	2yr	$150.00	15.00"	FLM	Primary	$150.00
(229)								

OUR FIRST CHRISTMAS TOGETHER   Ornament, Dated
520233	88	Boy and Girl in Package	Annual	$13.00	2.50"	FLW	Secondary	$15.00
(277)								

BABY'S FIRST CHRISTMAS   Ornament, Dated
520241 88 Girl in Sleigh   Annual $15.00 2.25" FLW   Secondary $25.00
(435)

REJOICE O EARTH   Figurine   Mini Nativity Addition
520268 88 Angel with Trumpet   UPP $13.00 3.00" FLW   Secondary $18.00
(67)   89   UPP   15.00   B&A   Primary   15.00
         90   OPEN   15.00   FLM   Primary   15.00

YOU ARE MY GIFT COME TRUE   Ornament, Dated
520276 88 Puppy in Sock   Annual $12.50 2.50" FLW   Secondary $30.00
(436)   [NOTE: Special 10th Anniversary Commemorative Piece.]

MERRY CHRISTMAS, DEER   Plate, Dated   Third Issue "Christmas Love" Series
520284 88 Girl Decorating Reindeer   Annual $50.00 8.25" FLW   Secondary $70.00
(438)

HANG ON FOR THE HOLLY DAYS   Ornament, Dated   Birthday Collection
520292 88 Kitten Hanging on to   Annual $13.00 3.50" FLW   Secondary $30.00
('400)   Wreath

MAKE A JOYFUL NOISE   Figurine   Easter Seal Raffle Piece   Individually Numbered
520322 89 Girl with Goose   1,500 $500.00 9.00" B&A   Secondary$1000.00
(5)

JESUS THE SAVIOR IS BORN   Figurine
520357 88 Angel with Newspaper   UPP $25.00 4.50" FLW   Secondary $30.00
(437)   89   and Dog   UPP   30.00   B&A   Primary   30.00
         90   OPEN   30.00   FLM   Primary   30.00

CHRISTMAS IS RUFF WITHOUT YOU   Ornament, Dated   Birthday Collection
520462 89 Puppy Resting on Elbow   Annual $13.00 2.75" B&A   Secondary $30.00
(470)

WISHING YOU A PURR-FECT HOLIDAY   Ornament, Dated   Birthday Collection
520497 90 Kitten with Ornament   Annual $15.00 2.75" FLM   Primary $15.00
(521)

LORD, TURN MY LIFE AROUND   Figurine
520551 90 Ballerina   UPP $35.00 5.75" B&A   Secondary $45.00
(493)   90   OPEN   35.00   FLM   Primary   35.00

MY HEART IS EXPOSED WITH LOVE   Figurine
520624 89 Nurse X-raying Boy's Heart   UPP $45.00 5.25" FLW   Secondary $50.00
(458)   89   UPP   45.00   B&A   Primary   45.00
         90   OPEN   45.00   FLM   Primary   45.00

A FRIEND IS SOMEONE WHO CARES   Figurine
520632 89 Mouse Wiping   UPP $30.00 4.25" FLW   Secondary $35.00
(449)   89   Clown's Tears   UPP   30.00   B&A   Primary   30.00
         90   OPEN   30.00   FLM   Primary   30.00

I'M SO GLAD YOU FLUTTERED INTO MY LIFE   Figurine
520640 89 Angel with Butterfly Net   UPP $40.00 5.75" FLW   Secondary $75.00
(447)   89   UPP   40.00   B&A   Primary   40.00
         90   OPEN   40.00   FLM   Primary   40.00

EGGSPECIALLY FOR YOU   Figurine
520667 89 Girl with Hen & Easter Egg   UPP $45.00 4.75" FLW   Secondary $50.00
(455)   89   UPP   45.00   B&A   Primary   45.00
         90   OPEN   45.00   FLM   Primary   45.00

YOUR LOVE IS SO UPLIFTING   Figurine

520675	89	Boy Holding Girl at Fountain	UPP	$60.00	6.50"	FLW	Secondary	$70.00
(454)	89		UPP	60.00		B&A	Primary	60.00
	90		OPEN	60.00		FLM	Primary	60.00

SENDING YOU SHOWERS OF BLESSINGS   Figurine

520683	89	Boy with Newspaper	UPP	$32.50	5.50"	FLW	Secondary	$35.00
(450)	89	over Head	UPP	32.50		B&A	Primary	32.50
	90		OPEN	32.50		FLM	Primary	32.50

BABY'S FIRST PET   Figurine   Fifth Issue "Baby's First" Series

520705	89	Boy with Baby Feeding Dog	UPP	$45.00	5.25"	FLW	Secondary	$50.00
(461)	89		UPP	45.00		B&A	Primary	45.00
	90		OPEN	45.00		FLM	Primary	45.00

JUST A LINE TO WISH YOU A HAPPY DAY   Figurine

520721	89	Dog Pulling Boy's	UPP	$65.00	6.50"	FLW	Secondary	$70.00
(456)	89	Fishing Line	UPP	65.00		B&A	Primary	65.00
	90		OPEN	65.00		FLM	Primary	65.00

FRIENDSHIP HITS THE SPOT   Figurine

520748	89	Two Girls Having Tea	UPP	$55.00	5.25"	FLW	Secondary	$60.00
(453)	89		UPP	55.00		B&A	Primary	55.00
	90		OPEN	55.00		FLM	Primary	55.00

JESUS IS THE ONLY WAY   Figurine

520756	89	Boy at Crossroads	UPP	$40.00	6.00"	FLW	Secondary	$45.00
(464)	89		UPP	40.00		B&A	Primary	40.00
	90		OPEN	40.00		FLM	Primary	40.00

PUPPY LOVE   Figurine

520764	89	Two Puppies	UPP	$12.50	2.10"	FLW	Secondary	$15.00
(465)	89		UPP	12.50		B&A	Primary	12.50
	90		OPEN	12.50		FLM	Primary	12.50

MANY MOONS IN SAME CANOE, BLESSUM YOU   Figurine

520772	89	Indians in Canoe	UPP	$50.00	5.00"	FLW	Secondary	$60.00
(457)	89		UPP	50.00		B&A	Primary	50.00
	90		OPEN	50.00		FLM	Primary	50.00

WISHING YOU ROADS OF HAPPINESS   Figurine

520780	89	Bride & Groom in Car	UPP	$60.00	4.50"	FLW	Secondary	$65.00
(460)	89		UPP	60.00		B&A	Primary	60.00
	90		OPEN	60.00		FLM	Primary	60.00

SOMEDAY MY LOVE   Figurine

520799	89	Bride with Dress	UPP	$40.00	5.50"	FLW	Secondary	$45.00
(446)	89		UPP	40.00		B&A	Primary	40.00
	90		OPEN	40.00		FLM	Primary	40.00

MY DAYS ARE BLUE WITHOUT YOU   Figurine   See "Nobody's Perfect!" Section

520802	89	Girl with Paint & Ladder	UPP	$65.00	7.00"	FLW	Secondary	$70.00
(462)	89		UPP	65.00		B&A	Primary	65.00
	90		OPEN	65.00		FLM	Primary	65.00

WE NEED A GOOD FRIEND THROUGH THE RUFF TIMES   Figurine

520810	89	Grandpa with Cane & Dog	UPP	$35.00	5.00"	FLW	Secondary	$40.00
(452)	89		UPP	35.00		B&A	Primary	35.00
	90		OPEN	35.00		FLM	Primary	35.00

YOU ARE MY NUMBER ONE   Figurine

520829	89	Girl Holding Trophy	UPP	$25.00	6.00"	FLW	Secondary	$25.00
(448)	89		UPP	25.00		B&A	Primary	25.00
	90		OPEN	25.00		FLM	Primary	25.00

THE LORD IS YOUR LIGHT TO HAPPINESS — Figurine
520837	89	Bridal Couple Lighting	UPP	$50.00	4.75"	FLW	Secondary	$50.00
(466)	89	Candle	UPP	50.00		B&A	Primary	50.00
	90		OPEN	50.00		FLM	Primary	50.00

WISHING YOU A PERFECT CHOICE — Figurine
520845	89	Boy Proposing to Girl	UPP	$55.00	5.80"	FLW	Secondary	$55.00
(459)	89		UPP	55.00		B&A	Primary	55.00
	90		OPEN	55.00		FLM	Primary	55.00

I BELONG TO THE LORD — Figurine
520853	89	Orphan Girl	UPP	$25.00	5.10"	FLW	Primary	$25.00
(463)	89		UPP	25.00		B&A	Primary	25.00
	90		OPEN	25.00		FLM	Primary	25.00

SHARING BEGINS IN THE HEART — Figurine — Special Events Piece
520861	89	Girl with Chalkboard	Annual	$25.00	5.75"	FLW	Secondary	$70.00
(467)	89			25.00		B&A	Secondary	30.00

HEAVEN BLESS YOU — Figurine
520934	90	Baby with Bunny and	OPEN	$35.00	3.50"	FLM	Primary	$35.00
(221)		Turtle						

TO MY FAVORITE FAN — Figurine — Birthday Collection
521043	90	Gorilla and Parrot	UPP	$16.00	2.50"	B&A	Secondary	$40.00
(501)	90		OPEN	16.00		FLM	Primary	16.00

HELLO WORLD! — Figurine — Birthday Collection
521175	89	Kangaroo with Baby	UPP	$13.50	3.25"	FLW	Secondary	$18.00
(451)	89		UPP	13.50		B&A	Primary	13.50
	90		OPEN	13.50		FLM	Primary	13.50

THAT'S WHAT FRIENDS ARE FOR — Figurine
521183	90	Crying Girls Hugging	OPEN	$45.00	6.00"	FLM	Primary	$45.00
(520)								

HOPE YOU'RE ON THE TRAIL AGAIN — Figurine
521205	90	Girl on Hobby Horse	UPP	$35.00	5.50"	B&A	Primary	$35.00
(494)	90		OPEN	35.00		FLM	Primary	35.00

HAPPY TRIP — Figurine
521280	90	Girl on Roller Skates	UPP	$35.00	5.75"	B&A	Secondary	$45.00
(499)	90		OPEN	35.00		FLM	Primary	35.00

MAY ALL YOUR CHRISTMASES BE WHITE — Ornament
521302	89	Girl Tying Snowball with	UPP	$13.50	3.25"	B&A	Secondary	$15.00
(477)	90	Ribbon	OPEN	13.50		FLM	Primary	13.50

YIELD NOT TO TEMPTATION — Figurine
521310	90	Girl with Apple	UPP	$27.50	5.50"	B&A	Primary	$27.50
(505)	90		OPEN	27.50		FLM	Primary	27.50

FAITH IS A VICTORY — Figurine
521396	90	Girl Wearing Boxing Gloves	UPP	$25.00	5.50"	B&A	Primary	$25.00
(496)	90		OPEN	25.00		FLM	Primary	25.00

I'LL NEVER STOP LOVING YOU — Figurine
521418	90	Girl with Letters Y O U	UPP	$37.50	5.50"	B&A	Secondary	$45.00
(511)	90		OPEN	37.50		FLM	Primary	37.50

LORD, HELP ME STICK TO MY JOB — Figurine
521450	90	Girl with Account Books	UPP	$30.00	5.75"	B&A	Secondary	$35.00
(503)	90	and Glue	OPEN	30.00		FLM	Primary	30.00

TELL IT TO JESUS   Figurine
| 521477 | 89 | Girl on Telephone | UPP | $35.00 | 5.25" | B&A | Secondary | $40.00 |
| (476) | 90 | | OPEN | 35.00 | | FLM | Primary | 35.00 |

THE LIGHT OF THE WORLD IS JESUS   Musical   TUNE: White Christmas
| 521507 | 89 | Girl by Lamppost | UPP | $60.00 | 7.00" | B&A | Primary | $60.00 |
| (475) | 90 | | OPEN | 60.00 | | FLM | Primary | 60.00 |

OUR FIRST CHRISTMAS TOGETHER   Ornament, Dated
| 521558 | 89 | Bride and Groom in Car | Annual | $17.50 | 2.75" | B&A | Secondary | $25.00 |
| (460) | | | | | | | | |

GLIDE THROUGH THE HOLIDAYS   Ornament
| 521566 | 90 | Girl on Roller Skates | OPEN | $13.50 | 3.50" | FLM | Primary | $13.50 |
| (499) | | | | | | | | |

DASHING THROUGH THE SNOW   Ornament
| 521574 | 90 | Girl Pushing Doll in Sled | OPEN | $15.00 | 3.00" | FLM | Primary | $15.00 |
| (367) | | | | | | | | |

DON'T LET THE HOLIDAYS GET YOU DOWN   Ornament
| 521590 | 90 | Boy with Christmas Tree | OPEN | $15.00 | 2.25" | FLM | Primary | $15.00 |
| (471) | | | | | | | | |

SWEEP ALL YOUR WORRIES AWAY   Figurine
| 521779 | 90 | Girl Sweeping Dust Under | OPEN | $40.00 | 5.25" | FLM | Primary | $40.00 |
| (502) | | Rug | | | | | | |

GOOD FRIENDS ARE FOREVER   Figurine
| 521817 | 90 | Girls with Flower | UPP | $50.00 | 5.50" | B&A | Primary | $50.00 |
| (492) | 90 | | OPEN | 50.00 | | FLM | Primary | 50.00 |

LOVE IS FROM ABOVE   Figurine
| 521841 | 90 | Boy Whispering to Girl | UPP | $45.00 | 5.50" | B&A | Primary | $45.00 |
| (510) | 90 | | OPEN | 45.00 | | FLM | Primary | 45.00 |

THE GREATEST OF THESE IS LOVE   Figurine
| 521868 | 89 | Angel Holding | UPP | $27.50 | 5.25" | B&A | Primary | $27.50 |
| (483) | 90 | Commandments | OPEN | 27.50 | | FLM | Primary | 27.50 |

EASTER'S ON ITS WAY   Figurine
| 521892 | 90 | Boy Pulling Girl and Lily | UPP | $60.00 | 5.25" | B&A | Primary | $60.00 |
| (508) | 90 | in Wagon | OPEN | 60.00 | | FLM | Primary | 60.00 |

WISHING YOU A COZY SEASON   Figurine
| 521949 | 89 | Boy by Stump | UPP | $42.50 | 5.25" | B&A | Secondary | $50.00 |
| (480) | 90 | | OPEN | 42.50 | | FLM | Primary | 42.50 |

[NOTE: All B&A marks have SWeet decal error inside stump.]

HIGH HOPES   Figurine
| 521957 | 90 | Boy with Kite | UPP | $30.00 | 5.25" | B&A | Primary | $30.00 |
| (498) | 90 | | OPEN | 30.00 | | FLM | Primary | 30.00 |

MAY YOUR LIFE BE BLESSED WITH TOUCHDOWNS   Figurine
| 522023 | 89 | Boy Playing Football | UPP | $45.00 | 4.25" | B&A | Primary | $45.00 |
| (473) | 90 | | OPEN | 45.00 | | FLM | Primary | 45.00 |

THANK YOU LORD FOR EVERYTHING   Figurine
| 522031 | 89 | Boy Having Dinner | UPP | $55.00 | 5.25" | B&A | Primary | $55.00 |
| (472) | | with Turkey | OPEN | 55.00 | | FLM | Primary | 55.00 |

THERE SHALL BE SHOWERS OF BLESSINGS   Figurine
| 522090 | 90 | Boy and Girl in Garden | UPP | $60.00 | 5.50" | B&A | Secondary | $65.00 |
| (500) | 90 | | OPEN | 60.00 | | FLM | Primary | 60.00 |

DON'T LET THE HOLIDAYS GET YOU DOWN   Figurine
522112	89	Boy with Christmas Tree	UPP	$42.50	4.25"	B&A	Secondary	$45.00
(471)	90		OPEN	42.50		FLM	Primary	42.50

WISHING YOU A VERY SUCCESSFUL SEASON   Figurine
522120	89	Boy with Box, Puppy & Bat	UPP	$60.00	6.00"	B&A	Primary	$60.00
(478)	90		OPEN	60.00		FLM	Primary	60.00

BON VOYAGE!   Figurine
522201	89	Boy & Girl on Motorcycle	UPP	$75.00	6.50"	B&A	Primary	$75.00
(474)	90		OPEN	75.00		FLM	Primary	75.00

HE IS THE STAR OF THE MORNING   Figurine
522252	89	Angel on Cloud	UPP	$55.00	6.00"	B&A	Primary	$55.00
(481)	90	with Manger	OPEN	55.00		FLM	Primary	55.00

TO BE WITH YOU IS UPLIFTING   Figurine
522260	89	Giraffe with Baby Bear	UPP	$20.00	4.25"	B&A	Primary	$20.00
(484)	90		OPEN	20.00		FLM	Primary	20.00

THINKING OF YOU IS WHAT I REALLY LIKE TO DO   Figurine
522287	90	Kneeling Girl with Bouquet	UPP	$30.00	4.50"	B&A	Primary	$30.00
(504)	90		OPEN	30.00		FLM	Primary	30.00

MERRY CHRISTMAS, DEER   Figurine
522317	89	Girl Decorating Reindeer	UPP	$50.00	5.50"	B&A	Secondary	$55.00
(438)	90		OPEN	50.00		FLM	Primary	50.00

HIS LOVE WILL SHINE ON YOU   Figurine   Special Easter Seal Piece   Easter Seal Lily on Decal
522376	89	Girl Holding Easter Lily	Annual	$30.00	5.75"	FLW	Secondary	$35.00
(443)	89			30.00		B&A	Secondary	35.00

OH HOLY NIGHT   Figurine, Dated
522546	89	Girl Playing Violin	Annual	$25.00	4.75"	B&A	Secondary	$30.00
(482)								

OH HOLY NIGHT   Thimble, Dated
522554	89	Girl Playing Violin	Annual	$7.50	2.25"	B&A	Secondary	$15.00
(482)								

OH HOLY NIGHT   Bell, Dated
522821	89	Girl Playing Violin	Annual	$25.00	5.50"	B&A	Secondary	$25.00
(482)								

OH HOLY NIGHT   Ornament, Dated
522848	89	Girl Playing Violin	Annual	$13.50	3.25"	B&A	Secondary	$35.00
(482)								

HAVE A BEARY MERRY CHRISTMAS   Figurine   "Family Christmas Scene" Series
522856	89	Teddy in Rocker	UPP	$15.00	3.75"	B&A	Primary	$15.00
(469)	90		OPEN	15.00		FLM	Primary	15.00

MAKE A JOYFUL NOISE   Ornament
522910	89	Girl with Goose	UPP	$15.00	3.25"	B&A	Secondary	$20.00
(5)	90		OPEN	15.00		FLM	Primary	15.00

LOVE ONE ANOTHER   Ornament
522929	89	Boy & Girl on Stump	UPP	$17.50	3.50"	B&A	Secondary	$20.00
(8)	90		OPEN	17.50		FLM	Primary	17.50

FRIENDS NEVER DRIFT APART   Ornament
522937	90	Kids in Boat	OPEN	$17.50	2.50"	FLM	Primary	$17.50
(219)								

I BELIEVE IN THE OLD RUGGED CROSS   Ornament
522953 89   Girl with Cross   UPP $15.00 3.50"   B&A   Primary $15.00
(224)   90   OPEN 15.00   FLM   Primary   15.00

ISN'T HE PRECIOUS   Figurine   Mini Nativity Addition
522988 89   Girl with Broom   UPP $15.00 3.75"   B&A   Primary $15.00
(189)   90   OPEN 15.00   FLM   Primary   15.00

SOME BUNNIES SLEEPING   Figurine   Mini Nativity Addition
522996 90   Bunnies   OPEN $12.00 1.75"   FLM   Primary $12.00
(431)

MAY YOUR CHRISTMAS BE A HAPPY HOME   Plate, Dated   Fourth Issue "Christmas Love" Series
523003 89   Family Christmas Scene   Annual $50.00 8.50"   B&A   Secondary $60.00
(479)

THERE'S A CHRISTIAN WELCOME HERE   *See "Nobody's Perfect!" Section
523011 89   Angel outside Chapel   OPEN $45.00 4.00"   UM*   Primary $45.00
(491)

PEACE ON EARTH   Ornament, Dated   First Issue "Masterpiece Ornaments" Series
523062 89   Children by Lamppost   Annual $25.00 4.25"   B&A   Secondary $75.00
(341)

JESUS IS THE SWEETEST NAME I KNOW   Figurine   Nativity Addition
523097 89   Angel with Baby   UPP $22.50 4.75"   B&A   Primary $22.50
(468)   90   Name Book   OPEN 22.50   FLM   Primary   22.50

BABY'S FIRST CHRISTMAS   Ornament, Dated
523194 89   Boy in Sleigh   Annual $15.00 2.50"   B&A   Secondary $20.00
(432)

BABY'S FIRST CHRISTMAS   Ornament, Dated
523208 89   Girl in Sleigh   Annual $15.00 2.50"   B&A   Secondary $20.00
(435)

YOU HAVE TOUCHED SO MANY HEARTS   Figurine   Easter Seal Raffle Piece   Individually Numbered
523283 90   Girl with Hearts   2,000 $500.00 9.00"   B&A   Secondary $600.00
(161)

THE GOOD LORD ALWAYS DELIVERS   Figurine
523453 90   Mother-to-Be with Baby   UPP $27.50 5.50"   B&A   Primary $27.50
(497)   90   Book   OPEN 27.50   FLM   Primary   27.50

THIS DAY HAS BEEN MADE IN HEAVEN   Figurine
523496 90   Girl Holding Bible and   UPP $30.00 5.50"   B&A   Primary $30.00
(506)   90   Cross   OPEN 30.00   FLM   Primary   30.00

GOD IS LOVE DEAR VALENTINE   Figurine
523518 90   Girl Hiding Valentine behind   UPP $27.50   B&A   Primary $30.00
(509)   90   Her Back   OPEN 27.50   FLM   Primary   30.00

I'M A PRECIOUS MOMENTS FAN   Figurine   Special Events Piece
523526 90   Girl with Fan   Annual $30.00   B&A   Primary $30.00
(490)   90   30.00   FLM   Primary   30.00

MAY YOUR CHRISTMAS BE A HAPPY HOME   Ornament, Dated
                                      Second Issue "Masterpiece Ornament" Series
523704 90   Family Christmas Scene   Annual $27.50 4.50"   FLM   Primary $27.50
(479)

TIME HEALS   Figurine
523739 90   Nurse at Desk with Clock   OPEN $37.50 5.50"   FLM   Primary $37.50
(518)

BLESSINGS FROM ABOVE   Figurine
523747   90   Boy and Girl Kissing under   OPEN $45.00   6.50"   FLM   Primary $45.00
(495)   Mistletoe

BABY'S FIRST CHRISTMAS   Ornament, Dated
523771   90   Baby Girl with Pie   Annual $15.00   2.75"   FLM   Primary $15.00
(516)

BABY'S FIRST CHRISTMAS   Ornament, Dated
523798   90   Baby Boy with Pie   Annual $15.00   2.75"   FLM   Primary $15.00
(517)

WISHING YOU A YUMMY CHRISTMAS   Plate, Dated   First Issue "Christmas Blessings" Series
523801   90   Boy and Girl at Ice Cream   Annual $50.00   8.25"   FLM   Primary $50.00
(358)   Stand

ONCE UPON A HOLY NIGHT   Bell, Dated
523828   90   Girl with Book and Candle   Annual $25.00   5.75"   FLM   Primary $25.00
(519)

ONCE UPON A HOLY NIGHT   Figurine, Dated
523836   90   Girl with Book and Candle   Annual $25.00   5.50"   FLM   Primary $25.00
(519)

ONCE UPON A HOLY NIGHT   Thimble, Dated
523844   90   Girl with Book and Candle   Annual $8.00   1.50"   FLM   Primary $8.00
(519)

ONCE UPON A HOLY NIGHT   Ornament, Dated
523852   90   Girl with Book and Candle   Annual $15.00   3.25"   FLM   Primary $15.00
(519)

NOT A CREATURE WAS STIRRING   Figurine   Set of 2
524484   90   Mouse on Cheese and Kitten   OPEN $17.00   2.75"   FLM   Primary $17.00
(514)

ALWAYS IN HIS CARE   Figurine   Special Easter Seal Piece   Easter Seal Lily on Decal
524522   90   Girl Looking at Sleeping   Annual $30.00   5.00"   B&A   Primary $30.00
(507)   90   Chick in Egg   30.00   FLM   Primary   30.00

HAPPY BIRTHDAY DEAR JESUS   Figurine   Nativity Addition
524875   90   Teddy Bear in Package   OPEN $13.50   2.25"   FLM   Primary $13.50
(513)

CHRISTMAS FIREPLACE   Figurine   "Family Christmas Scene" Series
524883   90   Fireplace with Stockings   OPEN $37.50   4.50"   FLM   Primary $37.50
(512)

WE'RE GOING TO MISS YOU   Figurine
524913   90   Girl and Melting Snowman   OPEN $50.00   5.50"   FLM   Primary $50.00
(515)

GOOD FRIENDS ARE FOREVER   Figurine   Special Events Piece   Special Rosebud Decal Understamp
525049   90   Girls with Flower   Annual   5.50"   B&A   Primary   *
(492)
            * Very desirable, one per Center for 1990 Events.

OUR FIRST CHRISTMAS TOGETHER   Ornament, Dated
525324   90   Bride and Groom in Car   Annual $17.50   2.50"   FLM   Primary $17.50
(460)

THE ENESCO PRECIOUS MOMENTS COLLECTORS' CLUB

SYMBOLS OF CHARTER MEMBERSHIP

BUT LOVE GOES ON FOREVER   Figurine
E-0001   81   Boy & Girl Angels   MemOnly $20.00   5.00"   NM   Secondary $175.00
(39)   on Cloud   TRI   Secondary   160.00
                                                                HRG   Secondary   160.00

BUT LOVE GOES ON FOREVER   Plaque
E-0102   82   Boy & Girl Angels   MemOnly $15.00   5.00"   TRI   Secondary $80.00
(39)   on Cloud   HRG   Secondary   75.00

LET US CALL THE CLUB TO ORDER   Figurine
E-0103   83   Club Meeting   MemOnly $25.00   5.75"   HRG   Secondary $70.00
(158)   FSH   Secondary   65.00

JOIN IN ON THE BLESSINGS   Figurine
E-0104   84   Girl with Dues Bank   MemOnly $25.00   4.50"   HRG   Secondary $65.00
(205)   FSH   Secondary   60.00
                                                                CRS   Secondary   55.00

SEEK AND YE SHALL FIND   Figurine
E-0105   85   Girl with Shopping   MemOnly $25.00   5.25"   CRS   Secondary $50.00
(104)   Bag   DVE   Secondary   45.00

BIRDS OF A FEATHER COLLECT TOGETHER   Figurine
E-0106   86   Girl with Embroidery   MemOnly $25.00   5.75"   DVE   Secondary $50.00
(295)   Hoop and Bird   OLB   Secondary   45.00

SHARING IS UNIVERSAL   Figurine
E-0107   87   Girl Sending Package   MemOnly $25.00   5.00"   OLB   Secondary $45.00
(336)   to Friend   CED   Secondary   40.00

A GROWING LOVE   Figurine
E-0108   88   Girl with Flowerpot   MemOnly $25.00   4.50"   CED   Secondary $45.00
(399)   and Sunflower   FLW   Secondary   40.00

ALWAYS ROOM FOR ONE MORE   Figurine
C-0109   89   Girl with Puppies   MemOnly $35.00   4.50"   FLW   Secondary $40.00
(444)   in Box   B&A   Secondary   35.00

MY HAPPINESS   Figurine
C-0110   90   Girl at Table with Figurine   MemOnly $35.00   4.50"   B&A   Primary $35.00
(489)   FLM   Primary   35.00

SYMBOLS OF MEMBERSHIP

BUT LOVE GOES ON FOREVER   Plaque   See "Nobody's Perfect!" Section
E-0202   82   Boy & Girl Angels   MemOnly $15.00   5.00"   UM   Secondary $85.00
(39)   on Cloud   TRI   Secondary   70.00
                                                                HRG   Secondary   70.00

LET US CALL THE CLUB TO ORDER   Figurine
E-0303   83   Club Meeting   MemOnly $25.00   5.75"   HRG   Secondary $65.00
(158)   FSH   Secondary   60.00

JOIN IN ON THE BLESSINGS   Figurine
E-0404   84   Girl with Dues Bank   MemOnly $25.00   4.50"   HRG   Secondary $60.00
(205)   FSH   Secondary   55.00
                                                                CRS   Secondary   50.00

SEEK AND YE SHALL FIND   Figurine
E-0005   85   Girl with Shopping   MemOnly $25.00   5.25"   CRS   Secondary $45.00
(104)   Bag   DVE   Secondary   40.00

BIRDS OF A FEATHER COLLECT TOGETHER   Figurine
E-0006   86   Girl with Embroidery   MemOnly $25.00   5.75"   DVE   Secondary $45.00
(295)   Hoop and Bird   OLB   Secondary   40.00

SHARING IS UNIVERSAL   Figurine
E-0007   87   Girl Sending Package   MemOnly $25.00   5.00"   OLB   Secondary $40.00
(336)   to Friend   CED   Secondary   35.00

A GROWING LOVE   Figurine
E-0008   88   Girl with Flowerpot   MemOnly $25.00   4.50"   CED   Secondary $40.00
(399)   and Sunflower   FLW   Secondary   35.00

ALWAYS ROOM FOR ONE MORE   Figurine
C-0009   89   Girl with Puppies   MemOnly $35.00   4.50"   FLW   Secondary $35.00
(444)   in Box   B&A   Secondary   35.00

MY HAPPINESS   Figurine
C-0010   90   Girl at Table with Figurine   MemOnly $35.00   4.50"   B&A   Primary $35.00
(489)   FLM   Primary   35.00

MEMBERSHIP PIECES

HELLO LORD, IT'S ME AGAIN   Figurine
PM-811   81   Boy on Telephone   MemOnly $25.00   4.75"   TRI   Secondary $435.00
(78)   HRG   Secondary   425.00

SMILE, GOD LOVES YOU   Figurine
PM-821   82   Girl with Curlers   MemOnly $25.00   5.25"   HRG   Secondary $250.00
(117)   FSH   Secondary   240.00

PUT ON A HAPPY FACE   Figurine
PM-822   83   Boy Clown Holding   MemOnly $25.00   5.50"   HRG   Secondary $195.00
(159)   Mask   FSH   Secondary   185.00
                                                                                              CRS   Secondary   180.00

DAWN'S EARLY LIGHT   Figurine
PM-831   83   Girl Covering Kitten   MemOnly $25.00   4.50"   FSH   Secondary $90.00
(160)   CRS   Secondary   85.00

GOD'S RAY OF MERCY   Figurine
PM-841   84   Boy Angel with   MemOnly $25.00   4.75"   FSH   Secondary $75.00
(206)   Flashlight   CRS   Secondary   60.00
                                                                                              DVE   Secondary   60.00

TRUST IN THE LORD TO THE FINISH   Figurine
PM-842   84   Boy with Racing Cup   MemOnly $25.00   5.50"   CRS   Secondary $75.00
(207)   DVE   Secondary   70.00

THE LORD IS MY SHEPHERD   Figurine
PM-851   85   Girl Holding Lamb   MemOnly $25.00   5.50"   DVE   Secondary $80.00
(293)   OLB   Secondary   75.00

I LOVE TO TELL THE STORY   Figurine
PM-852   85   Boy with Lamb   MemOnly $27.50   3.50"   DVE   Secondary $70.00
(294)   and Book   OLB   Secondary   65.00

GOD BLESS OUR YEARS TOGETHER   Figurine
12440   85   5th Anniversary Piece   MemOnly $175.00   5.50"   DVE   Secondary $245.00
(249)

GRANDMA'S PRAYER   Figurine
PM-861   86   Praying Grandma   MemOnly $25.00   4.50"   DVE   Secondary $90.00
(305)   OLB   Secondary   85.00
                                                                                              CED   Secondary   80.00

<u>I'M FOLLOWING JESUS</u>   Figurine
PM-862   86   Boy in Car   MemOnly $25.00   4.25"   OLB   Secondary $95.00
(320)   CED   Secondary   90.00

<u>FEED MY SHEEP</u>   Figurine
PM-871   87   Girl Feeding Lamb   MemOnly $25.00   4.75"   CED   Secondary $60.00
(366)   FLW   Secondary   55.00

<u>IN HIS TIME</u>   Figurine
PM-872   87   Boy Waiting for   MemOnly $25.00   4.10"   CED   Secondary $50.00
(375)   Seed to Grow   FLW   Secondary   45.00

<u>LOVING YOU DEAR VALENTINE</u>   Figurine
PM-873   87   Boy Painting   MemOnly $25.00   5.50"   OLB   Secondary $35.00
(321)   Valentine   FLW   Secondary   35.00

<u>LOVING YOU DEAR VALENTINE</u>   Figurine
PM-874   87   Girl Drawing   MemOnly $25.00   5.25"   OLB   Secondary $35.00
(322)   Valentine   FLW   Secondary   35.00

<u>GOD BLESS YOU FOR TOUCHING MY LIFE</u>   Figurine
PM-881   88   Girl Painting Butterfly   MemOnly $27.50   4.75"   CED   Secondary $50.00
(439)   FLW   Secondary   45.00

<u>YOU JUST CANNOT CHUCK A GOOD FRIENDSHIP</u>   Figurine
PM-882   88   Boy Rescuing Puppy   MemOnly $27.50   5.00"   FLW   Secondary $45.00
(442)   from Trash Can   B&A   Secondary   40.00

<u>YOU WILL ALWAYS BE MY CHOICE</u>   Figurine
PM-891   89   Girl with Ballot Box   MemOnly $27.50   4.75"   B&A   Secondary $35.00
(485)

<u>MOW POWER TO YA</u>   Figurine
PM-892   89   Boy Pushing Lawn Mower   MemOnly $27.50   4.75"   B&A   Secondary $35.00
(486)

SHARING SEASON ORNAMENTS   (Gift to Club Members for signing up new members)

<u>BIRDS OF A FEATHER COLLECT TOGETHER</u>   Ornament
PM-864   86   Girl with Embroidery   MemOnly $12.50   2.25"   OLB   Secondary $190.00
(295)   Hoop and Bird

<u>SHARING SEASON ORNAMENT</u>   Ornament
PM-009   87   Brass Filagree -   MemOnly $ 3.50   2.75"   UM   Secondary $25.00
(376)   Kids on Cloud

<u>A GROWING LOVE</u>   Ornament
520349   88   Girl with Flowerpot   MemOnly $15.00   2.80"   FLW   Secondary $110.00
(399)   and Sunflower

<u>ALWAYS ROOM FOR ONE MORE</u>   Ornament
522961   89   Girl with Puppies in Box   MemOnly $15.00   2.80"   B&A   Secondary $75.00
(444)

THE ENESCO PRECIOUS MOMENTS BIRTHDAY CLUB

SYMBOLS OF CHARTER MEMBERSHIP

OUR CLUB CAN'T BE BEAT   Figurine
B-0001   86   Clown with Drum   MemOnly $10.00   3.50"   DVE   Secondary $85.00
(304)   OLB   Secondary   80.00
                                                                      CED   Secondary   75.00

A SMILE'S THE CYMBAL OF JOY   Figurine   See "Nobody's Perfect!" Section
B-0102   87   Clown with Cymbals   MemOnly $15.00   4.50"   OLB   Secondary $60.00
(364)   CED   Secondary   55.00

THE SWEETEST CLUB AROUND   Figurine
B-0103   88   Pippin Popping out   MemOnly $15.00   4.50"   FLW   Secondary $35.00
(440)   of Cake   B&A   Secondary   30.00

HAVE A BEARY SPECIAL BIRTHDAY   Figurine
B-0104   89   Teddy Bear with Balloon MemOnly $20.00   4.50"   B&A   Secondary $20.00
(487)   FLM   Primary   20.00

SYMBOLS OF MEMBERSHIP

A SMILE'S THE CYMBAL OF JOY   Figurine   See "Nobody's Perfect!" Section
B-0002   87   Clown with Cymbals   MemOnly $15.00   4.50"   OLB   Secondary $55.00
(364)   CED   Secondary   50.00
                                                                      FLW   Secondary   50.00

THE SWEETEST CLUB AROUND   Figurine
B-0003   88   Pippin Popping Out   MemOnly $15.00   4.50"   FLW   Secondary $30.00
(440)   Of Cake   B&A   Secondary   25.00

HAVE A BEARY SPECIAL BIRTHDAY   Figurine
B-0004   89   Teddy Bear with Balloon MemOnly $20.00   4.50"   B&A   Secondary $20.00
(487)   FLM   Primary   20.00

MEMBERSHIP PIECES

FISHING FOR FRIENDS   Figurine
BC-861   86   Raccoon Holding Fish   MemOnly $10.00   2.50"   OLB   Secondary $110.00
(335)   CED   Secondary   110.00

HI SUGAR!   Figurine
BC-871   87   Mouse in Sugar   MemOnly $11.00   2.60"   CED   Secondary $80.00
(398)   Bowl   FLW   Secondary   75.00

SOMEBUNNY CARES   Figurine
BC-881   88   Bunny with Carrot   MemOnly $13.50   3.00"   FLW   Secondary $45.00
(441)   B&A   Secondary   45.00

CAN'T BEE HIVE MYSELF WITHOUT YOU   Figurine
BC-891   89   Teddy Bear with Bee   MemOnly $13.50   2.50"   B&A   Primary $13.50
(488)   and Bee Hive   FLM   Primary   13.50

NOTES

WE JUST WANTED YOU TO KNOW......

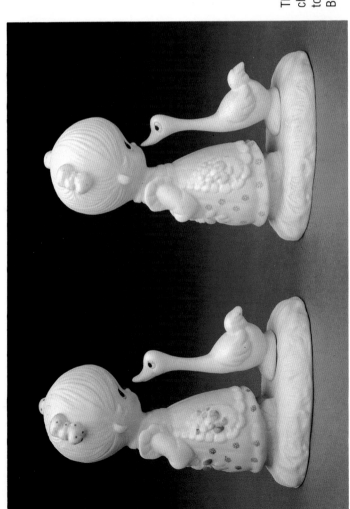

These side-by-side Goose Girls illustrate the changes in coloration from a NO MARK *(left)* to subsequent annual symbols including the BOW & ARROW *(right)*.

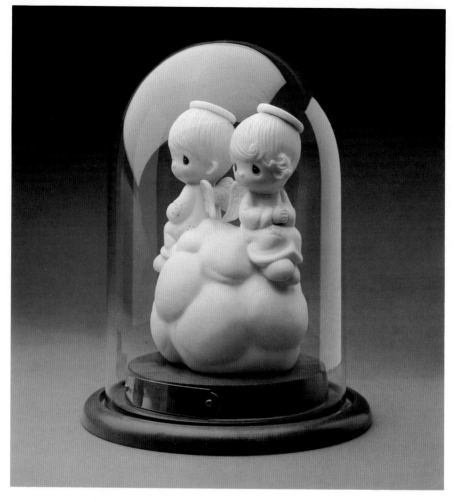

E-7350   RETAILER'S DOME
In 1984, Enesco gave a gift to PRECIOUS MOMENTS Collectors' Centers of a 6"
boy & girl on a cloud figurine, enclosed in a 9" dome, complete with an engraved
plaque bearing the Center's name. The enclosed card read:

Dear Valued Collectors' Center,
Teamwork, mutual respect, understanding and caring; these are some of the ingredients that
contribute to success. Your commitment to The Enesco PRECIOUS MOMENTS Collection
has meant a great deal to us and to the thousands of collectors, nationwide, who have taken
these very special, inspirational figurines to their hearts. We share together the burden of
responsibility and concern for our PRECIOUS MOMENTS customer/friends, and for this
dedication, we at Enesco, are most grateful. Because 1984 marks not only the 25th
anniversary of Enesco, but also the 5th anniversary of The Enesco PRECIOUS MOMENTS
Collection, we decided to commemorate these events in a special way. To that end, we have
created a unique memento for you to display proudly in your store. It is a symbol of our
sincere appreciation for your efforts and carries with it our pledge to continue to thank you,
everyday, for your confidence and support.
Sincerely, Eugene Freedman, President, Enesco Imports Corporation

103004   WE BELONG TO THE LORD

Known to collectors as "The Damien-Dutton Figurine," *We Belong To The Lord*, was
a limited piece - the edition limit unannounced. The figurine was produced by Enesco
and is the only piece to date crafted with a special <u>incised</u> symbol (DIAMOND). The
figurine was paired with a Bible, printed by Thomas Nelson Publishers, and the set
was offered to collectors by the Damien-Dutton Society for Leprosy Aid, Inc. via
direct mail. The following card was included in the front of the Bible:

Dear PRECIOUS MOMENTS Collector,
Thank you for your purchase of the PRECIOUS MOMENTS Bible and porcelain bisque figurine.
We know you'll enjoy these beautiful collectible treasures and also know that you have
contributed to the fight against leprosy throughout the world. These treasured collectibles will
grace your home and the homes of your children and grandchildren for years to come. We
pray that worldwide leprosy will be eliminated in the years ahead, and through the help of good
friends like you this dream is a possibility. That's our goal and your purchase is helping make
it a reality.
May God bless you and yours, Sincerely, Howard E. Crouch, President

196

This photo illustrates the evolution of the box. Line drawings were later added to the labels, sometime in 1983.

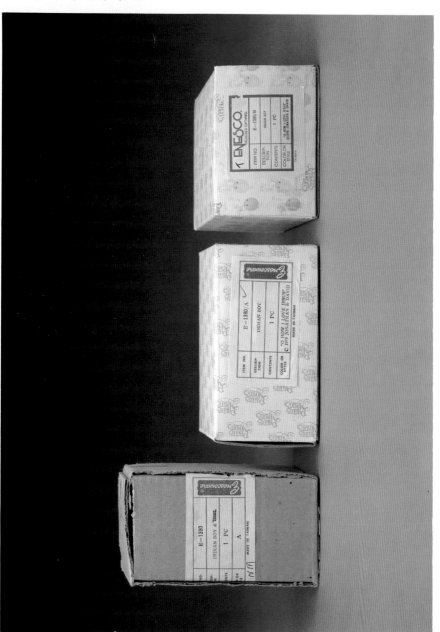

NOBODY'S PERFECT!

A GUIDE TO VARIATIONS AND PRODUCTION RARITIES

As with all things made by human hands, PRECIOUS MOMENTS collectible porcelains exist with variations. Some differences in shape and color occur naturally as a result of firing and painting. There are also pieces with variations caused by human error.

E-9268   NOBODY'S PERFECT
The first HOURGLASS pieces produced are known as "Smiling Dunces" or simply "Smiley" and appeared with a smile *(right)*. The "O" shaped mouth *(left)* is the normal piece. The GREENBOOK Market Price for "Smiley" is $475.00.

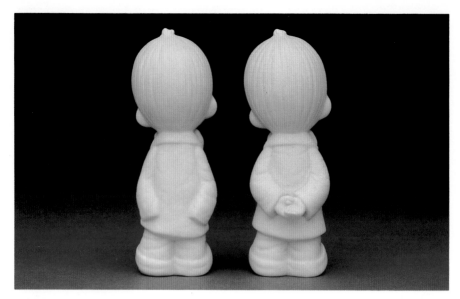

E-2837   GROOM

Termed the "No Hands Groom," during the first year of production (OLIVE BRANCH), this piece was produced with no hands. The mold was changed for the subsequent years to show the boy's hands. The GREENBOOK Market Price for the "No Hands Groom" is $45.00.

E-9261 & E-9262   SEEK YE THE LORD

All pieces with the FISH annual symbol do not have the word "he" in the incription on the graduates' scrolls capitalized. Refer to the Listings for GREENBOOK Market Prices.

E-2395   COME LET US ADORE HIM

Known as the "Turban Nativity," the shepherd holding a lamb was replaced in some HOURGLASS sets with a shepherd wearing a turban. Both of these pieces are included in the above photograph. "Turban Boy" shepherds were also shipped individually to retailers as replacement pieces, so collectors were sometimes able to add the "Turban Boy" as a twelfth piece to this eleven piece mini Nativity Set. The GREENBOOK Market Price for the "Turban Nativity" is $175.00. The GREENBOOK Market Price for the individual "Turban Boy" piece is $60.00.

111465
RETAILER'S WREATH

On some wreaths, the ornament, *Have A Heavenly Christmas*, has "Heaven Bound" upside-down (*photo*). The GREENBOOK Market Price for the wreath with the upside-down "Heaven Bound" ornament is $250.00.

111155   FAITH TAKES THE PLUNGE

At some point during the1988 production of *Faith Takes The Plunge*, the expression on the face was changed from a smile to a "determined frown." The smiling piece is often referred to as the "Smiling Plunger." GREENBOOK Market Prices are: Smiling with CEDAR annual symbol - $50.00 and Smiling with the FLOWER annual symbol - $40.00.

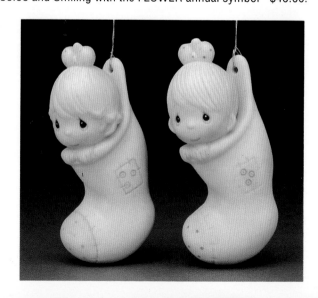

115231   YOU ARE MY MAIN EVENT
The balloon strings on this piece are metal wires covered with colored paper. The first CEDAR TREE pieces produced had pink strings - the rest of the production (balance of CEDAR TREE & FLOWER) had white strings. "Pink Strings" is the coveted piece. The GREENBOOK Market Price for "Pink Strings" is $105.00.   P.S.   Don't immerse this piece in water!

E-2362   BABY'S FIRST CHRISTMAS
UNMARKED pieces exist in four variations:
• Straight hair and no title *(right)*
• Curly hair and no title *(left)*
• Straight hair with the title, "Baby's First Christmas"
• Curly hair with the title, "Baby's First Christmas"

Subsequent pieces (CROSS through FLOWER) were curly hair with the title.

The straight hair, with or without the title, is considered the variation. The GREENBOOK Market Price for "Straight Hair" is $75.00.

E-5214   PRAYER CHANGES THINGS
Referred to as "Backwards Bible," the first production of this piece had the words
"Holy Bible" inscribed on the *back* cover. Pieces with this error exist in NO MARK and
TRIANGLE versions. Reportedly, NO MARK and TRIANGLE pieces also exist where the
title is placed correctly, but may be considered extremely rare. It is our understanding
that the original artwork for this piece was incorrect. The majority of HOURGLASS
pieces have the correctly placed title. GREENBOOK Market Prices are as follows:

	BACKWARDS	CORRECT
NM	$ 130	Very rare
TRI	120	Very rare
HRG	115	95

E-4724   REJOICING WITH YOU
Advertised as "No E" or "Bibl Error," during the first years of
production the "E" was missing from the word "Bible." It appears
as though all NO MARK, TRIANGLE, and HOURGLASS pieces have
this variation.

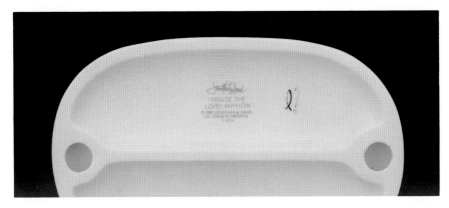

E-9254   PRAISE THE LORD ANYHOW

During 1983, it appears as though some experimentation was being done in applying annual symbols to pieces. Incision has been the standard method throughout the history of the Collection, but during 1983, the FISH appeared as part of the understamp <u>decal</u> on many pieces. During the course of the year, it also appears that pieces were produced which did not have a FISH at all - incised or decal. When this occurred on E-9254, we can only theorize an attempt was made to correct it by actually drawing the FISH on the bottom of the piece. This "inked" symbol can be washed off, creating an "Unmarked" piece. The GREENBOOK Market Price for the "erasable inked fish" is $125.00.

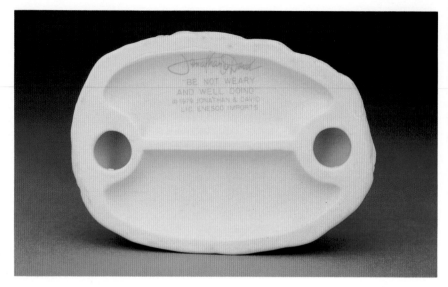

E-3111   BE NOT WEARY IN WELL DOING

Pieces exist in NO MARK versions with an error on the Inspirational Title. Instead of "Be Not Weary In Well Doing," they read "Be Not Weary **And** Well Doing." The black and white boxes in which the incorrect figurines were shipped also have the incorrect title on the label. The GREENBOOK Market Price for "...And Well Doing" is $135.00.

E-5379
ISN'T HE PRECIOUS

With the opening of a new production facility in Indonesia, numerous pieces of *Isn't He Precious* "whiteware" were inadvertently shipped to retailers.

12238
MINI CLOWNS

"CLOWNS" was misspelled
"CROWNS" on the understamp
decal of some sets . The
GREENBOOK Market Price for
the set of four with the
"CROWNS" title error is
$185.00.

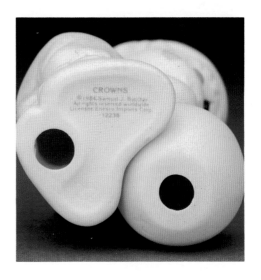

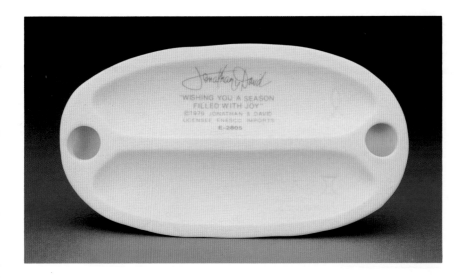

The above is an example of a "double mark." Double marks are only known to exist in
the TRIANGLE & HOURGLASS and HOURGLASS & FISH combinations.

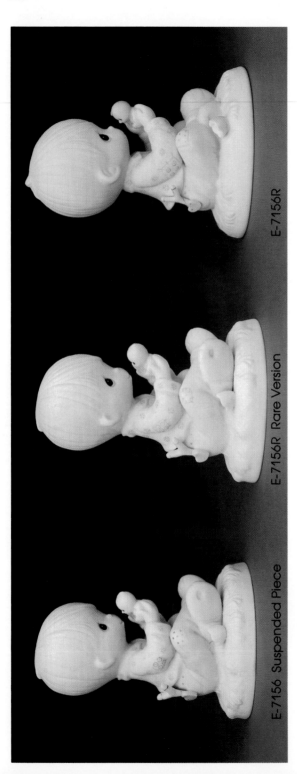

E-7156 Suspended Piece

E-7156R Rare Version

E-7156R

E-7156R   I BELIEVE IN MIRACLES

First introduced in 1982 as E-7156 *(left)*, the original version of this figurine had the boy holding a yellow chick. E-7156 was suspended in 1985, and in 1987 was re-sculpted and returned to production as E-7156R *(right)*. Among the changes made was the addition of the incised "Sam B" on the base of the figurine, and a change in the color of the chick - from yellow to blue. The re-sculpted piece is also considerably larger than the original version.

During the early part of production in 1987, the molds from the suspended piece, E-7156, were pulled and used along with the molds for the new re-introduced piece, E-7156R. Shipments of figurines crafted from the old suspended mold but with the new blue painting of the chick were made before the error was discovered *(middle)*. These pieces are the rare version (All rare versions have the CEDAR TREE annual symbol). The GREENBOOK Market Price for the rare version is $250.00.

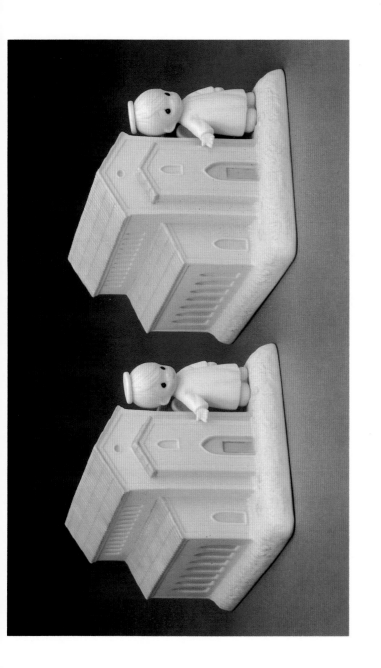

523011   THERE'S A CHRISTIAN WELCOME HERE

UNMARKED pieces of this figurine, known as the "Chapel Figurine," exist with and without an eyebrow on the angel boy (bangs cover where the second eyebrow would be). Several pieces are also in existence which are missing the wings on the angel boy. The GREENBOOK Market Price for the "Without Eyebrow" piece is $125.00.

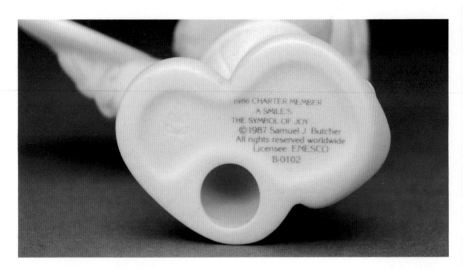

B-0102/B-0002   A SMILE'S THE CYMBAL OF JOY
The original Inspirational Title for these pieces was "A Smile's The <u>SYMBOL</u> Of Joy."
The GREENBOOK Market Price for the "Symbol Error" is $85.00.

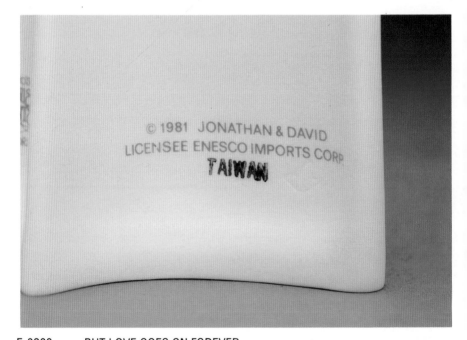

E-0202   BUT LOVE GOES ON FOREVER
Termed the "Canadian Plaque Error," approximately 750 pieces of this 1982 Symbol Of
Membership Piece were produced in 1985 and shipped to Canada. These pieces are
stamped "TAIWAN" and have the DOVE annual symbol. The GREENBOOK Market
Price for the "Canadian Plaque Error" is $160.00.

NOBODY'S PERFECT! - Pieces Not Pictured

E-1374B   PRAISE THE LORD ANYHOW
On this retired piece, the dog can be found with either a brown nose or a black nose. It has also been found with different flavors of ice cream - chocolate, strawberry or vanilla.

E-1374G   MAKE A JOYFUL NOISE
This is a favorite of collectors when the girl and the goose touch. The goose and girl are in different positions on different pieces due to shrinkage during firing.

E-1377A   HE LEADETH ME
This piece exists with the incorrect Inspirational Title -- "He Careth For You" is on the bottom of some NO MARK figurines. This is one of the most difficult to find of all the variations.

E-2013   UNTO US A CHILD IS BORN
An early issue of the GOODNEWSLETTER stated that this piece had the inscription placed on the book incorrectly - reading across both pages instead of down each page. However, it appears as though the incorrect version was never produced.

E-3117   WALKING BY FAITH
There are some pieces which do not have "Holy Bible" inscribed on the Bible.

E-5629   LET THE HEAVENS REJOICE
Some pieces are without the patch on the angel. The GREENBOOK Market Price for "No Patch" is $225.00.

E-9282   ESPECIALLY FOR EWE
The original title for this piece was "Loving Ewe."

100536   I PICKED A VERY SPECIAL MOM
The original Inspirational Title for this piece was "I Picked A Special Mom."

102903   WE ARE ALL PRECIOUS IN HIS SIGHT
Although the Fall 1987 GOODNEWSLETTER stated the Inspirational Title, "We Are All Precious In His Sight," was "missing" from the understamp on "some" figurines, to date, figurines with the title appear to be nonexistent. Because of the statement in the GOODNEWSLETTER, all who own the piece without the title, and, again, that's everyone, are under the mistaken impression they own a variation. We repeat: no pieces are known to exist with the title. Variations do exist, however, in the color of the pearl, and in the placement of the oyster shell on the girl's hand.

520802   MY DAYS ARE BLUE WITHOUT YOU
This piece is reported to exist with three variations of the mouth - smiling, "upside-down" smile, and round mouth.

WHAT & WHEN -
An Introductions Cross-Reference Table

By definition, this is a table of introductions, broken down by year and product type. All 1990 introductions included in this edition of the Guide are accounted for, i.e., those available to us at press time.

Experienced collectors should note that although 558125, the art-plas stocking hanger, is included in the Guide, it is not incorporated in these numbers. On the other hand, PM-009, the brass filagree Club Sharing Season Ornament is included since it was the 1987 piece in a continuing series. Those collectibles that were originally introduced as a set with a single Enesco Item Number and were later assigned individual Enesco Item Numbers (for example E-9267 - a set of six animals - became E-9267A through E-9267F) are counted as individual pieces in the year the set or collection was originally introduced.

YEAR	FIG	PLATE	BELL	MUSC	ORN	DOLL	THMBL	FRAME	CNDL CLMB	BOX	NITE LITE	CLUB FIG	CLUB PLQ	S/S ORN	B/C FIG	TOTALS
1990	32	1	1	4	10	4	1					2				55 *
1989	39	1	1	1	10		1					4		1	3	61
1988	43	1	1	2	12	1	1					4		1	3	68
1987	43	1	1	2	10	1	1					6		1	3	69
1986	46	3	1	3	14	3	5				1	4		1	2	83
1985	32	3	1	4	8	4	4	4				5				65
1984	40	5	1	1	6	3						4				60
1983	44	6	1	2	13	1		1		6		4				78
1982	31	7	6	8	12	2		9	1	1		1	2			80
1981	24	4	7	6	9	2			1		1	2				56
1980	24			5												29
1979	21															21
TOTALS	419	32	21	38	104	20	13	14	2	7	2	36	2	4	11	725

The following table takes the above data one step further, exploring the current market status of the yearly introductions. It is important to note that all 1990 introductions to date are counted in the STILL IN PRODUCTION column.

YEAR	PIECES INTRODUCED THAT YEAR THAT ARE NOW:			PIECES INTRODUCED THAT YEAR THAT WERE:			STILL IN PRODUCTION	TOTALS
	RETIRED	SUSPENDED	DISCONTINUED	LIMITED ED.	ANNUALS	CLUB PCS.		
1990							55	55*
1989				1	12	8	40	61
1988				1	13	8	46	68
1987				1	13	10	45	69
1986	3	12		3	15	7	43	83
1985	2	18			13	5	27	65
1984	5	17		3	5	4	26	60
1983	8	34		3	4	4	25	78
1982	8	48		5	3	3	13	80
1981	3	34		3	2	2	12	56
1980	6	11	1				11	29
1979	7	9					5	21
TOTALS	**42**	**183**	**1**	**20**	**80**	**51**	**348**	**725**

* 1990 Introductions to date, at press time

I received my first PRECIOUS MOMENTS figurine, E-1379A, "Love Is Kind," as a Christmas gift in 1979, gave "God Loveth A Cheerful Giver," E-1378, to a roommate as a Christmas gift, but didn't keep one for myself, and my fascination with PRECIOUS MOMENTS began. Over the next two years, I added a few pieces to my collection, and joined the PRECIOUS MOMENTS Collectors' Club in 1981 as a Charter Member. In 1981, I became serious about my collection, and as my interest in the PRECIOUS MOMENTS Collection grew, I constantly hounded Collectors' Centers for information about the collectible, trying to become as knowledgeable as possible about the Collection and the artist. My collection currently includes all PRECIOUS MOMENTS collectibles to date plus many "Nobody's Perfect!" pieces.

Armed with a degree in English and Journalism, and a great deal of research on the Collection, I began *Precious Insights* in 1988 in an effort to share with others the knowledge I'd gained .

I frequently speak at Collectors' Clubs and retail events and served on the Enesco PRECIOUS MOMENTS Collector Advisory Board, October, 1989.

Advice To The New Collector

One of the questions most commonly asked by the new collector is how to start a collection and what pieces they should concentrate on purchasing first. There are various ways of beginning your collection, and most new collectors will make their decision based on one or more of these ideas.

First of all, what do I want to collect? Just figurines? Figurines and ornaments? Just ornaments? Just pieces I like? Everything?

Secondly, how serious am I going to be about my collection? Do I want to collect by annual symbol, or do I just want the pieces, no matter what their annual symbol is?

Third, what can I afford?

One of the very first things a new collector should invest in when beginning a collection is the Club membership. Because the Club issues pieces which are available only to members, if you feel you want these pieces in your collection, you should enroll as soon as possible. With your membership in the Club, you will receive the Symbol of Membership for the year in which you enroll (this year's piece is *My Happiness*). There is no additional charge for this figurine - the price is included in your Club membership fee.

Enrolling in the Club will entitle you to purchase the Membership pieces from the Club which are announced twice a year and available only to active members. The Club sends a coupon with your name, address, and membership number to you when the piece is made available. Each Club Membership is sent one coupon which has an expiration date. You must redeem this coupon at an authorized PRECIOUS MOMENTS Center before the deadline printed on the coupon, and you may only receive one figurine per membership. Over the years, all figurines in the "membership" category have appreciated in value, so if for no other reason, they are a good investment. PM-811, *Hello, Lord, It's Me Again*, depicting a little boy with a "Dear Jon" letter and a telephone is the first Membership piece ever crafted, and while it originally retailed for about $25, it is now valued at $425 on the Secondary Market.

As a new collector, you will want to have as much information in hand as possible when you venture out to purchase pieces for your collection. Take your GREENBOOK. If you are concerned with collecting by annual symbols, you will find the Guide a ready reference to help you find the oldest piece possible. Even though you may not be concerned about the annual symbols on all pieces you collect, when possible you should purchase the oldest annual symbol available on your retailer's shelf. If the piece has been introduced during the last two to three years, and you are willing to work at it a bit, you should be able to find the piece in its original annual symbol. Original annual symbols generally appreciate in value faster than do pieces produced during later production.

...continued on next page

Advice To The New Collector continued

As new pieces are introduced to the PRECIOUS MOMENTS Collection each spring, some pieces will exist with the previous year's annual symbol incised on them. Annual symbols are changed at the beginning of the calendar year, but in order to meet production and shipping deadlines, the artisans begin crafting the new introductions during the previous year. These pieces are the annual symbols to purchase if possible, since these are the "original" annual symbols for spring introductions. In some cases, such as the angel boy with butterfly net, *I'm So Glad You Fluttered Into My Life*, introduced for Spring 1989, the previous year annual symbol (FLOWER) pieces are extremely rare, which immediately drove the value up considerably.

If you would like to have an "original annual symbol" collection, you will find that you must go to the Secondary Market for many pieces for your collection. For a new collector with "original annual symbol" as a goal, try working "backwards" through the Collection. Pick up pieces with their "original" marks from the retailers while they are still available. A bit of searching should allow you to obtain the pieces you want which were introduced during the current year and possibly the previous two to three years in their original annual symbols. Purchasing these pieces as soon as possible will save money in the long run, as you will not have to pay secondary market prices to get the marks you want.

When you are able to do so, begin with your favorite pieces and purchase them on the Secondary Market. Again, the more recent productions will be lower in price now than later, so working backwards may again be to your advantage. When purchasing pieces on the Secondary Market, be aware of how the prices increase from year to year on hard-to-find items such as "Free Puppies," and other Retired, Suspended and Membership pieces.

When pieces are retired from the PRECIOUS MOMENTS Collection, DO NOT PANIC! Final shipments of the retired pieces are made to retailers after the retirement announcement is sent to collectors. (For almost every retirement since 1981, this information has been sent to collectors in the Club's GOOD-NEWSLETTER - watch your mailbox in late July - early August). As you visit retailers trying to locate the pieces you need, have them put your name on their list to reserve the pieces when they come in. Most retailers reserve these pieces on a first-come, first-served basis and will call you if they have the pieces you want when the final allotment arrives. Have your name on lists at several retailers - if you reserve a piece, but find it somewhere else, let the retailer know so they can make it available to another collector.

One last word of caution - do not overbuy, whether you find duplicates of retired pieces, suspended pieces, or original annual symbols. Selling pieces is expensive - advertising and searching for buyers may cost you more than the profit you can make reselling pieces for which you paid retail price. Concentrate first on putting your dollars into your own collection. After you've had some experience in collecting and in purchasing pieces on the Secondary Market you'll be much more knowledgeable about what to buy and what not to buy, and will have much greater success purchasing for resale on the Secondary Market.

NOTES

The End Is In Sight

Even at an early age I was a collector. My collecting experiences are varied as I have collected stamps, coins, cards, comics, and toy figurines — just to name a few. In 1987, after many years of buying figurines as gifts for my younger sister, Annie, I started collecting PRECIOUS MOMENTS after purchasing the First Edition GREENBOOK. Collecting PRECIOUS MOMENTS has become a way to meet great friends and a way for me and my fiancé, Sylvia, to share special moments.

Since my article in the last edition of the GREENBOOK, I have received many letters and calls from collectors all over the country. I also have spoken at several local events.

I particularly enjoy all aspects of the Secondary Market and am currently trying to add to my collection of rare pieces.

Insights On Oversights

RETIRED VS. SUSPENDED

In the past, many collectors were convinced that the pieces to buy for future investment, because they would not be produced again, were the retired pieces. Retired pieces traditionally have been announced by Enesco in July or August each year. This announcement is made exclusively to members of the PRECIOUS MOMENTS Collectors' Club via the GOODNEWSLETTER. When pieces are retired, retailers may receive a retirement allotment - a predetermined number of the newly retired pieces - to meet the demand of their collectors.

As with retired pieces, when a piece is suspended, an announcement is made to collectors, usually in the GOODNEWSLETTER. Possibly the most important factor causing pieces to be suspended is to allow production room for new introductions to the Collection. The distribution of suspended pieces varies slightly from that of retired pieces. Although the suspended pieces are usually announced mid-year, outstanding retailer orders appear to be filled, and at the end of the calendar year, no further pieces are produced.

By definition, suspended pieces can be brought back into production at any time. Because of this, secondary market dealers (and collectors buying for potential investment) had for a long time been purchasing retired, limited edition, Club, and membership pieces but were never too keen on suspended pieces, afraid they would get stuck with pieces when they were re-introduced. And, on the other side of the fence, collectors were unwilling to pay more than the last suggested retail for suspended pieces, fearing if the piece were re-introduced their investment would be devalued. In the meantime, suggested retails for the ongoing pieces were increasing. So you had the situation of suspended pieces trading for less than they would be retailing for, had they not been suspended.

Then came the summer of 1987, and the only return from suspension to date, out of the nearly 200 pieces currently on the suspended list. The re-introduced *I Believe In Miracles* (E-7156) was re-designed, re-sculpted and assigned a new Enesco Item Number, E-7156R. Consequently, many collectors consider these figurines to be two different pieces, and have both pieces in their collection. The re-introduction and re-sculpting of *I Believe In Miracles* demonstrated to collectors that suspended pieces might never again be seen in their original mold, and so the unprecedented demand for suspended pieces began.

PRECIOUS MOMENTS ORNAMENTS

Ornaments is another area that has seen a dramatic increase in investment potential and popularity. Here, the PRECIOUS MOMENTS collector competes

...continued on next page

Insights On Oversights continued

with the ornament collector. Ornament collectors move from collectible to collectible, looking strictly for the ornaments from that collection. PRECIOUS MOMENTS ornaments are particularly attractive to the ornament collector because there are many dated pieces and the detail and quality are exceptional while reasonably priced. The influx of ornament collectors into the PRECIOUS MOMENTS market has had a tendency to cause shortages, especially on the dated pieces. Suspended ornaments, which include the traditional designs (Nativity, Three Kings, Angels on Cloud, etc.) are among the most difficult pieces to find of all PRECIOUS MOMENTS on the Secondary Market.

In 1987, as part of a wreath contest which the PRECIOUS MOMENTS Collectors' Club conducted, a "Dealer Wreath" was available to retailers who chose to participate in the contest. These wreaths have several interesting attributes which may command a serious collector's attention. The ornaments on the wreath have a very unique feature - all have two hooks on the back rather than a single hook on the top. They also contain the retired piece, E-0534, *To Thee With Love*. Additionally, some wreaths are in existence which have the ornament *Have A Heavenly Christmas* (12416) with an upside-down "Heaven Bound" decal on the plane. This variation is extremely rare, especially since the wreath itself is not easy to locate as many retailers appear to have taken them apart and sold the ornaments individually.

ADDITIONAL PIECES THAT WERE AVAILABLE
EXCLUSIVELY TO RETAILERS

In 1984, Collectors' Centers received, as a gift from Enesco, E-7350, *But Love Goes On Forever*. Known to collectors as the "Dealer Dome," the 6" tall figurine with a CROSS annual symbol comes in a glass dome with a wooden base. The wooden base has a plaque inscribed with the store's name. This is a beautiful and rare piece and in great demand by collectors.

In 1986, retailers were invited to purchase a nine piece 9" Nativity Set, identical to the regular sized *O Come Let Us Adore Him*, which was re-sculpted and re-introduced with a new product number (104000) that same year. Many stores sold their 9" sets to collectors for around $400.00. Although a four piece 9" set was introduced to collectors (111333) in 1987, collectors prefer the "Dealer's Nativity" because of the additional lambs and shepherds which are not available for the other set. PRECIOUS MOMENTS figurines in the 9" size are attracting a great deal of attention due in part to the tremendous secondary market performance of the 9" Easter Seal raffle pieces. Many collectors are realizing that they can currently obtain a 9" nine piece Nativity Set for about half the price of either of the first two Easter Seal pieces. This is definitely one of the best bargains on the Secondary Market at this point in time.